MAKING THE MONSTER

MAKING THE MONSTER

THE SCIENCE BEHIND MARY SHELLEY'S FRANKENSTEIN

Kathryn Harkup

BLOOMSBURY
sigma

To my parents

Bloomsbury Sigma
An imprint of Bloomsbury Publishing Plc

50 Bedford Square
London
WC1B 3DP
UK

1385 Broadway
New York
NY 10018
USA

www.bloomsbury.com

BLOOMSBURY and the Diana logo are trademarks of Bloomsbury Publishing Plc

First published 2018

British Library Cataloguing-in-Publication Data
A catalogue record for this book is available from the British Library.

Library of Congress Cataloguing-in-Publication data has been applied for.

ISBN (hardback) 978-1-4729-3373-7
ISBN (trade paperback) 978-1-4729-3374-4
ISBN (ebook) 978-1-4729-3375-1

2 4 6 8 10 9 7 5 3 1

Typeset by Deanta Global Publishing Services, Chennai, India
Printed and bound in Great Britain by CPI Group (UK) Ltd, Croydon CR0 4YY

Bloomsbury Sigma, Book Thirty-one

To find out more about our authors and books visit www.bloomsbury.com. Here you will find extracts, author interviews, details of forthcoming events and the option to sign up for our newsletters.

Contents

Preface

On 4 November 1818, a scientist stood in front of the corpse of an athletic, muscular man. Behind him his electrical equipment was primed and fizzing with energy. The scientist was ready to conduct a momentous scientific experiment.

The final preparations were made to the cadaver – a few cuts and incisions to expose key nerves. No blood ran from the wounds. At that moment the thing on the table in front of the young scientist was just flesh and bone, from which all life had been extinguished. Then the corpse was carefully connected to the electrical equipment.

Immediately every muscle was thrown into powerful convulsions, as though the body was violently shuddering from cold. A few adjustments were made and the machine connected a second time. Now full, laborious breathing commenced. The belly distended, the chest rose and fell. With the final application of electricity the fingers of the right hand started to twitch as though playing the violin. Then, one finger extended and appeared to point.

The images conjured up by this account may seem familiar. Perhaps you have seen them on the silver screen when Boris Karloff's iconic creature twitched and stumbled into life. Or maybe you have read something like this in the pages of a novel written by the teenage Mary Wollstonecraft Shelley. But the description above is not fiction. It happened. Two experimenters, Aldini and Ure, made the dead move using electrical devices.

Mary Shelley's debut novel *Frankenstein* created more than just a monster. It was the start of a new literary genre – science fiction. But Mary Shelley's science fiction owes a lot to science fact. Written at a time of extraordinary scientific and social revolution, her novel captures the excitement and fear of new discoveries and the power of science.

PART ONE
CONCEPTION

CHAPTER ONE

Enlightenment

'But these philosophers, whose hands seem only made to dabble in dirt, and their eyes to pore over the microscope or the crucible, have indeed performed miracles.'

Mary Shelley, *Frankenstein*

Mary Wollstonecraft Shelley (née Godwin) was born on 30 August 1797 and died on 1 February 1851. The 53 years of her life were packed with scandal, controversy and heartache. It has been said that she 'embodies the English Romantic movement'. She was survived by her son Percy Florence Shelley, named after his father, the poet Percy Bysshe Shelley. Mary Shelley lived at a time of political, social and scientific revolution, all of which she drew upon to create her masterpiece, *Frankenstein*.

How did a teenager create a work of fiction that has enthralled, inspired and terrified for two centuries? Like the infamous monster of her creation, stitched together from an assortment of fragments, Mary's novel took a collection of oddments from her own life and weaved them together to make a work much greater than the sum of its parts. Scenery from her travels, people she met and numerous influences from books she had read made it into the final work.

The novel, first published in 1818, was to dominate her literary legacy just as the monster dominated the life of his creator, Victor Frankenstein. *Frankenstein* gave Mary fame, if not fortune, and was recognised early on as a classic of English literature. In 1831 it was included in a series of standard English novels and this second publication gave Mary the opportunity to revise and edit her work. It is this later edition that is more widely read, but this book will examine both editions.

Frankenstein is often cited as the first science-fiction novel, but there is much scientific fact to be found within its pages. This book looks at many of the influences on the novel and particularly the science behind the story. Mary's characters were inventions – although they were heavily based on real people – but the science her characters studied was very real. Even the alchemists that fascinated the fictional Victor Frankenstein were real people. Mary's science fact veered off into science fiction when Victor made his sensational discovery of the secret of life.

To understand how Mary pieced together her creation it is worth spending a little time looking at the political, social and scientific world that she grew up in as well as the people and experiences that made their way into the novel. The ideas and concepts explored in *Frankenstein* – science, life, responsibility – were at the forefront of philosophical and public debate in the century preceding the book's publication. There were many other influences from Mary's childhood that will be explored in subsequent chapters before we look at the scientific aspects of the novel and the character of Victor Frankenstein in detail.

The eighteenth century is known as the 'Age of Enlightenment'. A time when prominent thinkers began to examine and question not only political theory, but also religious authority and how radical principles might be used as a means of social improvement. One method of social improvement was education, increasing the knowledge – or 'Enlightenment' – of everyone, not just a privileged few. Immanuel Kant, a prominent German philosopher of the time, defined Enlightenment in 1784 as 'mankind's emancipation from self-imposed immaturity, and unwillingness to think freely for oneself'.

The century preceding Mary's birth was a time of political turmoil and political unrest was a feature of much of her early life. Over the course of the eighteenth century much of Europe moved away from a medieval system of government towards the modern system of statehood. The transformation was not simple or easy. Borders moved frequently, smaller estates were subsumed into larger nation states and wars were fought over land, and the control of that land. For example, when Mary was born and for the first 17 years of her life Britain was almost continuously at war with France.

Rulers sought to consolidate their power, many becoming the sole source of government over vast regions and peoples. Many rulers were influenced by the values of Enlightenment and sought to improve the lot of their subjects. Strange as it may seem to modern eyes, these individuals were welcomed by contemporary philosophes* and became known as 'enlightened despots'.

At the turn of the eighteenth century, under the rule of Louis XIV, France became the artistic, cultural and political leader of Europe. Other rulers copied not only the system of government, but also the fashions and architectural styles of the Sun King's magnificent court. French became the common language of diplomatic and scientific discourse for the following century.

Louis XIV was succeeded to the throne by his grandson Louis XV. It became apparent that rule by one person was only as good as that person, and Louis XV failed to live up to the role. France stagnated politically under Louis XV's reign, but it generated a wealth of intellectual ideas.

Many French philosophes contributed and collected together their ideas in the French *Encyclopédie*, published between 1751 and 1772. It was the collective work of not only philosophers, but also contributions from experts from various fields, including science and engineering. The 28-volume work, complete with over 70,000 articles and more than 3,000 illustrations, aimed 'to change the way people think'. It was a grand compendium of knowledge as

---

* Intellectuals of the eighteenth-century Enlightenment – not all of them were philosophers. This group of public intellectuals promoted a 'republic of letters' that crossed national boundaries and spread information and ideas on topics as varied as history, politics economics and social issues.

well as Enlightenment ideas and its influence spread not just through France but across Europe.

Political and social upheavals were not confined to Europe. In America, war had erupted between the indigenous population and French and British colonisers. It was a successful campaign from the British point of view. Agreements were made with indigenous peoples for the division of land, but the French were militarily and financially ruined. The war had doubled Britain's national debt and to recoup some of their losses, new taxes were imposed on the colonies. Americans became increasingly hostile to these unfair taxes and began to challenge the authority of a distant foreign government. Incidents such as the Boston Tea Party in 1773 raised tensions and in 1775 revolution began. It resulted in the complete separation of this new nation from the British Empire in 1783.

Attention on America also threw a spotlight on the treatment of slaves brought from Africa to American, and British, colonies to work. The Shelleys were known to deplore the slave trade, and *Frankenstein* has been interpreted as a comment on slavery through examining the treatment of a race of humans visibly different to those around them.

The wars in America also had an impact in France. The defeat and financial cost had weakened both the monarchy and government. As a result of the spread of Enlightenment ideas and huge social upheavals, attention was increasingly drawn to examining how society treated its fellow citizens. In France, while these same ideas had taken hold, the aristocracy had effectively blocked social reform and shored up their own privileged positions. Poor crop yields, increasing disparity between rich and poor, and many other factors, eventually led to a violent and bloody revolution. In 1789 the French Revolution began and led to the Napoleonic Wars, which had repercussions throughout Europe.

The French Revolution transformed French society and moved it towards a more democratic and secular government. The authority of one group of people over the majority, and the majority's unquestioning acceptance of the situation, was no longer seen as a divine right. A set of principles were established in the *Code Civil des Français*, which remains the

basis of civil law in France to this day and its influence on
legal systems spread far beyond the French border to Italy,
Germany, Belgium and the Netherlands. The *Declaration of
the Rights of Man and of the Citizen* gave greater freedoms and
protection to people of different faiths, black people,
homosexuals and women. Though it was never implemented
it has influenced liberal democracy globally.

◀ ▶

The eighteenth century brought about changes in geography
and politics, as well as cultural and intellectual attitudes
towards science. The medieval view of the world, explained
by divine revelation, gave way to an increasingly secular way
of understanding the universe in terms of universally
applicable laws. Tremendous progress in science was made
possible by three main changes in scientific method. Firstly,
experimentation and experience came to be seen as valid
methods of producing knowledge, as the limitations of the
Greek tradition of advancing knowledge by well-constructed
arguments became apparent.

Secondly, Isaac Newton, and others, had shown that
processes such as movement could be explained in purely
mathematical terms. There was no need for a god's direct and
continued intervention to make the planets move through
the heavens. The universe could be seen as a fantastic
mechanical operation. However, God was not completely
excluded from the universe; some 'prime mover' was often
invoked as the initiator of everything.

Thirdly, the Enlightenment was an era of instrumentation.
Devices, gadgets and gizmos of increasing complexity and
accuracy were being designed, built and utilised. In Newton's
mechanical universe, God was either a mathematician or an
instrument maker.

While borders within Europe were something of a
moveable feast during the eighteenth century, there was
increased interest in the world beyond. Humans were no
longer bound to the surface of the globe as hot-air balloons
appeared in the skies above London and Paris. During the
eighteenth century the known world had simultaneously

expanded with the discovery of new continents, and shrunk as increasing travel and trade brought exotic goods and fantastic tales from far-flung places back to Europe.

Rulers realised that trade was the best way to bring much-needed money into their countries. The Dutch, the most mercantile and one of the wealthiest nations in Europe in the eighteenth century, had established the Dutch East India Company to trade exclusively with the East, as well as other operations in South Africa and the Americas. Spices, silks and slaves were packed into vessels that sailed across the globe. Other countries tried to mimic the success of the Dutch East India Company but their efforts paled in comparison.

Exploration of distant lands is a prominent theme in *Frankenstein*. The novel is framed within Walton's scientific expedition to the North Pole. The North Pole was a complete unknown and a source of fascination for eighteenth-century natural philosophers. No one knew if the top of the world was land, ice or open sea. Proposed expeditions to the Arctic hoped to increase scientific knowledge, for example, discovering the cause of a compass needle's attraction, as well as reaping the economic benefits from shorter trade routes to Asia.

As explorers pushed further and penetrated deeper into new continents, maps had fewer unknowns and cartographers had less recourse to populate their blank spaces with fantastical creatures. Man's dominance over the globe is perhaps exemplified by a series of scientific experiments conducted between 1797 and 98. The global met the provincial in Henry Cavendish, the reclusive scientific genius who weighed the world in a shed in his garden on Clapham Common.*

The availability of increasingly sophisticated instruments particularly aided both explorers and natural philosophers. Telescopes, microscopes and numerous other devices were

---

* Cavendish actually determined the density of the earth at a time when people weren't sure if our planet was a solid sphere or hollow. The experiment itself involved measuring gravitational pull between different masses and has become a classic. It is well worth looking up the details of Cavendish's work as it is a triumph of skill and ingenuity.

designed and developed. Astronomers looked beyond the earth, and the boundaries of space were pushed back further than ever before with the addition of a new planet – Uranus – and comets to the solar system. Distant stars and nebula were observed and catalogued. What had once been the domain of the heavens was now mapped and mathematically defined.

At the start of the eighteenth century, science, or natural philosophy as it was known, was still ill-defined and almost all-encompassing in the variety of its interests. As the century progressed, one discovery seemed to lead to another. Fantastic experiments and staggering scientific achievements proliferated. Science began to advance from an ad-hoc process, often carried out by wealthy individuals who had time and money to indulge their interests, to a professional activity. The aims of science changed as well. It was no longer seen as a purely intellectual exercise. Practical applications of this knowledge became increasingly obvious. The enlightened aims of science became not only to expand human knowledge, but to apply this newly acquired knowledge to real life. Engineering came to the fore with the direct aims of industrial, medical and social improvement.

Science became the fashionable philosophy of the day, the talk of every well-to-do drawing room and social gathering. Societies were formed, not just in the capitals of Europe but in the provinces as well, where science was discussed and experiments performed. Coffee houses in London buzzed with the talk of recent discoveries in far-flung parts of the world. A new intellectual rigour was brought to scientific investigations and, importantly, new discoveries were disseminated to a wide audience through lectures and printed works. Scientific ideas were published, not just as papers for the benefit of learned societies, but as books that were purchased, borrowed and shared by a wide readership.

In London in 1801, the Royal Institution opened its doors to allow the general public to attend lectures on the latest scientific discoveries. Audiences and readers were in turn encouraged to not only learn about science but to do scientific experiments themselves. The philosophy of the English Enlightenment encouraged everyone and anyone to participate in further discoveries. Pamphlets and books were sold at low prices and contained clear, practical advice on carrying out experiments for relatively little cost. Scientific equipment, microscopes, chemistry sets and electrical devices were on sale in London shops.

The boundaries between different scientific disciplines at this time were very blurred. Geology, anthropology, engineering, medicine and astronomy were all areas of interest, but individual disciplines and specialisms began to distinguish themselves. At the beginning of the nineteenth century chemistry was to emerge as the most prominent science of its day.

Chemistry had long been associated with alchemists and quacks but in the late eighteenth and early nineteenth century a phenomenal series of discoveries allowed it to move from a collection of facts and experimental results to the beginnings of a coherent scientific philosophy. Chemists were beginning to search for deeper truths that could connect all the known facts. Newton had led the way when he connected the motions of planets with the simple observation of an apple falling to the ground – gravity linked them all. Could there be greater underlying principles that connected different chemical reactions and properties of compounds and elements?

Phlogiston, a mysterious fluid thought to be in all substances to a greater or lesser extent, was proposed as the cause of burning. The eminent French chemist Antoine Lavoisier, who we will meet again in later chapters, thought it was the presence of oxygen that gave some compounds their acidic properties. The increased rigour that had developed exposed these theories as seriously flawed, but progress was being made. Tables of chemical affinities were constructed that began to reveal similarities or groupings for different elements. Lavoisier, with Pierre-Simon Laplace (known as the French Newton), developed a new system of chemical naming that brought order and showed connections, where before there had been chaos and apparently isolated facts.

As new discoveries were made a whole host of new things – lands, plants, peoples, elements, manufacturing techniques and scientific processes – all demanded new names. The naming of things took on huge significance. For example, Lavoisier's naming of oxygen, meaning 'producer of acids', encapsulated his theory behind the element and how he believed it combined with other substances. When new branches of science emerged the practitioners of those experiments defined themselves by their work. Benjamin Franklin and Joseph Priestley referred to themselves as electricians. Sir Humphry Davy and Antoine Lavoisier were both identified as chemists. However, these identities were fluid. In the eighteenth century Franklin could simultaneously be a statesman, printer and natural philosopher. Priestley was also known for his writing on political, religious and educational themes.

None of these people – not even Mary Shelley's Victor Frankenstein – would have named themselves a 'scientist'. Surprising as it may seem, the word simply hadn't been invented yet. It was at a meeting of the British Science Association in 1833 that William Whewell proposed, almost jokingly, that as those who worked in the arts were known as artists, those engaged in scientific work might therefore be called scientists. But it was a few more years before the term became accepted and used regularly.*

Chemists at this time were identifying, isolating and naming new elements at a rapid rate; even the term 'element' was re-assessed and redefined. Everyday substances like water completely changed their identity – it was found to be the product of hydrogen and oxygen, not an element in its own right as had been believed since antiquity.

---

* In this book, for simplicity and ease of understanding, the word 'scientist' will be used even if it is not historically accurate for the time.

Thanks to the efforts of people such as Sir Humphry Davy, researcher and lecturer at the Royal Institution, the status of chemistry as a subject was raised to much higher levels of importance. Chemistry was becoming a professional occupation and a requirement for those studying for medical and other scientific, engineering, geological or agricultural careers. It is no surprise that Mary's character Victor Frankenstein took a course in chemistry when he enrolled at the University of Ingolstadt.

Driving a large part of scientific discoveries in chemistry was electricity. Scientists in the eighteenth century had completely re-evaluated electrical phenomena. At the start of the century static electricity was the only form of electricity that was known and could be produced on demand. Certain animals such as the torpedo fish could generate shocks, which many believed were electrical in nature, but no one was certain. Lightning looked like a much grander version of the sparks that could be made using static electricity but nobody could be sure that they were one and the same substance – that was until Benjamin Franklin devised a dramatic experiment.

In 1750 Franklin proposed that electricity could be drawn down from clouds in a lightning storm to prove that lightning was electrical in nature. French scientists conducted the experiment in 1752 and confirmed Franklin's hypothesis. Lightning storms provided the backdrop for many dramatic moments in Mary Shelley's life and she alludes to Franklin's experiment in *Frankenstein* when the young Victor witnesses a tree destroyed by lightning.

A great advance in electrical technology came in 1745 with the invention of the Leyden jar, a simple device that could store electric charge, meaning electricity could now be collected and supplied on demand. The later invention of the voltaic pile (what we would call the first battery) in 1800 gave an increased level of control and electrical power that allowed scientists to use electricity to probe the very essence of different materials, revealing a host of new elements. The voltaic pile was also used to animate muscles in dead frogs and paraplegic humans.

Connections had been made between electricity and weather, and electricity and materials. Experiments on animals also revealed a strong connection between electricity and life. It was therefore no real stretch of the imagination to see the potential application of chemistry and electricity to the medical sciences.

Medical and anatomical knowledge had stagnated in Europe for almost 1,500 years until anatomists, such as the sixteenth-century Andreas Vesalius, dared to explore the interior of human cadavers and document the extraordinary detail and beauty of the inner workings of the human body. In the seventeenth century the human body was seen increasingly as an organic machine, perhaps best exemplified by the seventeenth-century physician William Harvey's description of the heart as a pump. Mary Shelley's *Frankenstein* is the next logical step in the progress of this thought. The novel suggested that a creature could be manufactured from parts exactly as a machine could be made to function when all its components are correctly assembled.

In the second half of the eighteenth century, fascination with the human body and its construction saw a huge rise among medical students. Anatomy was made required knowledge for those hoping to qualify as medical doctors. In Britain, legally available corpses were restricted in number and to those teaching anatomy at official medical schools. Enterprising individuals set up private schools offering hands-on teaching in anatomy. The source material for their students was provided by resurrection men who stole corpses from graveyards in the middle of the night. It was anatomy schools and graveyards that provided Mary's character Victor Frankenstein with the raw materials for his creature.

In a world brimming with scientific ideas and with little or no defined specialisms, there was an inevitable melding of a fascination with electrical phenomenon and human biology – resulting in galvanism, the use of electricity to stimulate muscles. Sensational demonstrations on the corpses of recently hanged criminals appeared to show that electricity had the potential to reanimate the dead. The phenomenon of galvanism was discussed in private homes and fashionable gatherings as well as scientific societies; it was the subject of conversation, along with other medical and macabre topics, at the Villa Diodati when Mary was inspired to write *Frankenstein*. However, the nature of electricity as a substance or force was still heavily debated and some suggested that it might be similar to a life force or, in fact, life itself.

The nature and origin of life began to come into question towards the end of the eighteenth century. Previously it would have been unthinkable to look outside the biblical interpretation of the origin of man and all other creatures. In biology and botany the variety of species – but also the similarities that were apparent between them – hinted at some form of adaptation and progression. Erasmus Darwin, physician, inventor and grandfather to Charles Darwin, put forward tentative early theories of evolution, as he put it 'everything from shells', and speculated on the process of generation. However, he was careful not to exclude God from the process completely and emphasised the 'power of the Great First Cause' as the initiator for such processes.

Darwin even suggested that the strength of one species could evolve to result in the destruction of another – a similar fear to that expressed by Victor Frankenstein when he contemplated making a female creature as a companion for his first creation. In the preface to her 1831 edition of the novel, Mary Shelley cited Darwin as an influence when she conceived *Frankenstein*. She recalled an experiment in spontaneous generation (the apparent ability of some creatures to spontaneously come into existence without the need for parents) – a piece of ordinary vermicelli preserved under a glass case seemed to move and show signs of life. This was unexpected for a piece of food, but was probably caused by flies' eggs, too tiny to be seen with the naked eye, hatching maggots. Observations of what was thought to be spontaneous generation were certainly reported, but the experiment cited by Mary was erroneously attributed to Dr Darwin.

The pace of scientific advancement in the century before Mary's birth, and for some decades afterwards, was at once extraordinary, exciting and, to some, terrifying. When Mary was born, chemistry had only recently been dragged out of its alchemical terminology into a modern, systematic science. In 1789, Lavoisier had listed 33 chemical elements[*]; by the time Mary died, a further 27 elements had been added to the list and patterns were emerging that would soon lead to the first periodic table.

Science held the promise of improved manufacturing, novel materials and radical improvements for health and welfare. Such rapid advances and bold claims for science brought enthusiastic responses but also critics. It is precisely these hopes and fears that Mary Shelley used to such powerful effect in *Frankenstein*. In some ways, *Frankenstein* can be seen as the summation of the previous century's scientific achievements.

The social and political atmosphere at the turn of the nineteenth century also influenced science. At a time when France was in the throes of revolution and hostilities between France and Britain were at their peak, British scientific discoveries were promoted as showing superiority over French science. The character of Victor's secretive, isolated experiments went against Enlightenment principles of sharing scientific investigations and perhaps this is part of the reason for his downfall.

◆ ◢

The Enlightenment era also marked a change in attitudes towards education, and science education in particular. Different nations took a different approach but there was a general trend towards establishing institutions for teaching technical skills to supply workers, managers and directors for growing industrial activities. There were also attempts to increase the education of the general population and the

---

[*] Most, but not all, of these were elements as we would define them today; Lavoisier included light and caloric (heat) in his list alongside elements proper.

poorer classes. Though the results were mixed and largely failed to improve educational standards of poorer children (their time could be ill-afforded in schools when they could be helping at home or working) but the trend had been set and patterns established that would be developed in the nineteenth century.

Children of the upper classes and burgeoning middle class were encouraged to learn about science, and many books written specifically for children were published. Women were also introduced to the sciences and became authors of popular scientific books for children. For example, in the early nineteenth century Jane Marcet's series of *Conversations* – books of scientific discussions between two young pupils, Caroline and Emily, and their teacher, Mrs Bryant – proved enormously popular. Marcet's books, illustrated with sketches of scientific equipment drawn by herself, guided her readers through the basics of physics, astronomy, chemistry and botany, with the teacher figure encouraging her young pupils to question, discuss and share their ideas.

Marcet spawned imitators and plagiarists, and her books remained as standard works for teaching science for nearly a century. They were popular with boys and girls – no lesser figure than Michael Faraday was a young fan. However, Marcet specifically addressed the issue of educating girls in science. The fact that she needed to make such a statement in her books shows the controversy over the subject, but she argued in favour of science for girls and stated that public opinion supported her. That a woman should be knowledgeable in the chemical sciences was considered a social advantage.

Marcet was not unique in her contributions to science. Erasmus Darwin, when he set up a girls' school, wrote a curriculum that included chemistry and botany. The Scottish engineer James Watt, when he corresponded with his wife, included considerable technical detail. Lavoisier's young wife, Marie-Anne, learned English so she could translate papers from the Royal Society and other works by English scientists. She became her husband's secretary and his laboratory assistant, making detailed drawings and notes of his experiments, contributing significantly to his work. In 1787, Caroline Herschel became the first woman in Britain to receive a professional salary for scientific work, awarded to her by King George III in recognition of her reputation as an astronomer and 'comet hunter'.

Despite a few notable exceptions, though, it was generally not considered appropriate for women to be active investigators in a laboratory setting. However, their contributions behind the scenes were known and the presence of women at public lectures was noted and encouraged.

Mary Shelley was alive at a time of new opportunities for women in terms of education. Despite being born into a scandalous family set-up on a very restricted income, Mary had an enviable, though unconventional, childhood when it came to education and intellectual stimulation. Her childhood was filled with books and spent in the company of writers, artists, scientists and philosophers. It was no surprise, and was perhaps even expected, that Mary would become a writer. What no one could have predicted was that she would produce a creature like Frankenstein's monster.

CHAPTER TWO

Development

'We are fashioned creatures, but half made up.'
Mary Shelley, *Frankenstein*

Mary Wollstonecraft Godwin was born to remarkable parents and, consequently, remarkable things were expected of her. Mary's father, William Godwin, was for a few years the most celebrated and controversial writer in England. His best-known work, *Enquiry Concerning Political Justice: And Its Influence on Morals and Happiness*, was first published in 1793 but revised and republished several times. A radical book that argues against the institutions of government and marriage, it brought him fame, followers and a considerable amount of criticism. Mary's mother, Mary Wollstonecraft, was an extraordinary woman: intelligent, bold, a successful writer, translator and proto-feminist. Many of these qualities were to be inherited by her daughter Mary.

There were many other people who played an important part in Mary's early life, as well as events and experiences that would find their way into her novel *Frankenstein*.

William Godwin was born in 1756 to a middle-class family with strong Calvinist beliefs. In his early life he trained as a minister and had a brief stint preaching without much success. His sermons, though well written and passionate, were uninspiring and his congregation preferred it when he read his father's sermons instead of his own. Doubts over his religion and increasingly atheistic thoughts crept into his mind as he read the works of philosophers Rousseau, Holbach and Voltaire, and he became more political.

As a young man he had ideas of opening a school and produced a pamphlet to advertise to potential students. Though this contained many ideas on education it didn't include any of the information you might expect, such as details of teachers, class sizes or even fees. It was clear that Godwin was more of a philosopher than a practical businessman.

Though his career as a teacher failed to get started, his writing career began to take off and he found he could sustain himself, albeit modestly, on his income as a freelance writer, producing articles, reviews and pamphlets on education, politics and other topics. When he first met Mary's mother, Mary Wollstonecraft, he was 35 years old and living a happy bachelor life in north London surrounded by a group of friends and fellow intellectuals. His relationship with Wollstonecraft got off to an unpromising start, and when they finally became a couple, many years after their first meeting, it was all too short lived – less than two years.

Mary Wollstonecraft was born in 1759, the second of seven children, with a father who was known to beat his wife in drunken rages. He eventually squandered whatever money the family had on failed speculations, and so Wollstonecraft had no family income to live on and worked all her life to provide for herself and often sent money to her relatives.

A woman in her position had limited opportunities to earn an independent income. At the age of 19 she left home and found a position as a paid companion. Over the following nine years she worked to improve her situation and her independence. She tried her hand at running a school with her sisters Everina and Eliza, but the venture eventually broke up. Later, she obtained a post as governess to the daughters of Viscount and Lady Kingsborough in Ireland.

Her experiences in education, and desperate need for money after the failure of the school, led her to write a book, *Thoughts on the Education of Daughters*. Later on, in 1791, she also published *Original stories from Real Life*, her only novel for children.

In 1787, after being dismissed from her governess role and with nowhere else to go, Wollstonecraft took the incredibly bold step of moving to London to support herself as a writer. It was a brave move since few women could expect to earn an independent living in this manner.

Wollstonecraft began by writing reviews but, when she was told that she could expect a better income from translation, she worked to improve her basic knowledge of French, as well as learning German and Italian. Her translation work enabled her to make ends meet. She also published her own work through her friend and publisher Joseph Johnson. Johnson was a strong supporter of both young and female writers, and published books on a wide range of subjects, including medical texts by Erasmus Darwin and poetry by William Cowper, though he is best known for publishing works by radical thinkers such as Joseph Priestley and William Godwin.

Johnson hosted celebrated dinners where he could meet with and expand his network of writers. It was an eclectic group, not just radicals, who were drawn by the opportunity to discuss interesting ideas and introduce new acquaintances to a wider circle of intellectuals and thinkers. It was at one of these dinners, in 1791, that Mary Wollstonecraft first met William Godwin. They did not get along. Godwin had gone to the dinner to hear Thomas Paine, but the author of *Rights of Man* contributed little to the conversation, which the assertive Wollstonecraft tended to dominate.

Godwin and Wollstonecraft didn't meet again for five years. In the intervening time both continued to publish influential and respected works, and their fame grew. Wollstonecraft left England for France. She had commented and published views on the French Revolution and now went to witness the political upheaval for herself.

By 1791 the Revolution in France had been in progress for two years but had not yet reached its bloody peak. The events there were widely discussed in England and there was much concern among the British ruling class as to the potential repercussions at home. The Revolution was a huge influence on both of Mary Shelley's parents. At this point Wollstonecraft had gained some notice for *A Vindication of the Rights of Men*, which she had written in 1790 in response to Edmund Burke's *Reflections on the Revolution in France*. Although Godwin hadn't read Wollstonecraft's work, he had also been reflecting on events in France and begun to compose his great work, *Enquiry Concerning Political Justice*. Although this discusses important issues fought over in the Revolution, such as the role of government, Godwin only specifically mentioned the events in France to condemn the violence that had broken out there. His deeply radical work may have predicted the fall of government and argued against the need for civil laws, but it was passionately anti-violence and sought a slow, peaceful transition to a world governed by truth and natural justice.

Wollstonecraft was transformed by events in France into a radical political writer. There, she became friends with leading members of the Revolution and visited salons to discuss politics and radical ideas. In 1792, she explored the Revolution's implications for the other half of the world's population in *A Vindication of the Rights of Woman*. Women's rights became a cause and Wollstonecraft was its most prominent instigator.

In Paris, Wollstonecraft also met an American businessman and adventurer, Gilbert Imlay, and fell in love. The couple were quite open about their relationship and Imlay even officially described Wollstonecraft as his wife, not out of a sense of propriety but because English citizens were under a very real threat of imprisonment at that time and American status would prevent Wollstonecraft's arrest. When Wollstonecraft found she was pregnant the couple moved to a more rural setting away from the turmoil of Paris and attempted to settle into a more domestic life. Wollstonecraft was apparently happy but Imlay was not and was frequently absent.

On 14 May 1794 Wollstonecraft gave birth to a baby girl, named Fanny after a close friend of Wollstonecraft's from her youth. Imlay, however, was growing increasingly restless and spent longer and longer away. But Wollstonecraft was besotted and followed Imlay first to Le Havre then back to England. When it became clear that Imlay had found someone else and was no longer interested, she attempted suicide by taking an overdose of laudanum. Imlay saved her life. Wollstonecraft was still hopeful of reconciliation and when Imlay's business dealings in Scandinavia took a turn for the worse he dispatched Wollstonecraft, alone with her young daughter, to sort things out for him. Wollstonecraft perhaps saw it as an opportunity to win back his favour and although she successfully resolved Imlay's business difficulties it was clear when she returned to England that their relationship was over.

Devastated, Wollstonecraft made a second suicide attempt, pacing up and down Putney Bridge to let the rain soak her clothes before jumping into the Thames. Fortunately, she was seen and rescued.

Imlay moved back to Paris and Wollstonecraft's life, with the support of friends, started to improve. Writing helped her recovery and Wollstonecraft used her experiences of travelling alone in a foreign country with a young child to write *Letters Written During a Short Residence in Sweden, Norway and Denmark*, published in 1796. Godwin read the book and wrote, 'If ever there was a book calculated to make a man in love with its author, this appears to me to be the book.'

When Godwin and Wollstonecraft met again in 1796 they got on much better. The growing friendship developed into a romance, but their radical principles meant they had no intention of marrying and maintained separate households. However, on 29 March 1797, Godwin abandoned his principles of free love and married Mary Wollstonecraft at St Pancras Church, London*, with only his close friend James Marshall as witness. It was not quite the U-turn it may appear. Mary had found herself pregnant for a second time and, after the backlash she had encountered following the birth of

---

* There are now two St Pancras churches, one built since Mary Wollstonecraft's time and the original St Pancras, now known as Old St Pancras.

Fanny, it is not surprising she wanted a marriage to legitimise the birth.

However, they were still not quite the conventional couple. After the wedding they moved into adjoining houses so they could be close but still maintain their independent lives. They attempted to keep their marriage a secret from their radical friends but the news eventually leaked. Some friends welcomed the union, but others felt it to be a betrayal of their principles and turned their backs on them.

While the newly married couple awaited the birth of their 'William', the summer of 1797 put on a show of spectacular weather. Tidal surges and waterspouts were seen at the coast. Torrential rain and powerful electrical storms swept the country. Although it wasn't known at the time, the unusual weather was probably due to particles thrown into the atmosphere by a distant volcanic eruption. Similar events would precede the birth of *Frankenstein*.

On 14 August 1797 a bright comet appeared in the night sky. Many would have seen this as a sign of troubled times ahead, but Godwin and Wollstonecraft called it their lucky star – something that Mary Shelley would herself reference in her later work. Unfortunately for the Godwins, the traditional view of comets as harbingers of bad news was more appropriate in their case. The comet was at its brightest on 16 August but faded rapidly and by 31 August it had disappeared completely.

On 30 August 1797 Mary Wollstonecraft went into labour. At 8 a.m. she sent a reassuring note to Godwin that she expected to 'see the little animal today'. Godwin went to his office as usual. Wollstonecraft, true to her radical beliefs, was attended by a female midwife having declined to have a doctor present at the birth. Fanny's birth had gone smoothly and she saw no reason why anything would be different this time.

At 11.20 p.m. Mary Wollstonecraft gave birth to a baby girl, whom she named Mary. Several hours later the midwife, evidently worried, told Godwin the afterbirth had not come away and that a doctor should be sent for. Mary had the placenta removed in pieces by the doctor. She described it as the worst pain she had ever experienced. Ten days later, after suffering periods of delirium and convulsions that shook the bed beneath her, she died of puerperal fever, an infection probably introduced by the doctor's own hands.

The 41-year-old Godwin was devastated by her death. He couldn't even face going to his wife's burial at St Pancras Church where they had been married six months earlier. In his grief he wrote *Memoirs of the Author of A Vindication of the Rights of Woman*, as a tribute to his late wife. His honesty and frankness about his wife's life, her affair with Imlay, her suicide attempts, won him no friends and, what he probably thought of as a tribute to a strong woman who had survived many adversities, came across as a slanderous account of an immoral life. Romantic poet Robert Southey described it as 'stripping his dead wife naked'.

Godwin was left with two young girls to look after, one of whom was not even his own. He was, however, devoted to the children. Godwin gave the three-year-old Fanny Imlay his own name and decided to hide her real parentage until she was old enough to understand about her mother's relationship with Imlay. However, raising two infant girls was a task he felt poorly equipped to carry out. The person most suited to it, the author of *Thoughts on the Education of Daughters* and *Original Stories from Real Life*, was dead.

When Mary was only 19 days old Godwin asked his friend William Nicholson (a scientist we will come across again in this story) to read her physiognomy*. The study of the facial features was used to determine personality traits, and at the time was a new and exciting science. When Mary cried, Nicholson found 'the mouth was too much employed to be well observed', but thought the shape of her head suggested 'considerable memory and intelligence', and no indication of 'sullenness' or 'scorn'. Nicholson was perhaps consoling the

---

* A system that was related to and led to the development of phrenology.

grieving Godwin and added the caveat that 'it would be silly to risk a character' on such a brief assessment.

In terms of educating the two young girls, at least Godwin had Wollstonecraft's books to draw upon, but his ideas on female ability varied from those of his wife. She thought 'the mind has no sex', but he differed. He firmly believed that both men and women were capable of huge potential, and that every child's individual character should be developed to the utmost. However, in the character of Fleetwood in his novel of the same name, he wrote that women were not capable of becoming Newtons or Shakespeares. Regardless, he made no difference between the primary education of male and female children and had high moral expectations of both sexes.

Though he did his best for the girls, Godwin's best option was to remarry. He had proposed to, and been rejected by, two women before a chance encounter led to his marrying a neighbour, Mary Jane Clairmont (referred to from now on as Mrs Godwin to avoid confusion with the other two Marys in Godwin's life). On 5 May 1801, Godwin made a note in his diary, 'Meet Mrs Clairmont' (the Mrs title was probably not an accurate reflection of her relationship with Mr Clairmont).

The couple were married on 21 December 1801, twice. The first marriage, between William Godwin and Mrs Mary Jane Clairmont, widow, took place in the presence of Godwin's close friend James Marshall. The couple then scurried away to another church, in secret, where William Godwin married Mary Jane Vial, spinster. Perhaps they were worried the first ceremony would not be valid because Clairmont was not her real name. The new Mrs Godwin may well have been pregnant at the time of the wedding, though the child did not survive. Mrs Godwin brought with her two children of her own, Jane (later known as Claire) and Charles. It is probable that the children had different fathers, meaning that of the five children living in the Godwin household, after the addition of William, born to the new Mr and Mrs Godwin in 1803, none shared the same two parents.

Godwin clearly cared very much for his second wife but the majority of his friends took a firm dislike to the new Mrs Godwin. Behind a polite facade reserved for visitors, she had a fearsome temper, she was deceitful, read other people's letters and spread gossip behind their backs. But her biggest crime seemed to be that she was not Mary Wollstonecraft, something she was painfully aware of and that may have spurred her more mean-spirited acts. Mary, who idolised the memory of her mother Mary Wollstonecraft, never got along with her stepmother. She would avoid household chores and escape the house to St Pancras churchyard to sit and read by her mother's grave.

Despite her drawbacks, however, Mrs Godwin had a nose for a good business opportunity and steered her husband towards starting a children's library, to capitalise on the increasing interest in children's education. The Juvenile Library would supply schools as well as individuals from the growing middle class. Mrs Godwin was also able to directly contribute several titles to the list by translating French and Swiss fairy tales, since she was a fluent French speaker*.

Godwin, too, contributed several titles published under pseudonyms to the library, reserving his own name for more scholarly work. Through his personal contacts, Godwin was also able to bring in a number of very well-respected authors, such as Charles Lamb and Thomas Holcroft, to contribute to the list of works. The Godwin household had the advantage of containing five children on which the new titles could be tested and it was a regular part of their lives to sit in a semicircle before Godwin listening to him read from the latest addition to the Juvenile Library.

At the turn of the nineteenth century there were many publications aimed specifically at children and several contained significant scientific content. For example, *The Juvenile Library* (nothing to do with the Godwins), a monthly publication issued between 1800 and 1803, that was collected

---

* It is thanks to her that the children's classic *The Swiss Family Robinson* by Johann David Wyss was introduced to English readers.

into a six-volume encyclopaedia for the education of both boys and girls, contained large sections on science and natural history. By comparison, the Godwins' Juvenile Library was the title of a series of books, the majority of which were adaptations of classic literature and history. There was little if any scientific content to these works but plenty of other material to inspire the young Mary Godwin.

William Godwin's contributions to the Juvenile Library were works on Greek and Roman mythology, English history and other topics that he felt made a good basis for his children's education, although their learning experience was much broader than this. Mary's education was conventional for the times in which she was living, in that she received little formal schooling and was educated at home, but the environment she grew up in was exceptional. Godwin had taught Mary to read and write her name by tracing the letters engraved on her mother's tombstone. Once she could read, Godwin did everything he could to encourage a love of reading. He was eminently successful in this respect as Mary was a voracious reader throughout her life, sometimes reading for up to 16 hours a day. Godwin had an extensive personal library and, after the Juvenile Library got under way, even more books filled the house. There were also specific books left for Mary's instruction. During her second pregnancy, Mary Wollstonecraft had written a series of lessons for Fanny and 'William'.

Mary had the added advantage over many contemporary young women of being born to intellectual parents with progressive thoughts about women's education, but Godwin's second marriage may have tempered how much of this he was able to put into practice. Godwin was frequently asked if he was raising his young family in the Wollstonecraft manner to which he would reply that, 'The present Mrs Godwin' did not accept all 'the notions' of their mother, and that neither of them had time enough 'for reducing novel theories of education to practice'.

The summer after Godwin met his second wife, Mary joined her elder sister at a day school, though this does not appear to have lasted long and Godwin continued to teach the girls at home. By contrast, Mary's brothers were sent away to boarding schools. Even Mary's stepsister Claire seems to have received a better formal education than Mary, spending some time at girls' schools. The expectation was that Claire would become a teacher. Mrs Godwin appears to have invested more time and resources into her own children's education than those of Mary Wollstonecraft.

Home education was the norm for girls, with heavy emphasis on feminine pursuits such as needlework, art and music. Mary had tutors in music and drawing, as well as a governess, Miss Maria Smith, to whom she was devoted. All young women were, however, expected to be knowledgeable in a range of topics so as to be able to engage intelligently in conversation, and there could have been few homes in England at the time like the Godwins' that could have provided such a rich and diverse education in stimulating conversation.

Whatever Mary may have lacked in terms of structured learning must have been more than made up for by the inspirational stream of visitors who came to the Godwins' house. In 1807 the Godwins moved to 41 Skinner Street, London, to provide a base for their publishing business, a family home and a shop, which also sold maps, stationery and toys, as well as books. Skinner Street was in a very insalubrious part of Holborn at the time, surrounded by slaughterhouses and within earshot of the gallows at the Old Bailey. The crowds would hurry past the shop on the way to a hanging and the bodies of murderers would be taken to the nearby College of Surgeons for anatomising.

Despite the less-than-fashionable address and the infamy brought upon the family by Godwin's memoirs of his first wife, many of his friends and acolytes still made the journey to visit him. Many also came to see Mary, the prodigal daughter of the two great radicals, and were impressed with her attractive appearance and evident intelligence.

Godwin's visitors included an extraordinarily diverse range of intellectuals, from medical men such as Anthony Carlisle, to scientists such as Humphry Davy, and artists like Henry James Richter and James Northcote (who painted Godwin's portrait). Politicians, philosophers and actors also stopped for supper as well as great writers such as William Wordsworth and

Samuel Taylor Coleridge. Mary and Fanny would creep into Godwin's study to listen to the conversations when they were supposed to be in bed. On one memorable occasion Mary, this time accompanied by her stepsister Claire, hid under the sofa to hear Coleridge recite his famous poem *The Rime of the Ancient Mariner*. It made such an impression on the young Mary that she could still recall the event many decades later and drew inspiration from the poem for her novel *Frankenstein*.

In addition to her extensive reading, and her tuition in music and drawing, there were also trips to London's art exhibitions, lectures (including a visit to the Royal Institution to hear Humphry Davy) and theatre visits, which particularly thrilled Mary. Moreover, when Godwin was invited to dine with friends he often took his young family with him.

Mary was very modest about her intellectual abilities and some have suggested that most of her education came as a result of meeting Percy Bysshe Shelley but, as I hope I have shown, she was on a par with Shelley and in some respects may have exceeded him, particularly in her knowledge of English literature and history, which Godwin was passionate about. Shelley on the other hand knew far more about the classics and science, and was a guide to Mary as she navigated her way through ancient Greek and Roman literature.

Shelley made much of the fact that he had published two novels while still at university. In fact, Mary had published at a much younger age and arguably had a more successful debut. Mary wrote 'stories' from a very young age, but it is believed that the 10-year-old Mary also wrote and had published an expanded version of a popular comic song *Mounseer Nong Tong Paw*. This was a very successful addition to the Juvenile Library and was republished several times, although she was not acknowledged as the author except in Godwin's private correspondence*. At home Godwin also

---

* Some doubt has been thrown on the true authorship of the poem. The young Mary may have provided the idea or basis for it and it could then have been expanded by a more experienced writer.

encouraged the family to sit and listen to oratories given by the young William. A crude pulpit was erected so he could address his small family audience properly. The contents of these little sermons were sometimes written by Mary.

Mary's home was doubtless an intellectually stimulating environment but it was not the happiest place. Mary idolised her father but he could be reserved and was strict as a teacher. Increasing antagonism between Fanny, Mary and their stepmother, as well as worries over money – despite growing sales of the Juvenile Library and, due to a legal confusion, living rent free, debts piled up – all added up to a tense household.

These stresses at home and the stormy relationship with her stepmother may have been contributing factors to a period of illness Mary suffered at the age of 14. A doctor treating her for weakness and skin eruptions on her arm recommended salt baths, and so Mary was packed off to stay in the seaside town of Ramsgate where she made some improvement. However, her return to Skinner Street saw a worsening of her condition and more drastic measures were taken.

On 7 June 1812, Mary, not yet 15, alone and with her arm in a sling, was put on board a ship bound for Scotland. Godwin wrote to an acquaintance, the radical dissenter William Baxter, describing the young girl Baxter had agreed to host for six months: 'She is singularly bold, somewhat imperious and active of mind. Her desire of knowledge is great, and her perseverance in everything she undertakes almost invincible.' At the dock, Godwin found a mother and daughter on board who he asked to watch over the young Mary until she disembarked at Dundee to the care of the Baxters.

It must have been a daunting adventure but Mary thrived in Scotland, where she formed close friendships with the Baxter girls, in particular Isabell. The Baxters took Mary on tours through Scotland, spending time in Edinburgh and St Andrews, and travelled up the Tay through the Grampians to Inverness. Scotland and the city of Dundee made a huge impression on the young Mary. Several Scottish sites were to

feature prominently in *Frankenstein*, although the remote
island Victor Frankenstein chooses as the location to build his
second creature is probably a product of Mary's imagination
rather than described from experience. Other aspects of her
stay also worked their way into the plot.

Dundee legend claims that Mary started writing *Frankenstein*
when she was living with the Baxters. Although this probably
isn't true, there were doubtless a few inspirational seeds sown
during her time in the city. Dundee at the beginning of the
nineteenth century was a huge port, from which ships set sail
for whaling expeditions and for scientific explorations of the
icy northern regions – the setting for the opening and closing
sections of *Frankenstein*. It was in Scotland, Mary recalled,
that she had allowed her imagination to run free, building
'castles in the air' and fantasy tales.

While Mary was revelling in her new Scottish life, back
home in Skinner Street Godwin had received a letter from a
new young acolyte. This was not unusual, many young men
had been inspired by Godwin and set up a correspondence
with the great man, but this letter was to have more
significance because it came from Percy Bysshe Shelley.
Godwin replied with encouraging words and in Shelley's
second letter the young radical let slip that he was heir to a
sizable estate a fact that made the terminally indebted Godwin
sit up and take notice.

Percy Bysshe Shelley was the eldest legitimate son of Sir
Timothy Shelley, second Baronet of Castle Goring, a Member
of Parliament and wealthy landowner. Shelley's somewhat
idyllic childhood had been spent at Field Place in West Sussex
where he could explore the rambling house and grounds,
inventing fantastic stories of giant snakes and alchemists to
entertain and scare his four younger sisters. Although he was
initially tutored at home, Shelley was sent to Syon House
Academy in west London at the age of 10 to receive the more
conventional education expected of a boy of his social status.
He hated the school, where he was ridiculed for his

country-bumpkin accent and other-worldliness, though there were silver linings to his cloudy school days.

At Syon House and then at Eton, Shelley came under the influence of Adam Walker. Walker toured the country delivering courses of lectures on science and specifically electricity. He was a strong advocate of the power of electricity to improve society and enthusiastically shared his knowledge. He published a book, *Syllabus of a Course on Natural Philosophy*, which was aimed at publicising his lectures but also contained detailed descriptions of electrical apparatus that allowed his readers to perform their own experiments. He was friends with Joseph Priestley, England's most famous electrician, and other members of the Lunar Society. This Birmingham-based society collected together people such as James Watt, Matthew Boulton and Erasmus Darwin for scientific discussions and informal experiments. When Walker wasn't on the lecturing circuit, or inventing marvellous machines, he taught at some of the most prestigious schools in England. Walker's showmanship and skill at scientific demonstrations must have served him well when he came to teach classrooms full of young boys. One of those boys, Percy Bysshe Shelley, was fascinated by what he saw and heard.

Shelley became an enthusiastic amateur scientist, a passion that remained with him for many years. One of Walker's assistants either sold, or helped Shelley to build, his own electrical machines. Shelley's sisters told stories of their young brother's clothes being stained and covered with burn marks from his latest chemical investigations. He was passionate about electricity and had his own galvanic battery constructed at Field Place. He would experiment on his sisters, convincing them to hold hands round the nursery table while he gave them electric shocks. One of his sisters later recalled being terrified at the sight of Shelley approaching her with 'a piece of brown packing paper under his arm, and a bit of wire and a bottle'. At his suggestion of curing her chilblains with electric shocks 'terror overwhelmed all other feelings'.

In 1804 Shelley went to Eton and received much the same treatment he had experienced at Syon House. He thus retreated into himself, refused to take part in the usual activities of the school, such as sports and fagging*, and was consequently bullied daily. Shelley's electrical experiments continued at Eton and an interest in ghost stories, magic and the occult also developed. He spent one night traipsing through the countryside convinced his spells had been successful and he was being pursued by the Devil. It's perhaps no surprise he was given the nickname 'Mad Shelley'.

At the age of 18 Shelley was sent to university at Oxford where he met his long-term friend and biographer Thomas Jefferson Hogg. Hogg was invited to Shelley's rooms in college where he found 'an electrical machine, an air-pump, the galvanic trough, a solar microscope ... conspicuous amidst the mass of matter'. Shelley would proclaim enthusiastically about the possibilities of science, and the huge power of electricity that would transform society, if only it could be tamed and controlled. Hogg described him at this time as 'the chemist in his laboratory, the alchemist in his study, the wizard in his cave'.

Shelley and Hogg's time at Oxford wasn't long though. Together, they wrote a pamphlet on the 'necessity of atheism', which led to their expulsion from the university on 25 March 1811. Shelley's father was so outraged that subsequent communication with his son was made through his solicitor. If Shelley didn't recant and submit unconditionally to his father's will he would be cut off from the family with only £200 a year allowance to live on (approximately £13,200 purchasing power today). Shelley stayed true to his radical principles and refused to recant, instead taking the £200 allowance, a meagre sum for someone of his status.

Five months after leaving Oxford in disgrace, the 19-year-old Shelley eloped to Scotland with the 16-year-old Harriet Westbrook. Harriet was the daughter of a successful coffee-shop owner and had been educated at a fine girls' school where she had met Shelley's sister Hellen. She was

---

*Younger students were expected to act as servants to senior pupils, who were often brutal in their treatment of the young boys.

intelligent, charming, but very young and clearly dissatisfied with her life at home with her father. Perhaps Shelley saw himself as rescuing a damsel in distress.

After their wedding the couple moved frequently, a pattern that was to continue for the rest of Shelley's life. They spent some time in the Lake District visiting the poet Robert Southey, as well as in the south-west of England and in Wales. They also made an ill-advised trip to Ireland, where Shelley attempted to involve himself in the Catholic cause for emancipation. His interests were increasingly political, particularly in radicalism. He had read *Political Justice* and works by Mary Wollstonecraft, but it was something of a surprise that he wrote to Godwin unannounced and unintroduced to seek his guidance.

Godwin firmly believed that wealth should be distributed to those who could make best use of it, a philosophy he had written about in *Political Justice*. So, he had no compunction in courting young Shelley and offering himself as a mentor in the hopeful expectation that, in return, Shelley would be able to alleviate his money worries. To this end, Godwin encouraged Shelley to reconcile with his family.

What started as an eager correspondence developed into regular calls at Skinner Street when Shelley and his wife Harriet came to London. News of the new acolyte and his visits were sent to Mary in Scotland but the two didn't meet for some time. When Mary returned to London for a six-month visit with Chrissy Baxter, one of William Baxter's daughters, it is possible she briefly met Shelley. On 11 November 1812, Shelley dined, along with his wife and sister-in-law, at Skinner Street. Mary and Chrissy had arrived only the day before and remained in London until June 1813, when they returned to Scotland. Mary and Shelley were not to meet again until Mary's return to Skinner Street in March 1814. At the same time Shelley resumed his visits to Godwin.

When Mary returned home in 1814 she was completely cured of any medical problems with her arm, and full of enthusiasm for Scotland; she even sported a tartan dress, unusual in London at the time. Shelley, meanwhile, was living increasingly apart from Harriet. His marriage was breaking down and by February 1814 he was spending weeks at a time away from his wife and his infant daughter Ianthe.

At Mary and Shelley's second meeting, on 5 May 1814, there was an instant attraction. It was Mary's intellect as much as her beauty that appealed to Shelley, and he described her as the finest scholar of any young girl he had ever met. She was also a young woman dissatisfied with living at home, and perhaps represented another opportunity for him to act as rescuer.

The couple spent more and more time together. Shelley would often join Mary on her retreats to her mother's grave at St Pancras churchyard. The couple were accompanied by Mary's stepsister Claire Clairmont, who was supposedly there as a chaperone, but often took herself away from the couple. It was here at Wollstonecraft's grave that they declared their love for each other and planned a life together.

Meanwhile, Godwin's hopes of financial support from Shelley had been initially frustrated. Unable or unwilling to reconcile with his family, Shelley was in no financial position to support Godwin directly, and so Godwin encouraged Shelley to obtain loans against the future security of his inheritance, at ruinous rates of interest. On 6 July 1814, after Shelley had signed papers securing one such loan, part of which was to go to alleviate Godwin's financial difficulties, he went for a long walk with Godwin and told him about his and Mary's plans to form a union. Given Godwin's advocacy of free love in *Political Justice* and his openness about his relationship with Mary Wollstonecraft before they were married, Shelley and Mary probably expected Godwin to give his blessing. Instead, Godwin was outraged and tried to separate the two, giving stern warnings to his daughter and Shelley. Shelley was barred from the house and Mary was told to cease all communication with the poet. Mary declared she would be faithful to Shelley, as she could love no other, but agreed not to see or encourage him.

But this was not the end of the matter. One afternoon after their forced separation, Shelley rushed into the schoolroom and said 'They wish to separate us my beloved, but death shall unite us,' before giving Mary a bottle of laudanum. He was also carrying a pistol. 'This shall reunite me to you,' he said. Mary calmed him down and he left, but shortly after a midnight ring at the doorbell awakened the household to the news that Shelley had taken an overdose of laudanum. The Godwins rushed out to save him but Mary stayed at home to fret. He survived the attempt.

All Godwin's efforts to keep the couple apart failed on 28 July 1814. Shelley waited outside Skinner Street with a carriage, while inside the house Mary packed her bags and left a note in Godwin's study. At 4 a.m. Mary walked out of 41 Skinner Street to the waiting carriage that sped the couple to Dover. To everyone's surprise Claire Clairmont left with them. From Dover they planned to travel to France. Clairmont explained she would be useful to them as she was the only one of the party who could speak French. It is likely she was also fleeing the tense atmosphere of the Godwin household, or perhaps she was already in love with Shelley, or perhaps it was a little of all three. Whatever her reasons for leaving, she was to remain with the lovers on and off for the next eight years.

The day of their escape was a blisteringly hot one and in the evening a storm broke over the channel as the trio made their crossing, with Mary lying on Shelley's lap suffering from seasickness (and perhaps the early stages of pregnancy). Thunder, lightning and torrential rain poured over them, but as their boat reached Calais the sun rose over their new adventure.

CHAPTER THREE

Elopement

'... we were on a voyage of discovery ...'
Mary Shelley, Frankenstein

A few days after arriving in France with Claire Clairmont, Mary and Shelley began a joint diary recording their new life together. Initially, both contributed to the descriptions of the scenery, local people and trials of their journey, but later it was Mary who took over the role of diarist. Later still, Mary used the diary as the main source material for her first published work as an adult*, *A History of a Six Weeks' Tour*, but the trio's journey also provided substance for *Frankenstein*.

The first two years of Mary's life with Shelley provided a huge amount of subject matter for her debut novel, not just her elopement (her first of many trips to Europe). A collection of pieces, ideas, scenery and characters were accumulating in Mary's memories that she would stitch together to make her monster. But all of this was years away. In the summer of 1814 Mary was embarking on an adventure with her beloved Shelley.

The couple's first journey together was full of anticipation. The novelty and excitement of travelling to new places kept them in good spirits despite limited finances. Europe had been largely closed to tourists for much of the previous 20 years due to war. The devastating results of these wars as well as revolutions in France were apparent to the travellers, but it did not put them off, caught up as they were in their own happiness.

---

* The book was actually published under Percy Bysshe Shelley's name but Mary was a co-author.

The trio's travels took them through war-ravaged France to Switzerland, much of the journey made on foot due to their very limited funds. Sprained ankles, uncooperative mules and surly drivers did little to dim their enthusiasm. They had hoped to stay in the Swiss mountains by one of the lakes but, with hardly any money left, they had no choice but to return to England by the cheapest means available – by boat via the Rhine. Along the river they passed bustling trading posts, busy towns and ancient crumbling castles. In early September 1814 they made a significant overnight stop at Gernsheim, just below Darmstadt, and a hill on top of which stands Castle Frankenstein.

The significance of the castle as inspiration for Mary's novel has been pored over for two centuries. There are certainly many coincidences and potential sources of inspiration for Mary's novel beyond the name of the castle.

Castle Frankenstein was built in the thirteenth century by Lord Conrad II Reiz von Breuberg, who, after building the castle, changed his name to von Frankenstein. Frankenstein simply means 'stone of the Franks' and would be a common way of naming an area owned by the Franks family, a fairly common German name. By the seventeenth century the castle had become a refuge and a hospital for those fleeing the war with France. On 10 August 1673 two refugees staying at the castle became the parents of the castle's most notorious inhabitant, Johann Konrad Dippel.

Dippel grew up to become a professional alchemist and was rumoured by the locals to have sold his soul to the Devil in a Faustian pact for material gain. Rumours abound about Dippel and his experiments, including stories that he had found the philosopher's stone* and had experimented with transferring souls. Whether he actually carried out this particular experiment is unknown, but he wrote in one of his books, *Maladies and Remedies of the Life of the Flesh*, about how,

---

* A material said to be able to transform base metals into gold and popularised in the twenty-first century by a certain boy wizard.

with the aid of a funnel, a soul could be transferred from one corpse to another.

Dippel became interested in alchemy and medicine when he was studying at Göttinghen in 1698. One of his professors described Dippel as an 'unintelligible writer, who was a chemist into the bargain, and whose brain seems to have been heated to a high degree of fermentation by the fire of the laboratory'.

Around 1700 Dippel began investigating potential new medicines and he focused his interests on animals. He produced an oil from the destructive distillation of animal parts. The medical use of animal, even human parts, already had a long history by the eighteenth century and many boasted of their benefits. The French chemist Pierre-Joseph Macquer wrote that animal oils had an excellent reputation in medicine. Peter Shaw, a physician and medical writer in the eighteenth century, described them as 'good in fevers, and grateful to the nerves'. Dippel claimed his oil was not just good for minor maladies, but that it was also a universal medicine capable of curing *all* diseases and even exorcising demons. He devoted a large portion of his MD thesis to discussing his oil's properties.

Among the experiments on corpses and attempts to turn base metals into gold, Dippel made a genuinely valuable contribution to modern science, though it owed more to chance than design. In 1704 Dippel was living in Berlin where a printmaker, Johann Jacob Diesbach, was making red Lake pigment from cochineal. Diesbach borrowed some salt of tartar from Dippel, who used it to produce his animal oil. When the salt was added to Diesbach's cochineal process, instead of the expected red colour a deep blue pigment was produced. The pigment was named Berlin Blue and later, when it was used to dye the uniforms of the Prussian Army, Prussian Blue. This pigment has been used by artists, printers and photographers, as well as in medicine to treat thallium poisoning and by pathologists as a stain to identify the presence of iron. Dippel's work was of medical benefit after all, though not in the way he predicted.

Dippel studied medicine at the university at Leyden. He graduated in 1711 and set up a medical practice near Amsterdam. However, just three years later he found himself imprisoned on the Danish island of Bornholm for his suspected involvement in a series of political intrigues. The remainder of his life was spent in Sweden and northern Germany. He was employed by the Duke of Wittgenstein-Gutzow and was provided with a laboratory at the duke's castle. It was here on 25 April 1734 that he was found dead at the age of 60, just months after he had predicted he would live for another 74 years. Some friends claimed he had been poisoned, perhaps deliberately by those who wanted to steal his alchemical secrets, or accidentally because of the state of his laboratory, but he probably died of a stroke.

The ruins of the Gothic Castle Frankenstein were a popular tourist destination in Mary's day. Tales of a resident alchemist carrying out macabre experiments on human cadavers can only have added to the attraction. It seems the obvious inspiration for *Frankenstein* except that, despite travelling within 10 miles of the castle, and stopping at the nearby towns of Mainz and Mannheim for several hours, there is absolutely no evidence that Mary ever visited the castle itself.

If she heard stories about the castle and its sinister occupants, which is quite possible if she talked to local people or fellow travellers on the boat, Mary made no mention of it in her diary or any other writing. She may have read about Dippel and his experiments but no definite link has ever been found. The parallels between Dippel, castle Frankenstein and the novel *Frankenstein* are so tantalisingly numerous that many feel that the visit *should* have happened even if it never did.

The Shelley party continued their journey and eventually arrived in Holland, almost penniless. From there they made the crossing to England, but by the time they landed they didn't have sufficient funds to pay their fare. The boatman was thus forced to follow them across London as they sought out bankers and friends who could loan them cash to cover the debt. Eventually Shelley begged the money from his estranged wife as Mary and Claire waited for hours in a carriage outside Harriet's house. It was a bad start to what was to be a dark part of Mary and Shelley's life together.

Financial embarrassments continued. Sir Timothy Shelley, outraged by his son's behaviour, cut off his allowance entirely. Sir Timothy was not the only one to take exception to the lovers' behaviour. The three were shunned by their friends and families. Rumours had spread that Godwin had sold Mary and Claire to Shelley for £800 and £700 respectively (over £52,000 and £45,500 respectively in today's money). Godwin and his wife cut off Mary and Claire completely: he wouldn't make contact with Mary for more than two years, even prohibiting visits from their siblings. Occasionally Fanny would send a note, or the younger William would contrive to make a brief visit, but in complete secrecy.

The next eight months saw Shelley borrow money where he could and even saw Mary and Claire pawn Shelley's prized microscope to pay for food. The trio moved lodgings several times to avoid creditors and for a while Shelley was forced to live apart from the women to hide from debt collectors. He returned to visit Mary on Sundays, the one day of the week he could not be arrested.

To compound Mary's woes, Shelley's wife Harriet gave birth to a healthy baby boy, named Charles, in November 1814. Shelley was delighted; the birth of a son and heir meant better prospects for obtaining loans. He visited Harriet and the baby but returned to Mary.

On 22 February 1815, two months premature, Mary gave birth to a daughter. The attending doctor did not expect the child to live, but Mary nursed her and the doctor was forced to concede that there might be hope. With the fragile baby still only days old the Shelley party moved again, with Mary walking to their new address carrying her newborn in her arms. On 6 March 1815 Mary noted in her diary 'find my baby dead'. Mary was understandably devastated; Shelley seemed less affected by the loss and continued with day trips into London with Claire.

A week after the death Mary dreamt about her daughter: 'Dream that my little baby came to life again; that it had been cold, and that we rubbed it before the fire, and it lived. Awake and find no baby. I think about the little thing all day. Not in good spirits.'

Claire's continued presence was also aggravating Mary, who wanted to be alone with Shelley. She pestered and pleaded with him to send Claire away but, because of the animosity with Skinner Street, there was nowhere for her to go. Eventually Claire was persuaded to move to lodgings near Lynmouth, alone. In May 1815 Mary drew a line in her diary and wrote, 'I begin a new journal with our regeneration'. This journal has since been lost and another journal picks up in July 1816, *after* the infamous party at Villa Diodati where *Frankenstein* was born.

Knowledge of the intervening period covered by the missing diary is therefore patchy but it saw Mary and Shelley travel to the West Country. Letters show the couple were staying in Torquay, a seaside resort known at the time as a destination for people suffering from consumption (tuberculosis). Shelley suffered from pains in his side and kidney pain on and off for much of his life, but at this time he thought he had consumption. In the early nineteenth century there simply wasn't any effective treatment for what is a bacterial infection, usually of the lungs. Before the knowledge of germ theory and antibiotics, all that could be done was to ease the suffering of the patient and try to delay the worst. Clean air and a warm climate were often recommended. In the summer of 1815 Shelley put himself under the medical supervision of William Lawrence.

Thankfully for Shelley he did not have consumption and he wrote to friends that he felt much better under Lawrence's care, and thus the Shelleys were treated periodically by the doctor for most of their lives. The doctor's relationship with the Shelleys developed beyond that of consultant physician. For example, Shelley attended Lawrence's wedding party. Moreover, Mary knew Lawrence from her childhood as he was one of Godwin's visitors at Skinner Street. Back then he was a newly qualified doctor but he was also very scholarly, and held strong views about the treatment of slaves and other radical policies, which perhaps attracted him to the Godwin household and to Shelley.

Lawrence was held in high esteem as a medical man. Later in his career he counted Queen Victoria as one of his patients and was elected president of the Royal College of Surgeons. He was an important figure in the writing of *Frankenstein* and may have contributed much to the appearance and development of the creature, as we shall see.

In 1815 Mary and Shelley found themselves a house in Bishopsgate, near their friend Thomas Love Peacock, who visited regularly. The couple set up home together and stayed for nine months (something of a record for them) and appeared to be very content. In early September of that year Shelley, Mary, Peacock and Charles Clairmont made a 10-day boating trip up the River Thames to visit Oxford. Shelley showed off his former rooms at the college where he had conducted his scientific experiments.

Although known for his poetry, and the scientific influences he incorporated into his poems, Shelley also wrote plays and essays. Most of his essays were political, but a wide range of topics were covered, including the principle of life. It was perhaps William Lawrence's influence that prompted Percy to write in his 1815 essay, *On a Future State*, 'but let thought be considered as some peculiar substance, which permeates, and is the cause of, the animation of living beings ... let it be supposed that his principle is a certain substance which escapes the observation of the chemist and anatomist.'

In the same year, Lawrence was appointed professor of surgery at the Royal College of Surgeons. As part of accepting this post Lawrence was required to give a series of lectures, which he delivered in March 1816. Though Mary was living at Bishopsgate, Shelley had taken lodgings in London as he was frequently in town on business and had the opportunity to see the lectures for himself, though he may have discussed the subject matter with Lawrence informally. These lectures were usually a formality, expressing thanks to colleagues and predecessors and looking over their work as well as the appointees' work. Lawrence took a controversial tack and launched into an attack on his mentor John Abernethy, a hugely influential surgeon and anatomist. The argument that ensued became known as the 'vitalism debate' and centred on the nature of life and the vital force.

Lawrence's argument was that life arose from the complexity of the organism, while Abernethy advocated the explanation given by John Hunter, Abernethy's mentor who we will hear more of in later chapters. Hunter believed that some kind of substance was needed to imbue an organism with life, but the nature of this substance was highly debated. It might be an electric fluid, or some other ethereal matter that was too subtle to be isolated or quantified. In many peoples' minds this subtle fluid equated to the physical manifestation of the soul. Lawrence argued that, however subtle this vital fluid might be, it should be able to infiltrate other materials, not just animal fibres, and if this was so, we should be able to use it to animate other materials. Everyday experience seemed to show that this did not happen, except perhaps in the fictional case of Frankenstein's creature, and so Lawrence questioned the existence of a vital fluid.

Debates on the nature of life were not confined to lecture theatres in London and the Shelleys' Bishopsgate home. It was widely discussed across Europe in scientific circles as well as in well-to-do salons and fashionable society. The Shelleys had the advantage of being closely associated with a few of those at the cutting edge of intellectual opinion on the matter and consequently were likely to be particularly well-informed on the topic.

In early 1816 Claire Clairmont, after living apart from Mary and Shelley for around nine months, was living with the couple again in their house at Bishopsgate. Perhaps tired of being in the shadow of her stepsister's romantic outlaw life, Claire had also decided on an adventure all of her own. She had set her sights on Lord Byron and took advantage of

Shelley's frequent trips to London to travel with him and introduce herself to the great poet.

At that time Byron was at the height of his fame, separated from his wife and daughter and living beyond his means in London. Claire established a correspondence with the poet, no mean feat when the poet's desk sagged under the weight of letters from adoring females. Through relentless flattery, coquettishness and boasting about being the stepdaughter of William Godwin and living with the poet Shelley, she gained an audience with him. At some stage they became lovers. Claire had ambitions for a permanent liaison but Byron was not interested.

Byron's marriage, separation and rumoured affairs were making life in England uncomfortable for him and as soon as the separation papers were signed he packed and left England. Claire was determined to follow him. Shelley had also decided to leave England, his health, the muted reception on the publication of his latest poem *Alastor*,* as well as continued financial worries, were probably contributing factors. Mary and Shelley had set their sights on Italy but, by whatever means, Claire ensured that Shelley and Mary's travel plans were changed to coincide with Lord Byron's.

Less than two years earlier the trio had set out on a similar trip to Europe, but this time there was a new addition to the party. In January 1816 Mary had given birth for a second time, to William (known as Willmouse), named after Mary's father in an attempt at reconciliation (it was not successful). The couple doted on the boy. On 2 May 1816 the Shelley party left England for Geneva and what was to become the most famous literary gathering in history.

The Shelley and Byron parties would have made very different spectacles as they travelled through Europe. Mary, Shelley,

---

* The poem has some parallels with *Frankenstein*: it also has its protagonist sleeping in charnel houses and coffins in the search for the answer to the ultimate question, much as Victor Frankenstein does during his studies at Ingolstadt.

Claire and baby William were a small domestic group travelling as quickly and cheaply as they could through France. Byron, on the other hand, travelled in flamboyant style that brought people out on to the streets to gawp at his personal carriage, modelled on Napoleon's and decorated with his family crest, followed by a train of smaller carriages carrying his clothes, books, dinner service and staff.

Byron had set off in the company of his usual entourage of servants, but there was a new addition to the retinue, John William Polidori, a young doctor with literary ambitions. Polidori was born into a respected family with literary connections. His father, Gaetano Polidori, had been secretary to Vittorio Alfieri, a dramatist and poet considered to be the founder of Italian tragedy. John Polidori was a brilliant doctor who had trained at Edinburgh, where he qualified at the age of only 19, the youngest his university had ever seen, and he was only 20 when he joined Byron. He had written his doctoral thesis on somnambulism (sleepwalking) but he also wrote fiction. Travelling with Byron, already acknowledged as one of the greatest poets of his generation, was a fantastic opportunity for the young man.

Unfortunately, Polidori was also vain and, in attempting to compete with the literary talents of Byron and Shelley, he fell short. While waiting to sail from Dover, Polidori had read to Byron and his friend John Cam Hobhouse a play he had recently written, a tragedy. The reading had Byron and Hobhouse in stitches. Polidori became the victim of Byron's vicious sarcasm and the butt of his jokes. He was eventually dismissed from Byron's employment as Byron could no longer stand his company, though he acknowledged that he was a good doctor with a promising career in medicine.

After his dismissal from Byron's employment, Polidori drifted and never really made the most of his early promise. Eventually he arrived back in England. He accumulated gambling debts and, on 21 August 1821, his body was found in his father's house. He had committed suicide by drinking prussic acid – cyanide. But all of this was still in the future. In the summer of 1816 Polidori was engaged in an exciting adventure with the most famous poet of his age and was soon to meet with even more literary talent.

Unknown to Byron, his publisher John Murray had paid Polidori £500 (around £40,000 today) to keep a diary of the pair's travels to be written up and published at a later date. It is from Polidori's diary, Shelley's Preface to *Frankenstein* and Mary's later recollections in her Introduction to the 1831 edition of the novel, that the critical weeks at Lake Geneva and Villa Diodati have been reconstructed.

Mary's account of the events differs from Polidori's. By the time Mary wrote her Introduction, Shelley, Polidori and Byron were all dead. Claire would not have wanted to be involved in anything even hinting at the incident at Villa Diodati, and her presence there was tactfully minimised or written out altogether in contemporary accounts. So Mary was free to romanticise events as she chose. Alternatively, she may have just misremembered the sequence of events.

Mary, Shelley and Claire all kept diaries, as did Byron off and on but, for the crucial summer of 1816, none but Polidori's has survived. The scandalous gossip that surrounded the party, known as 'The League of Incest, may have led the diarists to destroy their own notebooks in an attempt to draw a veil over the whole affair, though the gossip almost certainly made a lot more of the goings-on than really occurred.

As it turned out, Polidori's diary was not published until almost a century later in 1911, when his great nephew, William Michael Rossetti, stumbled across it in his mother's possession. His mother, Maria Francesca Rossetti, had transcribed the diary, editing out the most salacious entries and anything she considered 'improper' before burning the original. Fortunately, Rossetti had read the original and could recall some of the details that had been edited out.

When Byron's magnificent cavalcade arrived in Geneva, at the Hôtel Sécheron d'Angleterre, on 25 May 1816, everyone quickly knew about it, especially Claire, who had been waiting impatiently. Though the Shelley party left England after Byron, their route was more direct and they were settled in the hotel 10 days before Byron made his grand entrance.

Shelley and Byron first met on 27 May on the hotel's jetty. Shelley had just returned from a boating trip on the lake. Though Byron knew Claire intimately, and had probably been introduced to Mary by Claire when they were in London, this was the first time the two poets had met. They got on well immediately and dined together with Mary, Claire and Polidori the same evening. Polidori's first impressions of Shelley are telling: 'Percy Shelley, the author of *Queen Mab*, came; bashful, shy, consumptive; 26; separated from his wife; keeps the two daughters of Godwin, who practice his theories.' Shelley was 23 at the time and though not consumptive certainly had the appearance of it. Polidori was also under the impression that Mary and Shelley were married (Mary went by the name of Mrs Shelley for appearances' sake), but that Claire and Mary 'shared' Shelley. He was also aware that Claire was Byron's mistress. A few days later he understood the situation a little better – perhaps Byron had set him straight.

Within days of meeting the two parties were spending an increasing amount of time together and arranging to find houses near each other on the shores of the lake. Mary and Shelley were possibly a little in awe of Byron, and, though Byron and Shelley had similar aristocratic backgrounds, they had different interests, and this probably only inspired a wider range of topics of conversation and more interesting evenings spent in each other's company.

The Shelley party rented a small villa, Maison Chappuis, and Byron, still at Sécheron, would row across the lake to visit them in the evenings. On 10 June Byron moved into the much grander Villa Diodati, just a 10-minute walk through vineyards from Maison Chappuis. Claire was to take great advantage of Byron's proximity to sneak up to Diodati whenever the opportunity arose. Byron felt he had little choice in resuming his affair with her.

Byron kept unusual hours, getting up around midday, going for long rides on horseback and writing or entertaining until the small hours. Mary, Shelley and Claire adapted themselves to Byron's timetable. They would rise at an earlier hour but spent their mornings reading and studying, as was their custom, to leave themselves free to spend time in Byron's company later in the day.

Local gossip soon spread about the two households and how much time they were spending in each other's company. An enterprising hotelier across the lake bought telescopes that he set up on his hotel balcony to allow tourists to spy on the goings-on at Villa Diodati. The day bed linen that was hung out on Diodati's balcony caused a particular sensation, as the English gossips thought it was the young ladies' petticoats that they had spied through their telescopes. Byron and Shelley, however, did their best to keep to themselves and rarely went out to partake in society gatherings, preferring each other's company.

Mary would recall many years later, after the death of both Shelley and Byron, that this had been one of the happiest times of her life: 'We often sat up in conversation till the morning light. There was never any lack of subjects and, grave or gay, we were always interested.' Mary and Claire would have been present during Shelley and Byron's discussions even if they did not take an active part. Polidori would also have been part of these late-night conversational parties. It might have recalled the sister's experiences as children, sitting in Godwin's study listening to the intellectual conversations sparking round them.

That the conversation should turn to scientific matters is hardly surprising. It was the fashionable topic of the day and the company at Villa Diodati were well-informed. Polidori was a recent medical graduate with all the enthusiasm to impress the esteemed company he found himself in. He was also smitten with Mary and willing to show off at any opportunity. Shelley had a long-standing interest, some might say obsession, with all things scientific. Even Byron is known to have had a strong interest in science and would discuss scientific news and discoveries with his friend John Pigot, a medical student. Byron and Pigot would entertain each other with ribald jokes about the sex lives of plants they had read about in Erasmus Darwin's *The Botanic Garden*. Byron would also drop little scientific references into his correspondence.

These late-night discussions were hugely important in the build-up to *Frankenstein*'s conception and worth looking into in some detail. The paucity of information about the events that June, and the fact that the main source of information, Mary's Introduction, was written 15 years later, means it is difficult to piece together the exact sequence of events. Polidori noted in his diary on 15 June a conversation between himself and Shelley about 'principles – whether man was to be thought merely an instrument'. This is possibly the same conversation Mary later attributed to Byron and Shelley in her Introduction to the 1831 edition.

> *Many and long were the conversations between Lord Byron and Shelley, to which I was a devout but nearly silent listener. During one of these, various philosophical doctrines were discussed, and among others the nature of the principle of life, and whether there was any probability of its ever being discovered and communicated. … Perhaps a corpse would be reanimated; galvanism had given token of such things: perhaps the component parts of a creature might be manufactured, brought together, and endued with vital warmth.*

The scientific discussions probably happened over the course of several nights. There are other references to science in the Introduction and the Preface, and it can be assumed they were all topics of conversation during the evenings and nights at Diodati.

In the Preface to the novel, which Shelley wrote in 1817, there is only one reference to scientific matters: 'The event on which this fiction is founded, has been supposed, by Dr. Darwin, and some of the physiological writers of Germany, as not of impossible occurrence.' The physiological writers of Germany may be a reference to Johann Wilhelm Ritter, Christoff Heinrich Pfaff and Alexander von Humboldt, all enthusiastic experimenters in electricity and its effects on humans.

Ritter, like many natural philosophers in the late eighteenth century, experimented with electrical effects on frogs as well as himself and this may have contributed to his poor health early on in his life – he died when he was only 33. Ritter was the first to explain the effects of galvanic electricity as caused by chemical reactions rather than Galvani's 'animal electricity' or Alessandro Volta's theory of metals as 'electromotors'. These two opposing theories developed into a 'voltaic controversy' over how Volta's invention, the voltaic pile, actually worked, all of which will be explored in later chapters. It is Ritter's explanation that comes closest to the modern understanding of how the electric current is produced.

Pfaff was German–Danish physician, chemist and physicist, an acclaimed expert in electrical phenomena and Volta's greatest promoter in the German-speaking scientific community. He was an authority on galvanism and voltaic electricity, and championed the theory of metals as 'electromotors' in the voltaic debate.

Alexander von Humboldt was an indefatigable explorer, experimenter, collector and natural philosopher. His tireless enthusiasm for such a broad range of subjects gave him an incredible perspective across the breadth of the natural world. He has rivers, coastal currents, animals and even portions of the moon named after him. In many ways he is the epitome of Enlightenment philosophers, sharing his knowledge and passion through lectures and written works.

Inspired by the work of Galvani on animal electricity, Humboldt conducted more than 4,000 electrical experiments on frogs as well as himself, undoubtedly to the detriment of his health. When travelling in South America he took the opportunity to catch and dissect electric eels. Horses were driven into the pools to trigger shocks from the eels and exhaust them so they could be safely captured. Though several horses died in the process, the eels still retained enough electrical energy to give Humboldt and his companion, Aimé Bonpland, powerful shocks as they dissected the animals. The pair conducted every electrical experiment they could conceive of on the unfortunate animals, leaving the dissectors exhausted and weakened by their efforts.

However, the only named natural philosopher in *Frankenstein*'s Introduction and Preface, Dr Darwin, has already been mentioned in connection with Byron. Dr Erasmus Darwin, grandfather of Charles Darwin, was a physician, poet and inventor and was a very influential figure among the group that congregated at Diodati. Born in 1731 to the Darwin-Wedgewood family, he was a founder member of the Birmingham-based Lunar Society. He was also a lifelong friend of and correspondent with Benjamin Franklin. He lived in Lichfield in Staffordshire for many years, where he had a successful medical practice and also found time to invent speaking machines, as well as develop an early theory of evolution and write scientifically inspired poetry. In later life he developed firm ideas about the importance of educating women and helped to found two schools for girls. It is unsurprising that someone like this was of interest to William Godwin and the two met once when Godwin was travelling near Darwin's home.

Darwin published a number of works on a variety of topics – from botany to female education – but his poetical works *The Botanic Garden* and *The Temple of Nature* reached a much wider audience. The poems used scientific motifs and were accompanied by extensive prose notes explaining the scientific context of the poem. The format was to prove very influential on the Romantic movement and Shelley used the same arrangement in several of his own works.

Darwin's poems make several references to electricity, and the notes contain details about electric fish, Leyden jars and other electrical devices as well as the then current theories on the nature of electricity itself. The poems also discuss the possibility of electricity being the fluid that activates nerves. In addition to the scientific inclusions in his poetry, he wrote prose works including the medical work *Zoonomia*, which contains a passage on generation, the connectedness of different species and speculations on theories of evolution. Erasmus Darwin's ideas of evolution would be more fully developed by his grandson Charles, but Erasmus's contribution is notable because it pre-dates the work of one of the most famous early evolutionary theorists, Jean-Baptiste Lamarck.

Mary was certainly familiar with Erasmus Darwin and his work. Though her reading list does not include Darwin, the list is not complete. Both Byron and Shelley had certainly read The Botanic Garden and the fact that in Mary's Preface to the 1831 edition she mentioned a specific experiment – the spontaneous animation of a piece of vermicelli – and correctly stated that this was wrongly attributed to Darwin, indicates she was very familiar with his work. Mary's mention of this experiment also suggests that spontaneous animation was a topic of conversation at Diodati.

Spontaneous generation, and reproduction in general, had been the subject of speculation for millennia. Stories of homunculus, tiny fully formed humans, or other animals, that could be 'grown' into an adult, originated with the ancient Greeks who sought explanations for the appearance of maggots, flies and fleas from apparently nothing. Parents didn't seem necessary to the generation of these creatures.

Aristotle proposed the theory that some living things could be generated from non-living things because the inanimate matter contained pneuma or 'vital heat' (a term not too far removed from a spark of life). Aristotle's ideas persisted for nearly 2,000 years, only to be finally discredited by experiments carried out by Louis Pasteur in the nineteenth century. The theory of spontaneous generation was not just a niche scientific theory or only known to Greek scholars (Mary was fairly familiar with Greek and Shelley read several works by Aristotle, though possibly not his History of Animals). Spontaneous generation was also taken up by alchemists who talked of generating homunculus, soulless humans created from sperm without the contribution of females, usually grown in the soil.

Another example of spontaneous generation came from the barnacle goose – used as a symbol of the virgin birth before migration was understood – the birds seemed to appear from nowhere and were never seen to nest in Europe. The idea of parentless creatures even spread to popular culture in the Renaissance – Shakespeare made reference to spontaneous generation in *Antony and Cleopatra*, in which snakes and crocodiles formed in the mud of the Nile. In modern times the idea of bees spontaneously emerging from the head of a dead lion, which first appeared in the Bible, was used to advertise golden syrup in the UK. In addition, Mary may have had yet another source of information about spontaneous generation from Andrew Crosse.

Andrew Crosse lived at Fyne Court in Somerset and it has been suggested that Mary and Shelley could have visited him during their time in the West Country in 1815. This is, unfortunately, the period for which Mary's journal has been lost and so the visit can't be confirmed. Any evidence of their meeting Crosse is circumstantial.

At the age of 12 Crosse attended a series of scientific lectures, which included electrical phenomena, and he became enamoured of this new science. He continued his electrical studies at school, building his own Leyden jar when he was at sixth form. He also later constructed a voltaic pile at his family home. When his parents died he inherited the family estate at the age of 21. He abandoned his law studies and returned to the family home, able to indulge his combined interests of electricity and mineralogy.

He constructed vast electrical apparatus in the gardens and rooms of the house. A series of wires and spikes attached to trees were intricately arranged to attract and conduct atmospheric electricity, which he then used to charge rows of interconnected, or batteries, of Leyden jars. Such an arrangement would have been of great interest to Shelley who had speculated on the practical possibility of harnessing lightning for later use. Though Crosse did not often go out to mix in scientific company, his home was open to anyone who expressed an interest in science and he would enthusiastically give tours of his laboratory and explain his current experiments to anyone who knocked on the front door.

Crosse used his Leyden jars to store electricity until he required it. His main experiments, however, used voltaic batteries to pass electricity into bowls of water containing all manner of rocks, salts and other chemical additions. His aim was to investigate the possibility that crystals and mineral formations in caves and rocks were caused by electrical phenomena. To his surprise, in one set of experiments, he noticed not just crystals forming, but also tiny creatures emerging in some of the dishes after they had been electrolysed. It appeared he had generated life using electricity.

The creatures – insect like with bristly legs – continued to proliferate over the next few weeks and Crosse eagerly communicated his results in a paper delivered to the London Electrical Society. A local newspaper also reported the results, naming the creatures *Acarus crossii*, though Crosse referred to them as *Acarus electricus*. Crosse's discoveries caused a furore. Some scientists dismissed his discoveries, others tried to repeat them, some with apparent success. However, the ethical storm he created frightened off others from publishing their own results in support of Crosse.

Unfortunately for Crosse the creatures he thought he had created were probably cheese or dust mites that had contaminated his equipment. Unfortunately for the *Frankenstein* story, Crosse's experiments in spontaneous generation were conducted in 1836, nearly 20 years after the publication of the novel.

Whatever discussions Mary may have been part of at Villa Diodati on theories of spontaneous generation, she took the ideas and pushed them to the extreme when she had Victor Frankenstein create his monster.

The weather in the summer of 1816 also had a dramatic influence over the events at Villa Diodati. The previous winter had been poor and the bad weather continued into the summer. Mary described it as 'a wet, ungenial summer, and incessant rain'; Byron wrote to a friend of mists, fogs, rains and 'perpetual density'. Fires were lit at Villa Diodati in mid-June and on 16 June, the night after Polidori and Shelley's conversation 'on principles', the downpour was so tempestuous that the Shelley party were forced to stay the night at Villa Diodati rather than make the 10-minute walk back to Maison Chappuis.

The cause of the foul weather, unknown at the time, was a volcanic eruption. In April 1815 the Indonesian volcano Mount Tambora erupted. It was one of the most powerful eruptions in recorded history. Locally it had a devastating effect on the population, killing an estimated 10,000 people in the pyroclastic flow (more recent estimates have put the figure much higher) but an even greater number died due to starvation or disease in the months and years that followed.

The scale of the eruption was so vast that it had a global impact. The huge amounts of ash and debris blasted into the atmosphere created an eruption column that reached 43km (27 miles) up into the atmosphere. Larger debris continued to fall to the earth for weeks, but finer particles stayed in the air for months and were spread globally, creating spectacular sunsets in September 1815 that were visible as far away as London and recorded in some of J. M. W. Turner's remarkable paintings.

The long-term effect of the cloud of dust and ash, which coincided with a period of unusually low solar radiation, was that temperatures across the globe dropped by between 0.4 and 0.7°C. This may seem a tiny amount but the effect was devastating; 1816 was known as 'the year without summer', in Germany it was dubbed 'the year of the beggar', and in the United States 'eighteen-hundred and frozen to death'. On 4 June 1816 frosts were observed in New Hampshire and snow fell in Albany, New York, on 5 June. In Europe, harvests failed as crops were washed away by incessant rain. There were food riots in Germany and Welsh farmers travelled long distances to beg for food. A typhus outbreak occurred in the Mediterranean region.

Disruption to the Indian monsoon meant three crop harvests failed and a cholera epidemic began in Bengal. Contemporary reports describe appalling scenes, like something out of Dante's *Inferno* in their horror and scale. People, apparently in good health when they woke in the morning would suddenly drop dead the same afternoon. Bodies piled up along the banks of the rivers in the Ganges delta.

To get some idea of the horror and suddenness of the devastation you could read Mary Shelley's *The Last Man*, published in 1826, the first work of apocalyptic fiction. The novel sees a mysterious disease wipe out swathes of humanity, leaving a straggling band of survivors wandering across Europe in search of a safe haven. Mary would have heard about the calamity in India from Shelley's cousin Thomas Medwin's first-hand accounts. Medwin served in the army in India during the cholera outbreak and had been moved to renew his acquaintance with his cousin after finding a book of his poetry in a shop in Bombay.

Just as the ash cloud from Tambora had a global impact, so did the disease it brought in its wake. Cholera spread from India and slowly traced its way back to Java and Tambora, killing 125,000 people in 1819–20 – more than had died in the initial eruption. By 1830 the cholera epidemic had moved to Europe. In Paris, harlequins collapsed at masquerade balls. Such were the fears at the time, the victims were hastily buried in pits still wearing their costumes. Cholera reached Britain in 1832 and the outbreak in London was to claim the life of Mary's half-brother, William Godwin.

Switzerland, where the Shelleys were staying, was one of the European countries worst affected by the eruption. After the failed harvest of 1816, deaths exceeded births in both 1817 and 1818. It was only shipments of grain from Russia, which had been relatively unaffected by the Tambora ash cloud, that prevented a full-scale famine. The Shelleys themselves were relatively unaffected by food shortages. However, Mary and Shelley recorded in their diary sights of malnourished children they encountered on their trips around Geneva. Tiny, gaunt figures with enlarged necks played sullenly. The couple were so moved by what they saw they were tempted to try and adopt one of the children.

Protected from the worst effects of food shortages by their relative wealth and status, the spirits of the Villa Diadati party only seemed to be dimmed by the dismal weather. In the evenings spectacular lightning storms crashed around the peaks of the surrounding mountains. At some point the topic changed from science to something spookier. In a letter, Shelley made mention of an anecdote Polidori told that made his blood run cold. No details of the anecdote have been left to us but Polidori's experiences as a medical student had huge potential, and his literary leanings meant he could probably spin a good yarn. The Villa Diodati party had also found a French translation of a book of German ghost stories, *Fantasmagoriana: On Recueil d'histoires, d'apparitions, de spectres, revenans, fantômes, etc.*, and amused themselves by reading the tales aloud. Then, on 16 June, Byron proposed, 'We shall each write a ghost story.'

CHAPTER FOUR

Nascent

"Fran[kens]^{tein} comes"

Mary Shelley, *Journals*

Byron's challenge to write a ghost story was taken up enthusiastically by everyone at Villa Diodati. The wet weather and spooky stories continued over the following nights, fuelling the imaginations of the writers. Polidori wrote in his diary on 17 June, 'The ghost stories are begun by all but me.' But of the five stories that were started, only two were ever completed, and to everyone's surprise, it was not the established writers, Byron and Shelley, who made the most lasting contributions. Byron's challenge may not have produced much in quantity, but a simple, light-hearted challenge to alleviate the boredom of a miserable summer produced two of the most recognisable figures in Gothic and horror fiction: Frankenstein's monster and the vampire.

✝

The group continued to gather in the evenings at Villa Diodati and a few days after the writing competition had begun, on June 18, the supernatural theme continued. Byron read aloud Coleridge's *Christabel*, an unfinished poem with a strong supernatural horror theme, to the assembled party. At one point Shelley began shrieking and ran from the room. Polidori went after him to calm him down. Byron was astonished at Shelley's reaction to the poem, 'for he don't want courage', and Shelley loved late-night supernatural frights. He and Claire, after Mary had gone to bed, would often stay up late terrifying each other with ghost stories until Claire's imagination ran away with her and she became too scared to sleep. Mary was the composed and reliable one of the trio, and it would normally be her who was called upon to soothe Claire.

In her Introduction to the 1831 edition of *Frankenstein*, Mary claimed that it was not for several days after the challenge that inspiration came. Then, one night, perhaps the night of the *Christabel* reading, Mary had a frightening waking dream, 'I saw the pale student of unhallowed arts kneeling beside the thing he had put together. I saw the hideous phantasm of a man stretched out, and then, on the working of some powerful engine, show signs of life, and stir with an uneasy, half-vital motion.' Maybe the *Christabel* reading had a greater effect on her than she cared to admit. The fear she had experienced in her dream was exactly the kind of feeling she had been trying to capture for her story, and she promptly set about recording and expanding upon her dream.

Coleridge had cited a similar waking dream as the origin of his poem *Kubla Khan*. Horace Walpole also claimed the idea for *The Castle of Otranto*, the first and hugely influential work of Gothic fiction, came to him in a dream. Mary would have been reluctant to compare herself with Coleridge or Walpole, or sound like she was trying to imitate them, and made no mention of the dream when *Frankenstein* was first published in 1818. When she came to write the Introduction to the 1831 edition, maybe she wanted a Romantic inspiration for her great work rather than the reality of late-night discussions and scary stories at Villa Diodati. Or maybe it's the truth.

Whatever really happened over those few nights on the shore of Lake Geneva, the results were spectacular and rather unexpected. Mary's was the only story that made it to full-length novel and it is the one that has survived and thrived over the following two centuries. However much enthusiasm surrounded Byron's initial proposal, it soon waned.

There is no mention of Claire's story, what it was about and how much progress she made with it. The two established writers, Shelley and Byron, both started stories but did not complete them. Shelley's story apparently drew on his childhood experiences but nothing has survived. Byron's fragment of a story was appended to his poem *Mazeppa* when it was published in 1819. Mary talks of 'poor Polidori' writing a tale of a skull-headed lady, and he may have started with this idea but nothing came of it. However, Polidori, contrary to Mary's account in the Introduction, took up Byron's discarded tale and reworked it into a short story.

Polidori's reinvention of Byron's tale was published, unknown to either Byron or Polidori, in the *New Monthly Magazine* as *The Vampyre* in 1819. The Gothic tale of an aristocratic vampire, Lord Ruthven – a thinly disguised Byron – is credited as the first modern vampire tale and sparked its own literary subgenre, which was to culminate in the publication of *Dracula* 78 years later. When *The Vampyre* was published it was initially attributed to Byron himself but he disclaimed authorship as enthusiastically as Polidori claimed it when he heard of its publication.

⊤

The central idea of *Frankenstein* may have come to Mary in a waking dream but the concept of a man brought to life is not an original one. Quite apart from contemporary eighteenth-century scientific accounts of galvanism and spontaneous generation that she acknowledged in her Introduction, Mary had plenty of myths and stories to draw upon from her childhood. Godwin's education of his children paid a lot of attention to the classics of Ancient Greece and Rome. Shelley and Byron were also well versed in the classics from their own schooling.

The subtitle of *Frankenstein*, 'The Modern Prometheus', shows how strongly Mary drew upon classical mythology and folklore for inspiration. The Prometheus myth would have been taught to her as a child, probably from Godwin's own book, *The Pantheon* – on Greek and Roman myths.

The Prometheus myth exists in two versions. One has Prometheus stealing knowledge from the gods, and the other has him creating a man out of clay and stealing life-giving fire to bring his clay-man to life. In both versions of the tale, the theft of knowledge or fire outrages the gods. Prometheus had already displeased Zeus but this was the last straw. His punishment was to be chained to a rock and have a vulture

eat out his liver, only for the liver to grow back and the
process to be repeated each day for eternity.

The parallels with *Frankenstein* are obvious: a man tortured
in perpetuity for having the audacity to defy the gods and
create life. But Godwin gives a longer account of the legend
in *The Pantheon* and Mary may have used this additional
aspect of the myth as a prompt to think about the wider
implications of Victor Frankenstein's creation.

In *The Pantheon* Godwin tells that before Prometheus's
punishment, Jupiter (the Roman equivalent of the Greek god
Zeus) attempted to set a kind of honey-trap and ordered
Vulcan to create a female creature out of clay. Jupiter gave the
female life and the other gods gave her various attributes and
taught her all the finest qualities to make her a most attractive
and engaging individual. Because of her many gifts the female
creature was named Pandora. Jupiter also gave her a sealed
vase that was to be opened by her husband. Pandora was first
sent to Prometheus but he saw through Jupiter's plot and
rejected her. She was then taken to Epimetheus, Prometheus's
brother, who fell in love with her and married her. When he
opened the vase all the evils of the world were released leaving
only hope at the bottom.

The Prometheus legend was popular with Romantic writers
and Mary was not the only one to use this myth as inspiration.
Mary's own mother, Mary Wollstonecraft, saw the Promethean
legend as important inspiration for women of the revolution
who sought to throw off aristocratic and religious authority.
Byron published his poem *Prometheus* in July 1816 and Shelley
was to write his own interpretation of the Prometheus myth in
his epic lyrical drama *Prometheus Unbound*, published in 1820.
All had their own interpretation of the myth and many were
using it as a political and social metaphor.

The ancient Greeks are not unique in their myths of the
creation of man from clay. Stories of men and other creatures
being created from clay, or life created from non-living
matter, occur in many cultures around the world. In Hindu
tradition, the elephant-headed god Ganesha was created from
dirt. Creation of man from clay also occurs in Chinese,

Egyptian and Inca mythologies. Mary was thus tapping into a rich cultural seam and her story had the potential to resonate throughout the world.

Jewish stories of the 'golem' also have strong parallels with the *Frankenstein* concept and Mary may well have known of these and used them as inspiration. The golem was a clay figure moulded by a Rabbi and brought to life to carry out tasks in the household and to benefit the community. However, the story goes that each day the golem grows and becomes more difficult to manage until one day it rages out of control.

There are several versions of the story, or several occasions in Jewish history when a golem has been created, but the most famous is the sixteenth-century 'Golem of Prague'. This golem was moulded from clay by Rabbi Judah Loew ben Bezalel and, in one version of this tale, was brought to life with special incantations and prayers and by having the word *emet* (אמת, 'truth' in Hebrew) written on the creature's forehead. The powerful, mute golem had been created to protect the Jewish ghetto in Prague but he soon got out of control and threatened lives and homes in the Jewish quarter. Rabbi Loew rushed from the synagogue and erased the first letter from the word on the golem's forehead (א). The word now read *met* or 'death' and the creature disintegrated.

✝

Mary certainly had plenty of raw materials available to her to construct her story but she would continue to add to her store of influences and ideas during her time in Switzerland and through further reading.

After a gap of 14 months (the missing diary), Mary's journal picks up again on 21 July 1816, over a month after the date of Byron's challenge. On July 24 she notes 'write my story'. At the time Mary, Shelley and Claire were staying at Chamonix in the French Alps, and visiting glaciers and other local tourist attractions when the weather permitted. The diary entries are particularly long at this time as she and Shelley wrote down their impressions of the dramatic landscapes, mountains, glaciers and avalanches they were witnessing. The scenery clearly made a strong impression on Mary and particularly Glacier Montanvert (now known as Mer de Glace) on the slopes of Mont Blanc. It was here, on the frozen, fragile glacier that she was to set the dramatic confrontation between Victor Frankenstein and his creation.

On 21 August Mary wrote in her diary, 'Shelley & I talk about my story'. Shelley was encouraging her to develop her story into a full-length novel. Perhaps they also discussed the general plot and other details. The amount of input Shelley had into the final novel has been hugely debated in the centuries since its publication and no firm conclusion has been reached. It would be natural for the couple to discuss the work, Shelley was the established writer and had a more formal scientific education, and almost certainly contributed other ideas into the mix. But Mary was adamant in later years that the story was hers and hers alone. How much Shelley shaped and guided Mary to the final product will be discussed later. Mary continued to write throughout August.

The Gothic style of storytelling was already well-established in 1816 by books such as *The Monk* by Matthew Gregory Lewis and the novels of Ann Radcliffe, many of which Mary had read. Lewis stayed at Villa Diodati for a few days in mid-August and Shelley joined him and Byron to listen to his ghostly tales. These stories made such an impression on Shelley that he recorded them almost verbatim in the journal he shared with Mary.

Even Mary's father William Godwin had published fictional works, for example *St. Leon*, which involved Gothic themes such as alchemy and the secret of the elixir of life, and it is a clear influence on *Frankenstein*. Shelley's second attempt at a Gothic novel, *St. Irvyne*, written when he was a teenager, has a gigantic and hideous being giving out secret recipes for immortality. However, these works are fantasy, flights of imagination using supernatural or magical phenomena as plot devices. What is surprising about Mary's story is that, despite all the spooky stories told at Villa Diodati, the Gothic novels she enjoyed reading and the challenge to write a 'ghost story', what Mary produced is not in any way supernatural or ghostly.

As Shelley wrote in the Preface to the novel, 'The event on which the interest of the story depends is exempt from the disadvantages of a mere tale of spectres or enchantment.' It is precisely this fact that distinguishes it from other Gothic horror stories written at the time and the justifiable claim for the novel as a work of science fiction. It also calls into question the inspiration of the *Fantasmagoriana* and *Christabel*, both of which rely heavily on the supernatural.

Frankenstein stands out as something new and different because it tapped into contemporary advances in science. The terrifying spectacle of a creature brought to life from a collection of dead flesh, scavenged from dissection rooms and graveyards, was all the more terrifying because it felt all too possible. The scientific discussions at Diodati seem to have made a much bigger impression in terms of source material for Mary's 'story'. The supernatural tales perhaps contributed more to the creepy atmosphere that allowed Mary to imagine the horror of a creature constructed from cadavers and brought to life.

The company at Villa Diodati was a fantastic resource for Mary to tap into and ask any questions she may have had about the building and reanimating of Victor's creature. Polidori could have answered any queries about obtaining, dissecting and recombining human body parts and Shelley was a useful source of information about electrical experiments and chemistry. But Mary continued her own research when the Diodati group broke up later in the summer and the Shelley party returned to England.

T

At some point over the course of the summer Claire had revealed that she was pregnant. Byron wanted the child to be raised by a third party but negotiations between him and Shelley finally agreed on one or other parent raising the child: there was no possibility of Claire and Byron remaining a couple and raising the child together. On 28 August 1816 Mary was packing up Maison Chappuis so the party could travel back to England via Paris. By 10 September 1816 they were established in Bath, well away from London and the

Godwin household so they could keep Claire's pregnancy a secret. Mary and Shelley, together with their young son William, lodged separately from Claire, who was installed a short distance away under the name of Mrs Clairmont, whose husband was said to be away travelling on the continent, to keep up appearances.

Bath offered the Shelley group plenty of entertainment. It was a thriving city with theatres, public lectures and other social events, but the Shelleys largely kept to themselves. Mary had a drawing tutor and attended scientific lectures at the Literary and Philosophical Society Rooms, but much of her time was taken up with writing. In the autumn of 1816, Mary was probably focused on writing the first volume of *Frankenstein*, which establishes Victor Frankenstein's back story, his early education and his time at University.

The combined evidence of the stormy weather, the conversation topics at Diodati, together with Mary's waking dream, suggest she started her story at the point of 'a dreary night of November', when Victor took the momentous step of giving life to his creation. In the published novel this moment of reanimation does not occur until the opening of Chapter IV.

Through October and November 1816, Mary read Sir Humphry Davy's *Chemistry* as background research. The '*Chemistry*' Mary noted in her journal may refer to Davy's 1812 work *Elements of Chemical Philosophy* or an earlier publication of his first lectures at the Royal Institution. Both contain overviews of the history of chemistry from alchemy to present-day accomplishments. Whichever work it was that Mary was reading it probably inspired the descriptions of the lectures attended by Victor Frankenstein at Ingolstadt University (see Chapter 6).

Mary's story progressed well through the autumn, and she was writing almost every day from mid-October and throughout November. In a letter to Shelley written on 4–5 December, Mary wrote, 'I have also finished the 4 Chap. of Frankenstein which is a very long one and I think you would like it' – this is the chapter in which Victor discovers the secret of generation and life.

Mary was working at a time of enormous emotional stress. Claire, though she was in separate lodgings, was still an annoyance in her life. Mary's father still refused to communicate with her but continued to pester Shelley for money; and things were only set to get worse.

On 9 October a distressing letter arrived at Mary's lodgings from Fanny Imlay, Mary's half-sister. Fanny was the eldest child in the Godwin family, but the only child at Skinner Street without a natural parent living with her. Quiet and intelligent, she was usually the one who got caught in the middle by trying to appease everyone. She calmed troubled waters and soothed egos, but ended up being the butt of everyone's jokes. Her own talents would have shone in any other setting, but her undoubted intelligence paled when compared with Mary's. Her quiet nature and calm behaviour seems to have covered up a truly miserable existence. On 9 October 1816 Fanny had travelled to Bristol and written the heartbreaking note that Mary received the same evening.

Alarmed at what they read, Shelley rushed to Bristol but was too late. Fanny had left for Swansea where, on 10 October, at the Mackworth Arms Hotel, she was found dead of an overdose of laudanum. She had left a note wishing everyone ever connected with her 'the blessing of forgetting that such a creature ever existed'.

Godwin had also rushed after Fanny but turned back when he read the news of her death in a local newspaper. Fanny had to be identified by a necklace Mary and Shelley had bought her in Italy and the initials in her corset. Terrified of the shame it would bring on a family well used to scandal, the suicide was covered up at Godwin's insistence. Fanny was buried at Swansea in a pauper's grave with none of her family in attendance. Mary was devastated. Friends and relatives were told that Fanny had travelled to Ireland where she had caught a fever and died.

Two months after Fanny's suicide the body of Harriet, Shelley's estranged wife, was found in the Serpentine River. To add to the controversy, Harriet was heavily

pregnant at the time of her death, a fact that, out of respect
to Harriet, or plain embarrassment, Mary and Shelley never
revealed or discussed with anyone. Unfortunately their
behaviour, done with the best of intentions, led to
accusations that Shelley had driven his wife to suicide and
neither Mary nor Shelley felt they were able to correct or
explain themselves.

Shelley now applied to the courts for custody of his two
children by Harriet. In eighteenth-century England it was
natural for the father to have full custody rights in such
situations, as wives and children were almost classed as
property of the husband. Unusually, the case dragged on and
it was by no means certain that Shelley would win. His
avowed atheism and political radicalism were the main
factors counting against him, though his eloping with Mary
had certainly not helped.

In an attempt to improve his chances, and to repair the rift
between Godwin and his daughter, Shelley and Mary
reluctantly married on 30 December 1816. The Godwins
were in attendance, but Claire was still confined to Bath since
she was nearing the end of her pregnancy. The wedding
brought an end to the animosity between father and daughter,
with Godwin boasting to friends about Mary's marriage to
the heir of a wealthy baronetcy.

The newlyweds returned to Bath and told virtually no one
about the wedding. It was such an insignificant event in Mary's
mind that she wrote the wrong date of the wedding in her diary.
Years later many who encountered the couple still assumed they
were unmarried and as a result shunned their company.

†

Mary continued to write, almost daily, only interrupted by
Claire giving birth to a daughter, named Alba (after their
nickname of Albé for Byron, but she was later christened
Allegra at Byron's request), on 12 January 1817. Mary noted
in her diary 'four days of idleness'. The Godwins were kept
ignorant of Claire's daughter by a complicated series of moves
between Bath, London and Marlow involving friends of the

Shelleys', the Hunts, who had their own large brood of children. Alba's presence in the household was explained as her being the daughter of a friend. During February and March 1817, the Shelleys were establishing themselves at Albion House in Marlow, where they were joined by Claire and Alba.

The stay at Marlow was a productive time for both Mary and Shelley. It was here that Shelley wrote his poem *The Revolt of Islam* and edited *Mont Blanc* for publication. Some of the topics featured in *Frankenstein* were undoubtedly discussed while Mary was busy finishing her story in the spring of 1817.

By April, Mary had finished writing *Frankenstein* and was working on corrections. Shelley was deeply involved in Mary's novel at this stage, as is evidenced by sections of the draft and transcribed copies of the novel held at the Bodleian library. The manuscripts are heavily annotated in both Mary and Shelley's hand and it is from these documents that the degree of Shelley's involvement is inferred. Of the rough draft, there is approximately one half of the novel present, and about 1,000 words written by Shelley. The last 13 pages of the fair copy are entirely in his hand.

Assessments of Shelley's contribution to *Frankenstein* have ranged from that of 'minor collaborator' (by James Reiger) to the normal contributions made by a good editor (from Leonard Wolf). Much of what Shelley added to the rough draft clarifies, corrects or gives context to what Mary had already written. Other changes are creative additions or changes to 'baldness of style as necessarily occur in the production of a very young writer'.

Mary did not accept all of Shelley's changes and the value of Shelley's contributions to the quality of *Frankenstein* has been questioned (see Anne K. Mellor's biography). Modern readers may appreciate the straightforward narrative and find the more florid additions by Shelley detractions from the narrative. What is clear is that however involved in the writing Shelley was, and he may have contributed significantly to the style of the novel, the concept and content of the story are Mary's own.

In a final rush of activity, the corrections were finished and the novel transcribed, ready to be sent to prospective publishers. On Wednesday 14 May 1817 Mary wrote in her journal, 'write Preface – Finis'.

T

Mary and Shelley made a trip to London later that month, in part to take Mary's manuscript to John Murray, Byron's publisher. Murray talked of the novel favourably but in the end declined to publish it, much as Mary had expected. After all, it was not really in Murray's line. Other publishers were approached and more rejections arrived, one by return of post. In the end, *Frankenstein or The Modern Prometheus* found a home at Lackington, Hughes, Harding, Mavor & Jones. Lackington's specialised in publishing sensational novels, particularly those featuring necromancy and the occult. Although the novel was accepted in August, negotiations were still going on into September. Shelley bargained hard for a good deal on his wife's behalf and eventually fared better than he ever did for his own work.

When the proofs were ready they were sent directly to Shelley, and Mary gave him carte blanche to make any changes he deemed necessary. Mary was probably exhausted after an intense period of transcribing and correcting. She had given birth for a third time, just after her 20th birthday, on 2 September to a daughter, Clara Everina. She would have been busy with her newborn baby while Shelley continued the negotiations with Lackington's in London. Shelley probably took his wife's instructions literally and may have made further changes without consulting Mary.

On 31 December 1817 there was another new arrival. Mary noted in her diary, 'Fran[kens]^{tein} comes'; 500 copies of *Frankenstein*, dedicated to William Godwin, were printed and ready for their anonymous publication in March 1818.

PART TWO
CREATION

CHAPTER FIVE
Education

'In my education my father had taken the greatest precaution that my mind should be impressed with no supernatural horrors.'
Mary Shelley, *Frankenstein*

The waking dream that inspired Mary's *Frankenstein* centred on the moment of the creature's animation. With the encouragement of her husband she expanded her short story into a full-length novel. The moment of animation was moved to Chapter IV and the preceding three chapters form a considerable backstory of how Victor Frankenstein found himself following the dark path that led to his fatal experiment.

The novel is framed by the narrative of Captain Robert Walton, an adventurer leading a scientific expedition to the North Pole. Walton's scientific interest, which developed into an obsession that endangered not just himself but his whole crew, parallels Victor's own single-minded attitude to his research.

It is in the first few pages that we get our initial glimpse of the creature, a gigantic figure in the distance. A dark shape silhouetted against the blank, frozen landscape. When Victor was found, emaciated and exhausted, he was brought on board Walton's ship to recover. During his recuperation he told Walton how he came to be in the Arctic in pursuit of the 'daemon' the crew had seen the day before.

Walton's scientific voyage north reflects the interest in exploration during the Enlightenment era. The previous century had seen vast areas of the world being explored and mapped but there was still much to discover. No one had

reached the North Pole*. In the absence of facts about the
Arctic, theories abounded. One such was that the North Pole
was a frozen island surrounded by a sea, which resulted in
many people setting off in search of a sea route, the Northwest
Passage, which would lead around this great island to shorter
trade routes with the Americas, Russia and beyond. Others
believed the North Pole itself was an area of open sea
surrounded by a circular wall of ice. Some hoped the Arctic
would be a treasure trove of new species of animals and plants,
or even rocks and ores rich in valuable metals, including gold.
Yet more wondered about the source of the magnetic
attraction and went in search of what could cause all compasses
to point in the same direction.

The Earth itself was a vast unknown and many speculated
that it might in fact be hollow, with access to the vast interior
located at the poles. Decades after *Frankenstein*, the hollow
earth theory would be revived in Jules Verne's 1864 novel
Journey to the Centre of the Earth. The fact that the earth was a
solid mass had only been determined by Henry Cavendish's
experiments carried out between 1797 and 1798, just a few
years after the approximate dates for the setting of *Frankenstein*.

Few people, however, made serious attempts to reach the
North Pole even though expeditions were planned and
proposed by esteemed organisations such as the Royal Society.
It was a hugely risky undertaking and most of the sailing vessels
and crews were more interested in whaling, which was a reliable
source of income at the time. One whaling vessel, commanded
by Mr Ware and Captain Wilson, it is claimed, had pursued a
group of whales to 82° latitude and, finding the sea perfectly
free of ice, considered making the attempt to push further
north. The crew refused, fearing the ship would fall to pieces
when the Pole drew out all the ironwork from her.

---

* And no one would until 1926 when Roald Amundsen's group was
the first to fly over the pole in an aeroplane. The first group to set
foot on the North Pole was a Soviet team led by Alexander
Kuznetsov in 1948.

Some scientific expeditions would have departed from Dundee, where Mary had lived when she was a teenager, but many of the boats setting out from the Dundee quays would be heading north to hunt whales. Nevertheless, her time in the Scottish city would have provided a rich source of information about the landscapes and conditions in the Arctic.

Walton's expedition went in search of the mysterious land at the top of the world, 'there snow and frost are banished; and, sailing over a calm sea, we may be wafted to a land surpassing in wonders and in beauty every region hitherto undiscovered on the habitable globe'. He also talked of finding the source of the magnetic attraction. Mary, through her character of Walton, highlights some of the more common scientific interests and speculations about the North Pole.

Walton had set forth in good spirits but things changed when the reality of Arctic exploration set in. There were gales, fogs and vast sheets of ice that slowly encroached on the ship. When the fog cleared the crew spotted an enormous figure on a dog sled in the distance. The following day Victor was brought on board but it was two days before he had recovered the strength to speak and tell his tale.

♀

Victor Frankenstein has become the prototype for pretty much all subsequent depictions of mad or evil scientists. Many people have their impressions of Victor formed from film or theatre adaptations of Mary's novel, or the interpretations of the Frankenstein scientist type that followed from them. However, the idea you may have in your head of an hysterical, obsessive scientist with evil ambitions is very different from the character Mary Shelley created in 1816. The figure she depicted was certainly focused, perhaps even obsessive, about his scientific endeavours, but she did not portray Victor Frankenstein as mad. Victor's work may have been misguided, and lacking foresight, but Mary never showed his intentions to be evil. Nor is *Frankenstein* a very good example of science gone wrong. Victor's experiment in bringing life to an inanimate corpse was a complete success. It was his inability to foresee the potential consequences of his actions that brought about his downfall.

Mary often based her fictional characters on the people she knew. Byron and Percy Bysshe Shelley types make frequent appearances in her novels and short stories, and particularly clear examples can be found in her 1826 novel *The Last Man*. There were several people Mary knew who may have contributed to the complex character of Victor Frankenstein, but the most obvious was her husband. Shelley's early life and interests may well have been the template for Victor's backstory. Even the name Victor was the pen name Shelley used when he published his first collection of poems, *Original Poetry: by Victor and Cazire*, in 1810.

Shelley was born to an affluent family in Field Place, in Sussex, England. His fictional counterpart, Victor, was also born to an affluent family, but in Geneva, Switzerland. Mary also gave her character a similar education to the one received by her husband; going to school but keenly pursuing his personal interests independently. Inspiration for Victor's early obsession with discovering the hidden laws of nature may also have been drawn from Shelley's early interest in science. The 1818 edition of *Frankenstein* contains more information about Victor's formative scientific education than the revised 1831 edition, which has become the standard text.

As well as following the usual education in sciences provided by his school, Mary showed the young Victor as being amazed by scientific demonstrations he witnessed at the house of a friend of the family. Mary goes into few details about the demonstrations themselves but they included popular experiments of the time that would have been carried out in homes and salons across Europe. Perhaps Mary had taken her husband's enthusiasm for scientific experimentation, which he had shown at Oxford, as an example. One specific experiment that is mentioned in the text is the classic example that uses an air pump, immortalised in Joseph Wright of Derby's painting of 1768 now hanging in the National Gallery, London. This shows a family group

Figure 1 An Experiment on a Bird in the Air Pump: *a philosopher is demonstrating the formation of a vacuum by withdrawing air from a flask containing a white cockatoo. Mezzotint after J. Wright of Derby, c. 1780. The figure by the window may be a young Erasmus Darwin. Wellcome Library, London.*

clustered round a glass vessel containing a bird in evident distress as the air is sucked out. The experiment clearly demonstrated the presence in air of some component vital for life.

Other experiments described as part of Victor's early scientific education include, 'Distillation, and the wonderful effects of steam'. Rather than going into specific detail, Mary described Victor's education in vague terms. Victor was made to attend a series of scientific lectures, possibly like those Mary herself had attended when she was living in Bath. Perhaps to ensure Victor was kept fairly scientifically ignorant at this stage of the novel, or to avoid detailed descriptions of the lectures, Mary created an accident that prevented Victor from attending the lectures until the course was almost finished. A few chemical names were included, such as potassium, boron, sulphates and oxyds (oxides), but these words were used to alienate her character from the science of chemistry. Instead she had Victor become fascinated with alchemy.

An early interest in alchemy and alchemists is another parallel between Shelley and the fictional Victor. Mary has Victor's interest sparked by the discovery of a book by Cornelius Agrippa, a real-life alchemist we will hear more of later. Victor's father's disparaging remarks about Agrippa, 'sad trash', served to increase his interest in everything alchemical. The way Mary described it, Victor's introduction to science at school was tame and unsatisfying compared with the wonderful power and promises of the alchemists. Soon she had her fictional creation devouring everything he could find on Agrippa and others. Mary cited Victor's most important influences at this time as not just Agrippa but also the works of Albertus Magnus and Paracelsus – similar to the reading material favoured by the young Shelley. Importantly, in the novel, Victor noted that the experiments he had witnessed at the friend's house were noticeably absent from the works of his new favourite authors.

Shelley would have been an excellent source of information about and inspiration for alchemists and alchemy. When he was a child, he told tales to his four younger sisters of alchemists living in the attic of the family home. 'We were to go and see him "some day"; but we were content to wait, and a cave was to be dug in the orchard for the better accommodation of this Cornelius Agrippa,' one of Shelley's sisters was to recall many years later. According to his university friend Thomas Jefferson Hogg, Shelley spent his pocket money on a mixture of books on witchcraft, chemistry, galvanism and magic. He would stay up late watching for ghosts and tried to gain access to the vault at his parish church so he could stay there all night. At school he would recite incantations, perform electrical experiments, all the time mixing his scientific interests with his reading of the occult, and attempts to raise the Devil.

In contrast to Shelley, Victor's interests, when he was growing up, seem confined to the alchemists; his fascination with modern science came later. Victor's interest in alchemy

was significant in the development of his scientific pursuits
and worth looking at in some detail.

Y

Mary may have learned of alchemy and alchemists through
Shelley sharing with her his early enthusiasm for the subject,
but she may also have known something about them from her
father. In 1799 Godwin had published the fictional tale, *St.
Leon*, about a man who learned the secrets of alchemy: how
to produce gold and the elixir of life. His knowledge of these
secret arts brought him great wealth and eternal life, but also
caused him nothing but misery and he was forced to leave his
family and live an isolated existence. The novel has several
similarities with *Frankenstein*.

In 1834, Godwin published a non-fiction book titled *Lives
of the Necromancers* (16 years after *Frankenstein*), but his enthusiasm
for the subject clearly dated to a much earlier time. The full
title of Godwin's later work reflects eighteenth- and nineteenth-
century attitudes to alchemy: *Lives of the Necromancers or An
account of the most eminent persons in successive ages who have claimed
for themselves or to whom has been imputed by others the exercise of
magical powers*. It is a collection of every significant person in
history who has had some magical episode attached to them,
from Merlin to Richard III and many others you might not
expect. However, the book also includes Cornelius Agrippa,
Albertus Magnus and Paracelsus, the three real-life figures
Mary used to inspire her character Victor Frankenstein.

There had been a significant shift in attitude towards
alchemy and alchemists in the eighteenth century. The
scientific advances of the Enlightenment era had revealed a
rational universe underpinned by comprehensible, definable
and quantifiable phenomena. Rather than a place of mysteries
and the whim of gods, the universe was seen increasingly in
mechanistic terms. Those who summoned demons to help
reveal truths, or tried to transmute metals into gold were
ridiculed and considered by Enlightenment philosophers as
misguided at best. At worst, their behaviour was thought of
as criminal or against God. Gold was nothing more than gold

and could not be transmuted from other metals; even the human soul might be a tangible and measurable substance such as electricity. This eighteenth-century attitude to alchemists prevails to this day but it doesn't do justice to the history of alchemy; these earlier studies have contributed a huge amount to modern science.

♀

The popular view of alchemy is of delusional, obsessive crackpots stooped over bubbling vats of who-knows-what, trying to turn common metals into gold with the help of mysterious incantations, obscure ingredients and perhaps the assistance of the Devil himself. The philosopher's stone, the prized goal of many alchemists, was an object said to possess many of the abilities the philosophers sought. Not only would the stone be able to turn base metals into gold, but it would also have the power to cure all diseases and extend human life to hundreds, possibly thousands, of years. In this sense the stone is bound up with another alchemical goal, the elixir of life. This final quality was of particular interest to the young Victor Frankenstein, in the 1831 edition of the novel, but these alchemical elixirs were usually aimed at extending life, or curing illness, rather than creating life. Godwin claimed in his *Lives of the Necromancers* that the elixir could extend life indefinitely.

Alchemy also has a rich history as the precursor to modern chemistry. Alchemical processes have their origins in ancient Egyptian manufacturing techniques. Papyri from the third century AD describe processes relating to gold, silver, precious gems and textile dyes, techniques that probably date back to a much earlier time. They are technical documents with clear descriptions, so clear they have enabled modern scholars to reproduce the processes. In these early texts it is evident that these techniques relate to making *imitation* gold and silver effects. There were also methods detailing how to determine the true identity and purity of metals. It is clear that people at this time understood the difference between making something with the appearance of gold and real gold – the goal of transmuting one metal into another came later.

The titles of some of these texts are also misleading. For example, *Physical and Mystical Things* is better translated as *Natural and Secret Things*. The use of 'Secret' in the title is more likely to be a reference to the need to protect trade secrets rather than the 'mystical' influence of the supernatural or spiritual.

The first mention of the aim of *making* gold and silver, or transmutation from another metal, occurs around AD 300. Documents attributed to Zosimos of Panopolis described details of instruments and equipment necessary for what is essentially a focused programme of research into the nature of metals and other substances. Zosimos thought metals had two components: a solid body and a volatile spirit. It was the spirit that gave the metal its colour and other properties. Based on this logic it was not unreasonable that the spirit could be separated from the body and used to change another metal into something with the appearance and properties of gold. For example, water of sulphur (hydrogen sulphide dissolved in water) could be used to tinge the surface of silver a yellowy colour, giving the appearance of gold. Perhaps to protect his interests, Zosimos's writings use obscure language designed to disguise the true nature of his discoveries, a characteristic that developed and became the norm for alchemical writing.

The second major movement in alchemy was among Arabic scholars and experimenters. It is from this period we get the word 'alchemy'. The addition of *al* is the Arabic definite article. The origins of the '*chemy*' part has various theories including the Coptic word *kheme* meaning black, referring to the black Egyptian land of the Nile silt. An alternative theory has the origins in the Greek word *cheō* meaning 'to melt or fuse' in particular reference to metals. Both may be true and the word *chemy* therefore obtained a double meaning.

The most notable person involved in alchemy at this period was Jābir. Legends claim he was born in the eighth century, but modern analysis of his work suggests he wrote more in the style of ninth-century Arabic scholars. Given the mysterious nature of alchemical writing, and the sometimes deliberate subterfuge, much of Jābir's life and writing is still the subject of disagreement. Regardless, Jābir wrote detailed information about equipment, materials and practical techniques, but his major contribution to alchemy was the mercury–sulphur theory of matter. Jābir believed that all metals were formed from various combinations of mercury and sulphur, condensed underground in various proportions and purities to form different metals.

Gold and silver were seen as noble metals, perfect combinations of mercury and sulphur. The other known metals – iron, copper, lead, tin and mercury – were considered base, because they looked less appealing, and were susceptible to corrosion or tarnishing, evidence of their imperfection. These metals were not seen as elements in their own right but combinations of a simpler fundamental material. Yet the origins of the mercury–sulphur theory go back even further, to Aristotle and his theory of the four elements – fire, wind, earth and water – that made up all matter.

The four-elements theory of matter paralleled the four-elements theory of health, although the two notions were not explicitly linked at this stage. Good health was enjoyed by those who had the correct balance of four humours: black bile, yellow bile, phlegm and blood.

Greco–Egyptian alchemists used the word *xērion* to describe the powders they used to transmute metals. The word has medical origins referring to a substance that could heal wounds. Jābir translated *xērion* into Arabic, *al-iksīr*, which became elixir, and was used to refer to a substance with remarkable healing properties. If these substances could heal people, perhaps they could also heal imperfect metals to make gold and silver.

The use of the word elixir thus formed a link between alchemy and medicine. Increasingly, alchemists spent time investigating compounds that could have curative properties. Over time this developed into the notion of being able to extend life far beyond normal expectations.

Arabic contributions to science and philosophy, over a period of more than a thousand years, were tremendous. Significant advances were made in physics, astronomy, mathematics and chemistry. Techniques, instrumentation and apparatus became more advanced and scholars sought to understand how the universe, and everything it contained, functioned. Their ideas about the nature of matter and human disease were fundamentally flawed but their experiments in transmuting metals and healing disease were entirely reasonable and consistent with their understanding at the time. Contemporary European science, by comparison, was languishing far behind.

Alchemy arrived in Latin Europe on 11 February 1144: it was a Friday. This is the day, we are told, that Robert of Chester, living in Spain, finished his translation from Arabic of *On the Composition of Alchemy*. When Christian Europeans had more regular contact with Muslim scholars in the thirteenth century they discovered a wealth of scientific knowledge, from the work of Muslim scholars themselves, as well as Ancient Greek texts. Arabic scholars had preserved and translated these Greek texts into Arabic and these were then reintroduced to Europe, which had lost touch with much of the work of Ancient Greek philosophers – only fragments had survived.

European philosophers were quick to take up alchemy and over the next 600 years it would flourish in all its diverse forms. The early Middle Ages followed the traditions of Arabic interests in alchemy but this developed and branched out into a range of topics, the main part of which was transmutation of base metals into gold, though this was by no means the only thing Middle Ages alchemists were interested in.

Alchemy at this time incorporated a wide range of scientific investigations, into medicine, the nature of matter as well as transmutation. There was little distinction between these practices and what we would call 'science' today. The whole universe was open to investigation by whatever means. Although there were undoubtedly quacks and charlatans, what we would consider to be misguided alchemical experiments were carried out by highly regarded men of learning and scholarship, and did progress scientific knowledge, albeit based on flawed theories.

The sixteenth and seventeenth centuries are considered the golden age of alchemy when the likes of Robert Boyle and Isaac Newton spent huge amounts of time collecting alchemical works, repeating the experiments and conducting their own investigations. Newton, for example, devoted more of his time to alchemy than he did to gravity or optics and Robert Boyle has been described as both the first chemist and as the last alchemist. However, a distinction between alchemy and *chymistry**, was starting to appear, though the words continued to be used interchangeably for some time.

By the eighteenth century the gap had widened and a clearer distinction was being made between alchemy and chemistry. Eighteenth-century scholars and writers categorised alchemists as occultists who raised spirits and demons to assist them in their magical work. Alchemy was denigrated as backward thinking. Chemistry was a modern and rational science. As the science progressed, and phenomena could increasingly be understood in terms of well-defined scientific theories, rather than a spiritual explanation, alchemy and alchemists were mocked.

When Godwin published his *Lives of the Necromancers* in 1834, the emphasis was heavily on those involved in magic and the book makes no mention of alchemy as a serious study of the nature of things. It was this attitude towards alchemy and alchemists that formed the background when Mary was writing *Frankenstein*, providing the stark contrast between

---

* The older spelling of chemistry, *chymistry*, is a term used by many historians of science to distinguish between a range of practices that could be classified as chemical *and* alchemical but are definitely not what you expect from modern chemistry. It highlights a period of transition from an ancient to a modern understanding of chemistry.

Victor Frankenstein's early interest in the occult sciences and his later serious studies in science.

Through the voice of Waldman, Victor Frankenstein's chemistry tutor, Mary juxtaposed the old and new attitudes to chemistry thus:

The ancient teachers of this science promised impossibilities, and performed nothing. The modern masters promise very little; they know that metals cannot be transmuted, and that the elixir of life is a chimera. But these philosophers, whose hands seem only made to dabble in dirt, and their eyes to pore over the microscope or crucible, have indeed performed miracles. They penetrate into the recesses of nature, and shew how she works in her hiding places. They ascend to the heavens; they have discovered how the blood circulates, and the nature of the air we breathe. They have acquired new and almost unlimited powers; they can command the thunder of heaven, mimic the earthquake, and even mock the invisible world with its own shadows.

♀

The three alchemists that Mary chose as influences for Victor Frankenstein's early life – Albertus Magnus, Cornelius Agrippa and Paracelsus – were three of the more dominant names in the history of alchemy as it was viewed in the early nineteenth century. However, the interests of these three historical figures demonstrate the huge range of philosophies held by so-called alchemists. Interestingly, none of the three would have called themselves alchemists and all of them wrote dismissively about those who tried to turn base metals into gold.

The first of Victor's inspirational alchemists was Albertus Magnus, a thirteenth-century Dominican friar, bishop, theologian and philosopher who, in 1941, was made patron saint of natural philosophers. He is known as 'the Great' and 'Doctor Universalis' because of his extensive knowledge. He wrote on a range of topics including commentaries on the gospels, botany, minerals and the works of Aristotle, but some works on alchemy may be falsely attributed to him.

He was deeply involved in experimental science, so much so that some of his contemporaries accused him of neglecting his spiritual studies. His knowledge of natural philosophy was comprehensive and though he wrote about alchemy, it was as part of a theological argument dismissing the art of magic. However, this did not stop rumours starting that he had certain secret knowledge. After his death it was claimed that he had made the philosopher's stone and bequeathed it to his student Thomas Aquinas. Given his well-documented antipathy for such things, and the fact that Thomas Aquinas had died six years before his tutor, the story seems unlikely to be true.

In an age when many alchemical texts were written in a language designed to conceal knowledge, or only reveal it to those with sufficient understanding, many have read meaning into Magnus's work that was never there. Others, hoping to give credibility to their own theories, and improve sales of their books, claimed Albertus Magnus as author of, for example, *Secreta Alberti* and *Experimenta Alberti*.

Most interestingly from Victor Frankenstein's point of view, are legends that Albertus Magnus built a man from brass. The tale has many parallels with those of the golem (see page 71) as well as Mary Shelley's *Frankenstein*. According to the account given in Godwin's *Lives of the Necromancers*, Albertus is said to have laboured over the construction of his mechanical man for 30 years. The finished product was capable of answering all sorts of questions and was used to perform domestic chores in Abertus's house. Eventually Albertus's student, Aquinas, became so enraged at the automata's incessant talking that he beat it to pieces with a hammer. In his *Lives of the Necromancers*, William Godwin also claimed that there were some accounts of the mechanical man being made of flesh and bone but that, to him, this seemed unlikely.

The story of the mechanical man is not unique to Albertus Magnus. Similar tales of automata are credited to Francis Bacon, the English natural philosopher born in the sixteenth century, and Daedelus (of Greek mythology, who is said to have created the labyrinth that trapped the Minotaur, and

wings of wax and feathers for himself and his son Icarus).
Daedelus is also said to have animated statues, though many
debated if they were really some kind of automata, or if it was
all just a clever illusion.

☿

The second of Victor Frankenstein's alchemical heroes,
Cornelius Agrippa, was of considerably less help when it came
to science or anything that might relate to building a human,
mechanical or otherwise. Heinrich Cornelius Agrippa von
Nettesheim, to give him his full title, was a sixteenth-century
polymath. He had studied the work of Albertus Magnus when
he was a student at the University of Cologne. When he was
young he wrote *Three Books Concerning Occult Philosophy* and it
is these works that he is best known for. However, in a later
edition of the work he retracted much of his earlier writing
and claimed that his thinking had been erroneous.

The three books are a philosophical discussion on ritual
magic and its use in medicine, alchemy and scrying (fortune-
telling with crystal balls and mirrors etc.). It uses as its sources
theories on numerology, astrology and the kabbalah.
Although he didn't publish until very late in life, his work
was well known in manuscript form. Despite writing on such
controversial subjects, at a time of huge religious upheaval in
Europe (Agrippa was a contemporary of Galileo and Luther),
he does not seem to have been persecuted.

Many people, impressed by his knowledge, asked Agrippa to
cast their horoscopes, though he was well aware of the folly of
what he was doing and warned his patrons against relying on
such things. He begged that his patrons employed him for his
practical skills in medicine rather than his dubious talents at
astrology. He also wrote vehemently against the practice of
necromancy. Agrippa wrote relatively little on the practice of
alchemy, in terms of transmutation, and probably never carried
out experiments himself. Despite this, Agrippa became almost
a byword for alchemy, alchemists and the occult in the
eighteenth century.

Cornelius Agrippa would appear to offer Victor Frankenstein little in terms of practical help with his chemical knowledge and even less in terms of bringing life to the dead. Agrippa wrote about medicines but his theories of cures were based on numbers. For example, he thought a five-leaf grass (possibly *potentilla*) could be used to cure malaria because the disease was also linked to the number five. The same grass, he claimed, could also drive out demons as well as being used as a protection against poison. Unsurprisingly, it would have been of no practical use. However, Agrippa was exactly the kind of alchemist to appeal to the young Percy Shelley, who would have revelled in the ideas put forward in his earlier occult works. He is a great character to use to associate Victor with the strange and occult in readers' minds.

The third of Victor's alchemical poster boys was Philippus Aureolus Theophrastus Bombastus von Hohenheim, who liked to be known as Paracelsus meaning 'surpassing Celsus' (Celsus was a dominant figure in Roman medicine). Paracelsus was a German–Swiss philosopher who brought a new approach to medical and toxicological theory. He was also a contemporary of Agrippa but rejected his magic theories. Paracelsus's father was a chemist and physician from whom he received his scientific education, but he also had other tutors. He studied medicine at the University of Basel and received a doctorate degree from the University of Ferrera, but was not always in agreement with what he was taught. He spent much of his life wandering from town to town throughout Europe learning from 'old wives, gypsies, sorcerers, wandering tribes, old robbers'.

As can be gathered from his adopted name, Paracelsus was quite arrogant and was also known to have a temper. He was also argumentative and angered many of his contemporary physicians. He would have outbursts of abusive language, shouting down untested theories, and had no truck with people who placed titles above practice. He lectured in German when his colleagues all lectured in Latin, so that more people could learn from him. He publicly burned the works of Avicenna and Galen, the then authorities on human anatomy and medicine, and advocated learning from practical experience, by studying the patients in front of them rather than from abstract historical texts.

Paracelsus was influenced by medieval alchemy in the respect that he advocated a tripartite system of sulphur, mercury and salt, and three poisons that contributed to human disease. The *tria prima* also constituted the human identity: sulphur was the soul, salt was the body and mercury the spirit (thought, imagination and higher mental functions). He developed a biochemical theory of digestion and taught medicine to his students using analogies from chemistry, though this did not go down well with the student body.

Paracelsus attempted nothing short of an entire world view based on chemical processes (though his chemistry was very different from the modern science). Everything was due to chemistry; from the formation of minerals underground, to the processes within the body such as digestion and excretion. His holistic approach was unlike anything that had been seen before. He pioneered the use of chemicals and minerals as medicines and, though many of the compounds he advocated have been shown by modern science to have no medical benefit, he made significant contributions. For instance, Paracelsus found the combination of alcohol and opium was particularly effective in pain relief. His combination of pain-numbing compounds is known as laudanum and became a staple of medical treatments for centuries.

Though he revised old works and wrote new ones on medical matters, Paracelsus struggled to find anyone who would publish his radical manuscripts. Even when most of his work was published after his death they still invited controversy and the books were described as 'heretical and scandalous'.

Paracelsus's theories of creating a homunculus would have been of particular interest to Mary's character Victor. In his essay *On the Nature of Things*, Paracelsus wrote that such a creature could be produced if human semen was sealed in a flask and placed in a gentle heat to putrefy. After 40 days the contents of the flask would begin to move and produce a living being with a human form. The creature had to be fed with special preparations of human blood for 40 more weeks to develop into a homunculus. The homunculus looked like a human child, but had 'great knowledge and powers' because it was a product of 'art' (manufactured rather than produced by a natural process) and a 'pure' male, rather than a mixture polluted with female parts. Paracelsus had dire warnings for anyone who wanted to produce a 'pure' female. Using the same procedure, but with menstrual blood in the place of semen, the results would not be a woman with great knowledge and powers, but a terrifying basilisk.

As we have seen (pages 61–63), Paracelsus was not the first to put forward theories of 'artificial' or spontaneously generated life. Many alchemists were interested in the possibility of generating life or reanimating the dead. Some felt that spontaneous generation was only possible with simpler creatures and sexual reproduction was needed for more complex life. Bees were 'known' to be generated from the rotting carcasses of bulls; mice could be spontaneously generated from mud. Some went further and thought that plants and small animals could not only be resurrected but brought back to life in a new and improved form. For example, a tree would be burned to ashes, mixed with an oil specially extracted from the same species of tree, and the mixture left to putrefy. The resulting mess would be buried in fertile earth and in time a tree of the same species would grow but would be 'more powerful and noble' than before. A similar recipe could be used to produce enhanced birds and small animals. Still others had recipes for growing a human inside a human-shaped cast gently heated over a fire.

Paracelsus was writing at a time when the details of sexual reproduction were little understood. Though it was evident that a male and a female were necessary, the respective roles of the genders were anything but clear. Many believed that male sperm contained a complete human in miniature form ready to grow to a full-sized adult. Some even claimed they had seen the tiny creatures within the sperm with the aid of microscopes. The female contribution was to provide an environment and nutrition to allow the mini-human to grow. Taking sperm and providing an alternative growing environment was simply taking current accepted ideas and extending them to their next logical step.

Knowledge of reproduction had progressed little by the time Erasmus Darwin published his theories on the subject more than 200 years later, after Paracelsus wrote about his homunculus. Darwin accepted the idea of spontaneous generation of simple living organisms, such as mould and microscopic animalcules, without question and cited several examples in his notes in *The Temple of Nature*. Another previously mentioned work, *Zoonomia*, discusses human reproduction and the role of both men and women. Darwin adhered to the theory that sperm contained all the potential for a complete human but that a woman was necessary for its development into a baby. Both Mary and Percy Shelley were hugely influenced by Darwin.

Paracelsus was an excellent choice of inspiration for a fictional character who sets out on independent research to answer big questions, such as the nature of life. Paracelsus taught others to question accepted teaching for its own sake and to learn from observation and experimentation – exactly what Mary had Victor do when he later went to university. Though Paracelsus did much to overthrow the medical theories of his time, the system and underlying explanations for matter and disease, and how they could be cured with medicines was fundamentally wrong and of little use to his patients. However, his passion brought many followers and imitators to his way of thinking. To be associated with Paracelsus and his world view was to be considered an outsider or anti-establishment – something that would appeal to radical Romantics such as Mary and Percy Shelley – and fitted well with the character of Victor going against the scientific orthodoxy of his age.

In eighteenth-century thinking, the works of Albertus Magnus, Agrippa and Paracelsus would have been lumped together as occult sciences. In the Age of Reason, alchemy went into drastic decline. Dark, discredited, ineffectual alchemy was contrasted with enlightened, rational, powerful science.

However, not everyone was convinced by the promise of the new scientific movement and many continued to see alchemy as a viable method for investigating the unseen and the unusual, something that the Age of Reason did not offer. Late eighteenth-century supporters of alchemy criticised the 'idolatry of reason' and what they considered to be the excesses of the Enlightenment. This is in part what led to the Romantic movement and the anti-establishment reaction against a mechanical, all-powerful, rational world. It is this conflict of philosophical views that is played out so well in *Frankenstein*.

⚲

Victor Frankenstein's real-life counterpart, Percy Shelley, had his youthful obsession with the occult sciences slowly infused with a passion for modern science through his exposure to charismatic science tutors when he was at school. When Shelley was at Syon House he was taught by Adam Walker, one of the first popular scientific lecturers. As we saw in Chapter 2, Walker's compelling lecture style sparked Shelley's lifelong passion for science and electricity.

Later, when Shelley was studying at Eton, his scientific interests would be influenced by another great figure in his life, Dr James Lind, a semi-retired medical doctor*. In Thomas Jefferson Hogg's biography, he wrote about Shelley's affection for Dr Lind 'who he never failed to mention, except in terms of the tenderest respect'. Lind was 'well known among the professors of medical science' and corresponded with the likes of Benjamin Franklin and James Watt. He had been born and educated in Scotland and spent many years as a ship's surgeon.

By the time Shelley met Lind he was a widower, had retired to Windsor and was living in a house complete with laboratory filled with telescopes, galvanic batteries and other electrical equipment, evidence of his interest in all aspects of natural

---

* Not to be confused with his famous cousin, also James Lind, who wrote a treatise on scurvy and did much to eradicate the deficiency disease from the British Navy.

philosophy. Lind was well aware of Galvani's experiments on frogs since he corresponded with Tiberio Cavallo, a London-based Italian physicist, author of a popular treatise on electricity and a great promoter of Galvani's work. He also corresponded with Joseph Banks, president of the Royal Society, who supplied Lind with frogs so that he and Cavello could carry out their own investigations into electrical phenomena in animals. His experiments were even demonstrated in front of the royal family.

Lind certainly had an influence on Shelley's work and he even mentioned him in his poem *Prince Athanase*. The poem exists only as a fragment but is related to the completed poem *Alastor*. *Prince Athanase* was written during the Shelleys' productive period at Marlow in 1817, though Shelley continued to work on the poem in later years.

Apart from the interest in electricity and the influence on Shelley, there is another link between Lind and *Frankenstein*. Lind studied under William Cullen, a Scottish physician, chemist and a principal figure in the Scottish Enlightenment, whose popularity exerted huge influence over his students. Cullen was central to the codification of techniques of revival of drowned or otherwise asphyxiated persons. These techniques would have been useful to Captain Walton when he dragged Victor's emaciated, semi-conscious body aboard his ice-bound ship, or when breathing life into Victor's newly constructed creature. Cullen's work is mentioned in a textbook known to have been ordered by Shelley in 1812.

For a long time Shelley's interest in occult and modern sciences ran in parallel, resulting in extraordinary incidents, such as when he was found by one of his schoolmasters standing on a chair, surrounded by blue sparks and trying to summon the Devil. At Field Place a local tomcat was apparently wired up to a kite that was to be flown into a thunderstorm. During his Oxford days Shelley's bookshelves contained treatises on magic and witchcraft alongside those on galvanism and electricity.

The fictional Victor also had a similar mixture of interests in the 1818 edition of *Frankenstein*. However, in the 1831 one much of Victor's early interest in sciences, both occult and modern, had been significantly edited to give a clearer progression and distinct separation of the two interests.

The result was that Victor's interest in modern science was, by comparison, rather more sudden. Mary used a single dramatic incident, a 'miraculous change of inclination' in Victor's life to produce a complete conversion from his previous obsession with the occult.

The incident in question occurred when Victor was still young. A terrific lightning storm crashed overhead and a bolt of lightning struck a tree close to his house. The spectacular sight of the shredded stump of the tree sparked a curiosity about lightning and initiated a discussion about the nature of lightning and electricity. In the 1818 edition this conversation was between Victor and his father but in the 1831 version it was a natural philosopher who happened to be visiting the house that guided Victor towards an interest in electrical phenomena. This visiting natural philosopher may well be a fictional amalgam of Walker and Lind. Mary's changes to the text emphasised Victor's isolation from his family and corrects an apparent contradiction – earlier in the text, his father is described as having no interest in science.

The incident of the obliterated tree in *Frankenstein* also has a parallel with Shelley's early life. While at Eton, Shelley had been found near his school lodgings having blown up a tree stump with a home-made gunpowder device.

Until this point in the novel, Victor had been unaware of the laws of electricity and the subject of galvanism. From then on the works of Agrippa and Paracelsus 'suddenly grew despicable'. Victor's previous interest in alchemy was immediately thrown over in favour of modern science and he turned to books about mathematics and all branches of natural philosophy. Years later, when Victor was looking back on this point in his life, he recognised this as the moment when he could have avoided the catastrophes that lay ahead. However, 'Destiny was too potent, and her immutable laws had decreed my utter and terrible destruction.'

Inspiration

'The world was to me a secret which I desired to divine.'
Mary Shelley, *Frankenstein*

By the age of 17 the fictional Victor Frankenstein was an eager student of the modern sciences but he still retained an affection and interest for the alchemical arts. It was his experiences at university, and the influence of his chemistry professors, that nudged him towards his obsessive quest for the key to life, and ultimately to his death. As the world of scientific knowledge opened up to Victor, his focus narrowed to a single point: the manufacture of a creature.

∽

Mary seemed to deliberately isolate her character. In *Frankenstein*, following his family's wishes, Victor left his home to study natural philosophy at university. Rather than study in his native Switzerland, Victor elected to travel to Bavaria and the town of Ingolstadt.

Ingolstadt was an interesting choice for Mary to send her character to study, a real university but the source of several controversies. The university was founded in 1472 but in the eighteenth century it became the centre of the Illuminati (Latin for enlightenment), a secret society that has become the focus of a number of conspiracy theories. The society was founded in 1776 by Adam Weishaupt, a professor of law at Ingolstadt University. The Order of the Illuminati was a group of free thinkers who were notably anti-religious but also interested in ideas common to the English Enlightenment, such as egalitarianism. Members of the Order included the legendary writer Johann Wolfgang von Goethe as well as aristocrats and politicians.

Conspiracy theories about the Illuminati are nothing new. In 1797 and 1798 John Robison published *Proofs of a Conspiracy* and Abbé Augustin Barruel published *Memoirs Illustrating the History of Jacobinism*, which presented the theories that the Illuminati had been behind the French Revolution. Furthermore, Barruel believed the group continued to be a powerful influence whose aims were overthrowing governments, private property and religion. Modern scholars consider these conspiracy theories to be almost entirely the imaginings of the two authors, but at the time the books became an unexpected success, running to several editions and being translated into many European languages. Percy Shelley read *History of Jacobinism* avidly and shared his enthusiasm with Mary and Claire, who also read Barruel's work when they made their first European trip with Shelley in 1814.

Among Barruel's detailed description of the inner workings of the Illuminati are the society's attitudes towards science. Burruel claimed that the Order's aim was to accumulate scientific information and to use this immense stock of knowledge to form new theories and make new discoveries. All of these are laudable ambitions, but Barruel asserted that the results of these activities would be directed towards the destruction of society and a return to a free or savage state. Knowledge was to be kept secret and only shared with those among the sect who could put it to best use and bring about the sect's aims.

The society was short lived. By 1787 the Illuminati had effectively ceased to exist after an edict was declared in 1782 banning all secret societies. The Illuminati's letters and papers were seized and published. However, many people believed the society continued for years afterwards, and some believe they are still at work today, pulling strings and influencing events behind the scenes.

When Mary's character Victor arrived at Ingolstadt in the late 1780s or early 1790s memories of the Illuminati scandal would have been very fresh. Though *Frankenstein* contains no direct references to the Illuminati, nineteenth-century readers would have understood the references to the University of Ingolstadt in connection with secret societies and dangerous revolutionary practices.

Victor's choice of subject at university, natural philosophy, was also full of controversy during the years he was studying. The late eighteenth and early nineteenth centuries were a time when arguments raged over many aspects of science and some of the most hotly debated points had a direct impact on Victor's studies and, later, his ambition to create a creature. Life processes were beginning to be interpreted in terms of electrical and chemical phenomena, but experimental results were interpreted differently and battle lines were drawn along national as well as scientific lines. For example, theories of the nature of burning were broadly divided between the British, who supported the theory of phlogiston, and the French theory of oxygen. At a time when the two countries were at war, an individual's viewpoint on the subject would be strongly influenced by their nationality.

The perception of French science was often seen through the works of the towering scientific figure of Antoine Lavoisier. His involvement in a number of aristocratic committees, particularly the very unpopular *Ferme Générale*, responsible for many forms of taxation and its collection, resulted in his tragic death at the guillotine in 1794. However, even after his death, his scientific work was still discussed and became influential across Europe, transforming the philosophy of chemistry. He has been credited as nothing less than the father of modern chemistry.

With his wife Marie-Anne acting as laboratory assistant, translator, illustrator and scribe for his experiments, Lavoisier made huge contributions to the chemical sciences, not least discovering several elements. He also promoted an improved methodology for conducting experiments, as well as proposing an alternative system of naming and classifying chemicals – a system that is still in use today.

Before Lavoisier, substances had been named because of some characteristic they possessed rather than the elements

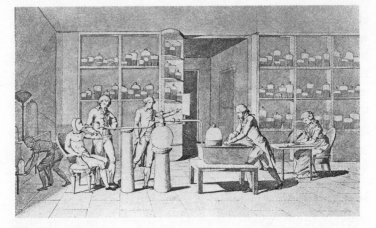

Figure 2 Lavoisier experimenting on the respiration of a man at rest, with his wife taking notes. By Édouard Grimaux, 1888. Wellcome Library, London.

they were composed of. There was no underlying system and, for the uninitiated, the names appeared almost random. Lavoisier himself summed up the situation after he had attended a series of lectures on chemistry when he was just a teenager, 'They presented me with words which they were in absolutely no condition to define for me, and which I could only acquire by the study of the whole chemistry. And so, in beginning to teach me the science, they supposed that I already knew it.'

With any developing discipline, as it becomes more established, specific words are needed to describe specific things. As more and more elements and compounds were being identified and isolated, the names of these substances proliferated. Lavoisier sought to bring order to the chaos. He proposed that the names of elements should have a Greek origin and the name should help to identify their character. Furthermore, that name should be retained as part of the name of any compound it formed with other elements. Most importantly, this would allow the participation of elements and chemical units in reactions to be followed clearly.

For example, he suggested the name hydrogen for the recently discovered inflammable gas because it was the creator ('gen') of water ('hydro'). The involvement of the element hydrogen when combined with chlorine in a solution would make hydrochloric acid. In the reaction of zinc with hydrochloric acid, the compounds formed would be named zinc chloride and hydrogen, showing that the chloride part of the reaction had swapped partners from the hydrogen to the zinc.

Zinc + **Hydro**chloric acid → Zinc chloride + **Hydrogen**
Zinc + Muriatic acid → Butter of zinc + inflammable air

In the old naming system, which had its roots in alchemy, the same reaction would be described as zinc reacting with muriatic acid and the compounds formed would be called 'butter of zinc' and 'inflammable air'. And these older names were just the ones used in Britain. Other countries would have different names for the same compounds, making communication and collaboration between natural philosophers across Europe all the more difficult.

The French naming system was very sensible, but many English scientists objected to adopting it because it carried with it a new theory of combustion. Lavoisier's oxygen theory flatly contradicted the phlogiston theory advanced by the German scientist Georg Ernst Stahl, and widely supported by British eighteenth-century natural philosophers such as Joseph Priestley and others. Priestley held fast to the theory that the mysterious substance phlogiston was the vital component in combustion even to his death.

The phlogiston theory followed the logic that materials containing more phlogiston burned more readily and released the phlogiston into the air. The mixture of nitrogen and carbon dioxide found in air after burning was therefore named 'phlogisticated air' and when Henry Cavendish, the reclusive natural philosopher, discovered the gas hydrogen, he named it 'inflammable air' and linked this substance directly with phlogiston itself.

On the face of it, the phlogiston theory made sense, but unfortunately it could not explain many experimental results. For example, some materials clearly gained mass when they burned. How was this possible when they were supposed to be losing phlogiston? Some tried to explain this away by attributing phlogiston with a negative mass, but other problems kept arising and the phlogiston theory could not be stretched to solve them all.

Lavoisier did away with these issues by proposing the oxygen theory of combustion. When substances burn they combine with oxygen. Conducting meticulous experiments in closed vessels proved that no mass was gained or lost in the process of combustion. The materials within the vessels had been transformed into new substances, the material being burned had gained oxygen, which it had taken from the air.

Lavoisier claimed the discovery of oxygen for himself, but the same substance had been discovered before by both Priestley and by the German–Swedish chemist Carl Wilhelm Scheele, who were working independently. Lavoisier's failure to acknowledge the work of Priestley or Scheele led to a certain amount of animosity between the scientists and an understandable resistance to adopting Lavoisier's new theories. Lavoisier may have been arrogant or inconsiderate but he was also right. However, his oxygen theory was not perfect*.

Lavoisier's oxygen theory of combustion still left some things unexplained, such as the heat that was generated by his chemical process. To fill the gap, Lavoisier proposed that there was a subtle fluid that was expelled from matter as it cooled and he called this fluid 'caloric'. Caloric was heat in the form of a substance, perhaps even Victor Frankenstein's 'spark', and though it explained many observed phenomena it was still not a complete theory. For many people caloric sounded a lot like phlogiston acting under a different name, and used it as the main point of attack on Lavoisier's combustion theory. Nevertheless, Lavoisier's insights into combustion were a major step forward.

---

* Lavoisier was not infallible; he named the new gas oxygen ('maker of acids') because he erroneously believed that all acids contained the new element. The acid theory may have been flawed but oxygen's name has stuck.

Phlogiston has been described as the last alchemical theory. Lavoisier, and others, had pushed chemistry firmly towards the realms of modern science even if the transition was not quite complete. With a solid, rational foundation, chemistry was now in a position to allow further insight into the nature of the world. If chemistry could be used to explain why some materials burned, perhaps it could be used to account for yet more phenomena.

When Lavoisier established that a burning candle and respiration *both* consumed oxygen to produce carbon dioxide, it led him to the hypothesis that it was slow combustion in the lungs that produced body heat*. Lavoisier's oxygen theory of combustion had taken something that was a chemical process that could be carried out in the laboratory and shown it had the potential to explain living processes, a brilliant illustration of the potential power of chemistry. If chemical processes could explain the warmth of living creatures what else could it achieve?

Though Lavoisier started a revolution in chemistry, he was building on ideas that had been around for some time. For example, the idea that oxygen, or at least some component of the air, was vital to life had been known for more than a century before Lavoisier. Robert Boyle's experiments with an air pump, carried out in the seventeenth century, had shown that animals placed in a vessel from which the air was extracted expired quickly. Something in the air kept them alive. Candle flames were also extinguished when they burned in a closed vessel. Observations on blood carried out during this time, when blood-letting was a common form of medical treatment, had shown that dark blood drawn from the veins developed a top layer of bright red blood and something in the air seemed to be the cause.

---

* We now know that the lungs are merely the means for absorbing oxygen into the blood, which transports it to individual cells where the actual respiration (the chemical combination of oxygen with glucose that produces energy) takes place.

Boyle's contemporary, the physician John Mayow, was the first to combine these observations into a coherent theory of respiration. He proposed that particles in the air were absorbed by the body that turned the blood red, and the circulating blood delivered the particles to the muscles. The muscles then used these particles in tiny explosions that had to be replenished with more particles. It explained everything, even why people breathed harder when the exerted themselves – they needed more particles to be supplied to the muscles. Unfortunately, Mayow's work didn't gain a wide readership and many of his ideas were independently reimagined by later scientists and philosophers. It is unlikely that Lavoisier knew of Mayow's work when he published his own theories on respiration.

In 1774, when Priestley made his discovery of a new gas, he called the substance 'vital air' or 'dephlogisticated air', because of its evident importance in combustion and supporting animal life. Scheele had named the new substance 'fire air' when he independently made the discovery in 1771. Experiments had shown that animals placed in vessels containing a pure sample of the new gas survived, and even thrived, for much longer than usual. But it was Lavoisier, 150 years after Mayow, who finally named these particles, or component of the air, 'oxygen'. The 1818 edition of *Frankenstein* makes it clear that the young Victor knew all about the vital component of air.

For a long time British natural philosophers resisted Lavoisier's new naming system. Many, such as Joseph Priestley and James Keir, held on to the cherished phlogiston theory. Others objected to Lavoisier's science because he used elaborate experiments of his own design that were difficult to replicate and verify. Lavoisier's authoritarian style of describing his findings also rankled with Enlightenment scientists in Britain. He was seen as taking science away from people, making it accessible only to a rich elite. The popular feeling was that 'the Englishman's mind was practical, down to earth; the Frenchman's, speculative and abstract'.

But resistance was futile. The elegance of the new system and the power to reveal underlying connectivity was overwhelming. Lavoisier had helped to shake off chemistry's dubious alchemical past and establish it as a separate scientific discipline. When Erasmus Darwin wrote *The Temple of Nature*, published posthumously in 1803, he used the new chemical names to demonstrate his modernity.

The character of Professor Krempe, one of Victor's chemistry tutors at Ingolstadt, has a lot in common with Lavoisier; a certain contempt for the old way of doing things, an arrogance in his certainty over the power of modern science and a strong sense of self-importance. Victor describes Krempe as conceited, but he came to value his lectures as he says they contained 'a great deal of sound sense and real information' despite his repulsive manners – he might have been a British scientist describing Lavoisier.

Victor's relationship with Professor Krempe did not get off to a good start. The professor was dismissive of Victor's early studies of the alchemists and told him, 'You have burdened your memory with exploded systems, and useless names.' Victor became despondent, not because of Krempe's dismissive attitude towards alchemy, he had already reached much the same conclusion, but because the books Krempe had recommended to him failed to inspire him.

Things changed when Victor met Professor Waldman. The professor became something of a mentor to Victor. Though Waldman's main interest was chemistry (it was the branch of natural philosophy he asserted had shown the greatest improvements), he maintained an interest in all branches of natural philosophy and recommended Victor do the same. To focus solely on chemistry would be to become a mere 'petty experimentalist'. Victor took him at his word, and applied himself with the same obsessive nature that he showed for the alchemists, but his studies now became focused on the works of the modern natural philosophers. He also attended lectures and got to know 'the men of science at the university'. What started as a matter of duty for Victor, developed into an 'ardent and eager' application to the sciences.

Mary described the moment of Victor's wholehearted embrace of modern science as coming with Waldman's opening lecture to the new students. Waldman traced the history of chemistry from the time of the ancients, through the interests of the alchemists and on to modern chemistry, highlighting the importance of others that had gone before. On the subject of alchemists, Waldman told the students 'these were men to whose indefatigable zeal modern philosophers were indebted for most of the foundations of their knowledge. They had left us an easier task, to give new names and arrange in connected classification the facts with which they in a great degree had been the instruments in bringing to light.' He provides a stark contrast to Krempe's attitude.

The character of Waldman and his lectures at Ingolstadt owe a lot to the British chemist Sir Humphry Davy. Mary knew Davy personally – he was one of the visitors to the Godwin household when she was a child – and she may also have attended his lectures at the Royal Institution. Davy and his published work undoubtedly found their way into *Frankenstein* in one form or another. In addition to Professor Waldman, Davy can also be seen in the character of Victor Frankenstein. Davy's career may have helped shape Victor's scientific attitude and education as well as his progression from amateur alchemist to a highly successful scientist.

Humphry Davy was a significant figure in Enlightenment science, and much of the changes in attitudes to science and scientific pursuits at the turn of the nineteenth century can be attributed to him. He played a huge role in the popularisation of chemistry, and electrochemistry in particular. Davy also helped move science, and principally chemistry, from a gentlemanly hobby to a professional endeavour capable of revolutionising industry and society.

Davy, born in Cornwall in 1778 to a family on a modest income, had little guided education in science. He never went to university, and was essentially a self-taught scientist learning from books and his own experiments. At the age of 16 he needed to decide on a profession to support his family after his father died. He chose medicine and apprenticed himself to Mr Bingham Burlase, a surgeon and apothecary in Penzance. Some of this apprenticeship would have included learning chemical concepts, and he was clearly an apt pupil who used his knowledge to amuse himself and his sister by making home-made fireworks. However, Davy's real interest in chemistry dated from when he was 19 and read Antoine Lavoisier's *Traité Elémentaire.*

In 1798 Davy was employed by Thomas Beddoes at his recently established Pneumatic Institute. Beddoes was intrigued by the possible medical benefits of the newly discovered gases oxygen and nitrous oxide (laughing gas, or N_2O), and had opened a clinic to establish their curative powers. Davy investigated the effects of nitrous oxide by experimenting on himself, patients and friends, including an enthusiastic Samuel Taylor Coleridge, who knew plenty about euphoric sensations from his opium addiction.

Breathing in nitrous oxide gas produced extraordinary results, 'A fullness of the heart accompanied by loss of distinct sensation and voluntary power, a feeling analogous to that produced in the first stage of intoxication.' However, personal experiences differed. Some had a sense of euphoria, others a 'sense of muscular power became greater', but some suffered unpleasant affects and many struggled to articulate the sensations produced and used analogies such as rebirth. Davy carefully documented and published the results in *Researches, Chemical and Philosophical, Chiefly Concerning Nitrous Oxide and its Respiration*, published in 1800.

Beddoes had founded the Pneumatic Institute, based on radical Enlightenment principles aimed at social progression, and gathered a lot of support from fellow radicals. However noble its aims, though, the ethos ran against establishment norms at a time of political unrest and this left the Institute, Beddoes and Davy's experiments open to ridicule in the conservative press. Davy's carefully collated accounts of the results of inhaling laughing gas gave them plenty of material to mock.

Today, we know that most of the treatments investigated and applied by Davy and Beddoes with the newly discovered

Figure 3 A lecture on pneumatics at the Royal Institution, *London. Coloured etching by James Gillray, 1802. Wellcome Library, London. Wellcome Library, London.*

'airs' were of little or no benefit. The only real exception was nitrous oxide, which may have briefly alleviated pain. Davy had noted that nitrous oxide dulled the senses, and even suggested the gas may have some future use in surgery, but he didn't make the link between these effects and anaesthesia. That connection was only made 45 years later by Horace Wells who used it in his dental practice. The failure to note the gas's potential as an anaesthetic was a significant oversight by Davy and his contemporaries. However, the research Davy carried out at the Pneumatic Institute, and the results he observed, would have been of interest to any potential Victor Frankensteins who might be trying to create a creature with apparently superhuman strength and resistance to pain.

In the same year Davy published the results of his nitrous oxide experiments, news reached England of Alessandro Volta's marvellous invention, the voltaic pile. This was the first battery, and the first instrument that could produce reliable, and sustained electrical current and will be the focus of Chapter 11.

Davy was quick to see the possibilities of electricity and began experimenting with Volta's invention at Beddoes Institute. He repeated many of the experiments that Volta and Luigi Galvani had conducted, which sparked the controversy over 'animal electricity' and would be of such importance to scientific progress as well as *Frankenstein*. Yet Davy's real successes with electricity came after he left Beddoes Institute for a more prestigious post in London.

Davy's time at the Pneumatic Institute had established his credentials as an experimenter and facilitated his move to the Royal Institution of Great Britain (RI), where he was able to fully develop his interests in electricity and electrochemistry. He arrived in London in early 1801 to take up the post of assistant lecturer in chemistry. The RI had been opened only the year before with the twin aims of scientific research and education. One of its express goals was to bring science to a wider public, 'diffusing the knowledge, and facilitating the general introduction, of useful mechanical inventions and improvements; and for teaching, by courses of philosophical lectures and experiments, the application of science to the common purposes of life'.

As well as research, part of Davy's role at the RI was to give lectures open to the general public. The first series of lectures he delivered was on the theme of galvanism. Davy was an engaging speaker who won over his audience with a clear narrative, lucid explanations of the science and impressive demonstrations. His inaugural lecture was widely and positively reviewed in the press, encouraging attendance at future lectures. Notably, the audience had a wide demographic and women were conspicuous by their presence in large numbers. This was seen as an encouraging sign, though some journalists joked that the women engaged in furious scribbling during his lectures were writing love letters to the charismatic Davy, rather than taking notes on the science. One of the young women in Davy's audience was a young Mary Godwin.

The popularity of Davy's lectures at the RI caused traffic jams and led to the road outside being turned into the first one-way street in the UK. It also meant the RI established a programme of popular public lectures that continues to this day. Transcripts of Davy's lectures were published to bring the science to even more people. Davy also wrote books on science, notably *Elements of Chemical Philosophy*, which contains an introduction to the science of chemistry that almost certainly inspired the fictional Professor Waldman's address to his fresh intake of students at Ingolstadt; Mary was reading Davy's work when she was writing the sections of the book where Victor is studying at Ingolstadt.

Davy's enthusiasm and charisma undoubtedly encouraged wider participation in the sciences by members of the public, and this extended to reading about the subject, discussing it at fashionable soirées and attending lectures. What few people could do was recreate Davy's experiments or develop their own variations or improvements. The flamboyant nature, and expense of the demonstrations Davy produced, meant they were beyond the means of the majority of amateur scientists.

Though Davy promoted the possibilities of science to transform society, he was careful to frame this within established social hierarchy and condemned the French Revolution. He had left the Pneumatic Institute and the radical politics of its founder behind him but remained friends with radicals such as Godwin and Priestley. Davy's star was ascending and he made sure nothing he said in public would threaten his meteoric rise to fame and scientific glory.

Davy was very conscious to take every opportunity for personal advancement. In 1807 he was asked to deliver the Bakerian lecture at the Royal Society, the most prestigious scientific organisation in Britain. Davy wasted no time and spent an intense period in the laboratory at the RI to produce something remarkable in time for the lecture. And produce he did. He used electricity from his powerful voltaic battery to isolate an element previously unknown to science – potassium, the first metal to be isolated by the process of electrolysis. A few days later, using the same methods he isolated sodium. In the space of a few weeks, Davy had made two new additions to the list of only 37 known elements. He would add a further four elements to the list the following year. The intensity of the work, the use of electricity and the single-minded goal of making a great scientific discovery that would bring fame is reminiscent of Victor Frankenstein's ambitions when he began work on his creature.

Davy announced his discoveries at the Bakerian lecture in dramatic style. In front of a prestigious audience, he recreated his laboratory experiments. On one such occasion Davy applied electrodes to a sample of potash (potassium hydroxide, or KOH). The electricity supplied from the voltaic pile pulled apart the elements that formed potash into pure potassium metal, which formed at one of the electrodes. Drops of the molten metal then dripped from the electrode and reacted with the moisture in the air, burning with a lilac flame as they fell. It must have been spectacular to witness and Davy's impressive lecturing technique soon won over his audience to his discovery. The scientific establishment, however, was not so easily convinced. As Davy built bigger batteries and carried out more spectacular public demonstrations he was seen as moving further towards the French style of scientific investigation.

To his detractors, Davy used his personality and his rapport with the audience to give credibility to his science. The huge and powerful equipment he had built to enable his discoveries could only by paid for and built by establishments such as the RI and were beyond the means of most experimenters. His discoveries could therefore not be tested by others, which called into question their validity. However, these detractors were in the minority. To the majority, Davy was the shining light of English science and his discoveries were held up as examples of British success and triumph over the French. Davy was richly rewarded for his work: he was awarded the Copley, Rumford and Royal medals, made president of the Royal Society and given a baronetcy, the first to be given to a man of science, among many other accolades and honours.

In *Frankenstein*, Victor's rapid academic rise during his time at university is impressive. Though he is shown to have applied himself to his studies with real earnestness and dedication, Mary clearly gave her character an aptitude for chemistry. He was soon the star student, and even made valuable novel contributions to the discipline. In fact, Mary made Victor such a gifted student that he quickly outstripped most of those around him and soon had little to learn from his academic mentors. Having surpassed his fellow students, and many of his professors, Victor was thus at a loss as to what to do next. There seemed no point in staying at Ingolstadt since there was little left at the university for him intellectually.

Although chemistry had been the main focus of his studies, as professor Waldman recommended, he had maintained an interest in other areas of natural philosophy and developed a particular interest in the human sciences. After a period of searching for something to occupy his mind, and debating on where to take his studies, he branched out from chemistry to medical matters.

Lavoisier had shown the relevance of chemistry to respiration and life. Others sought chemical explanations for different processes within the body, such as digestion. The study of chemical processes that denoted life has now developed into the huge scientific field of biochemistry, as well as the many specialisms within this area of science, but was in its infancy in the eighteenth century. This meant that the transition from chemistry to medicine and human sciences would not have been as abrupt or difficult then as it might be today. Natural philosophy was at the time an all–encompassing subject with very blurred and indistinct boundaries between different disciplines and so Victor would have easily been able to transition to a new area of study: the human, its structure and what principle endues it with life.

Mary had Victor study anatomy and physiology, which would have been a standard part of university learning, but, crucially, he is shown to branch out on his own. The character's earlier interest in alchemy and the alchemical notion that life came from death allowed a natural progression to independent research into the nature of decay, 'To examine the causes of life, we must first have recourse to death.' Victor went to graveyards, spent nights in crypts and charnel houses watching the minutiae of decomposition, 'I beheld the corruption of death succeed to the blooming cheek of life; I saw the worm inherited the wonders of the eye and brain.' From the description, it seems Victor witnessed the secret of life transfer from one body to another.

When a body decomposes there are, broadly speaking, five stages that it goes through: fresh, bloat, active decay, advanced decay and dry remains – a deceptively short list for what is a fantastically complex series of events. From Mary's descriptions of Victor's studies it is clear they would have made her character familiar with all the stages of decay. However, it is probably the active stage that was being referred to when Victor described 'death succeed to the blooming cheek of life'. This part of the decomposition process is when other animals, usually insects, become involved.

Blowflies are the first insects to be attracted to a corpse, drawn by the smell of gases and other volatile compounds produced in the initial 'fresh' stage of decay (discussed more in Chapter 8). These flies lay eggs on a corpse since it is a rich source of food for the emerging maggots. Other species will be attracted by products from the later stages of 'fresh' decay, such as rancid fats and ammoniacal compounds. Yet more fly species, such as house flies and flesh flies, colonise the body at the bloat stage. Within days, a dead body can swarm with life, writhing with activity as maggots and insects of different species compete for food.

Some insects, known as necrophagus species, will feed directly on the corpse, and included in this list are certain species of flies, ants, beetles and omnivorous insects such as wasps. This may be the origin of ideas of wasps and bees being spontaneously generated in rotting animal carcasses that were described in Chapter 5. Yet more insects and parasites are attracted to feed on the maggots and other insects that are feasting on the rotting remains. The whole seething mess of life can generate a considerable amount of heat.

Adventive species, such as some spiders and centipedes, will take advantage of this warmth and shelter created by the hive of activity, and will incorporate the rotting remains into their normal habitat.

Access to the corpse is key to insect colonisation of a body. Remains left in the open can be colonised very quickly. Bodies left indoors, such as those in the crypts that Victor would have been studying, can take a little longer for the insects to find – three or four days. The process will also be delayed by the lower temperatures typically found in crypts and underground vaults. Soil can also prevent access to the body if it is buried in the ground. A body more than 60cm (24in) under the soil may not be reached at all by egg-laying flies, in which case other decay processes dominate.

Initially, insects will gain entry into the body through wounds or orifices, followed by moist, creased areas of skin. Eyes are another easy access point, something Victor evidently noticed in his studies when he commented, 'I saw the worm inherited the wonders of the eye.'

The study of insects involved in decomposition has evolved into an important academic discipline and the examination of insects found on a corpse can give vital forensic clues to the time since death, as well as the history of the corpse since death. For example, if a body has been moved from inside to outside; if it has been buried; and likely locations of burial – all based on the species identified at the site, their stage of growth, or even how many generations have been produced.

In the eighteenth century it would not necessarily be appreciated that some insects had first laid eggs on a corpse and those eggs later appeared as maggots. The sudden and dramatic emergence of life from death, an abundance of life appearing within days, must have been astonishing to anyone well versed in the concept of spontaneous generation – as Victor Frankenstein would have been as a character created in the Enlightenment age.

As we have seen, Mary and Percy Shelley would have been well acquainted with the ideas of spontaneous generation of insects through reading either Aristotle's account or the discussion of it in Erasmus Darwin's work. Yet Mary's character Victor had apparently studied the whole transformation of death into life in more detail than anyone before him, because somewhere in the squirming, putrid mass of death and life he found the clue to life itself.

In one brilliant eureka moment, Victor knew the vital component, process, or spark that imbued all living creatures. 'I succeeded in discovering the cause of generation and life; nay, more, I became myself capable of bestowing animation upon lifeless matter.' He had found the thing that makes the difference between life and death, 'a light so brilliant and wondrous, yet so simple, that while I became dizzy with the immensity of the prospect which it illustrated, I was surprised that among so many men of genius who had directed their enquiries towards the same science, that I alone should be reserved to discover so astonishing a secret.' Despite two centuries of scientific effort since then, scientists still debate about what life itself might be.

Victor goes on to state, 'When I found so astonishing a power placed within my hands, I hesitated a long time concerning the manner in which I should employ it.' 'Astonishing a power' is something of an understatement.

It was at this point in the novel that Victor sat back to contemplate the enormity of his discovery. You might expect such a momentous finding to be shouted from the rooftops, but Victor kept his knowledge to himself. After ruminating on what to do with this knowledge, he decided to put it to practical use. Theory is one thing but Victor had to prove his theory to be true – an important part of the scientific method and philosophy of science. But not to share the enormous potential of such a fantastic discovery, even at an early stage, seems selfish and was wholly against the principles held so dear by Enlightenment scientists. Many, such as Joseph Priestley, stressed the importance of sharing ideas and incomplete experiments so that others might contribute to further understanding. By not disseminating his knowledge, and choosing to work alone, Victor Frankenstein demonstrated none of the collaborative ethos of Enlightenment science.

Victor had acquired incredibly powerful knowledge and was initially daunted at the prospect of being able to bestow life, up until then something only the Creator had been able to do. The desire to use his newly acquired power was too great and overwhelmed any calm analysis of the implications of what he was about to do. Victor barely paused to take breath. Swept up in the excitement, and giving scant consideration to the potential consequences, Victor decided to build a human-like creature. Full of grand thoughts of eliminating human disease and, perhaps, even the ability to resurrect the dead, he dismissed the idea of starting with something smaller and simpler. Even though he knew it would be immensely difficult, his first project would be to make a being like himself. Victor would create nothing short of a new species that he expected to love and worship him as its creator.

The complexity of the task and the difficulties ahead did little to dim his enthusiasm or rein in his ambition. He saw only the most positive outcomes, Victor pushed aside any doubts he may have had and embarked on his project.

CHAPTER SEVEN

Collection

'I collected bones from charnel-houses; and disturbed, with profane fingers, the tremendous secrets of the human frame.'
Mary Shelley, *Frankenstein*

Having decided to take the momentous step to build a creature, Mary allowed Victor to pause for only a brief moment to reflect on the difficulties ahead. He fully expected any number of problems and setbacks but he was undaunted and confident in his abilities to succeed. The first problem Victor would have faced was to obtain the raw materials for his work. Today, this would present enormous difficulties but at the end of the eighteenth century things were very different and there were a number of ways of collecting body parts. Mary lists Victor's sources as anatomy rooms, charnel houses and crypts.

The study of anatomy had seen a huge rise in popularity in the eighteenth century, resulting in the proliferation of anatomy schools in major cities across Europe. Until the sixteenth century, however, knowledge of how the body worked came from ancient texts. The accepted authority on anatomy was Galen, a second-century Greek natural philosopher living in the Roman Empire whose first-hand knowledge of human anatomy came from his time working as a physician to gladiators, whereby he would have been able to glimpse the inner working of the body through the wounds they sustained in combat. Only five gladiators died during his four-year post, a testament to his skills as a physician, but this also meant there were few opportunities for human dissection. Even with more subject matter, though, Galen would have been reluctant to dissect humans because it was considered taboo by the Romans.

Instead, Galen made do by dissecting hundreds of animals, from apes to pigs, and anything else he could get his hands on. He used his findings to develop theories, on not only the anatomy of the human body, but how it functioned and, crucially, how it didn't function when humans became ill. His successes allowed his career to progress to physician to several Roman emperors and his written work on human anatomy and pharmacology became the standard texts for 1,300 years, although notions about the human body and how it worked were lost for centuries after the fall of the Roman Empire. When they were rediscovered, his work acquired an authority that no one would challenge, even though Europeans were now more willing to dissect human cadavers.

The first major blow to Galen's dominance in medical theory came from Andreas Vesalius, professor of surgery and anatomy at the University of Padua from 1537. Vesalius taught mainly through dissection and encouraged his students to carry out their own dissections. His detailed explorations of the human body revealed errors in Galen's work and Vesalius began to suspect Galen had never actually dissected a human. Galen's kidneys looked more like those of a pig and the brain was that of a cow or a goat. In total, Vesalius found no fewer than 200 pieces of animal anatomy in Galen's human.

Vesalius set out to correct the errors. He employed skilled illustrators and craftsmen to immortalise his dissections in beautiful illustrations that were compiled into one of the most influential books on human anatomy, *De Humani Corporis Fabrica Libri Septum* (*On the Fabric of the Human Body*), published in 1543. It was a veritable Ordnance Survey of the human form and brought Vesalius international fame and glory, as well as a steady supply of cadavers courtesy of a judge at Padua's criminal court.

Galen's theories were by no means banished overnight. William Harvey, the seventeenth-century physician and anatomist, still experienced hostility when he challenged Galen's accepted theories of the function of the heart and blood in 1628. In a series of elegant experiments and clear descriptions in *Exercitatio Anatomica de Motu Cordis et Sanguinis in Animalibus*

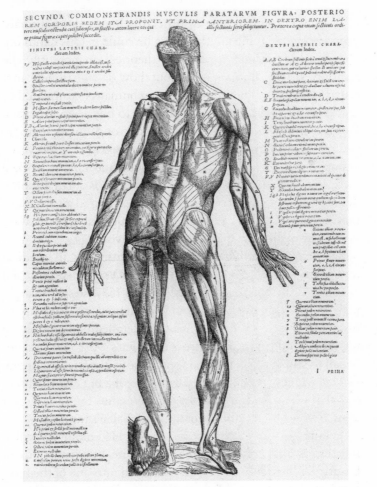

Figure 4 From Andreae Vesalii Suorum de humani corporis fabrica librorum epitome. *Woodcut by Jan Stephan van Calcar. Wellcome Library, London.*

(*An anatomical Essay Concering the Movement of the Heart and Blood in Animals*) Harvey showed that the heart was merely a pump with two distinct halves that circulated blood around the body. Galen's theory had blood being generated continuously in the liver and consumed by the organs of the body. The blood crossed from one side of the heart to the other through tiny holes or pores. The fact that no one had ever seen these pores was seen as a failing of the anatomists who searched for them, rather than of Galen's theory. Many of Harvey's critics did not even attempt to challenge Harvey's science; the fact that he had questioned Galen was enough to condemn him.

But attitudes were changing, and it became clear that the best way to understand human anatomy was from direct experience of dissection. Harvey was working in a very different environment to Vesalius. The number of cadavers available to anatomists in England in the seventeenth century was just six per year, and these were murderers executed at the gallows, although things were slightly different in Oxford, where Harvey was based for a time*. The university anatomists were entitled to dissect the bodies of any criminal executed within 21 miles of the university. Even so, Harvey's quest for knowledge and lack of human material led him to dissect his own sister and father when they died. Surprisingly, Harvey did not like the idea of having his own body dissected after his death and requested his corpse be wrapped in lead to protect it from other anatomists.

Vesalius may have been at the start of a shift in attitude towards modern theories, but the coming centuries saw broader, and more fundamental changes to the understanding of how the body and the universe worked. *De Humani Corporis Fabrica* was one of the first steps towards a mechanistic view of the body and Harvey's *De Motu Cordis* was a further step towards humans being described as machines.

Harvey was a contemporary of Descartes and Hobbes, both of whom saw the universe and everything in it in very mechanistic terms. Celestial bodies moved around in space like the workings of a clock and the body was increasingly being viewed as nothing but an 'earthen machine' of organic pumps and levers. It was a monumental shift in scientific attitude without which novels like *Frankenstein* could never have been created.

---

* In the seventeenth century the University of Oxford was allowed to make some of its own laws, both civil and criminal.

Dissection, rather than studying ancient texts, was thus increasingly seen as the preferred method for learning anatomy. By the eighteenth century the combined factors of a growing interest in human anatomy and demands for good doctors swelled the number of anatomy students. Physicians and surgeons were required to pass examinations in human anatomy and in order to do so, students paid for lectures from surgeons attached to hospitals or at private anatomy schools. More and more anatomy schools opened, but in the first half of the eighteenth century the only corpses legally available for dissection were the six handed over from the gallows every year.

In 1752 Parliament passed the Murder Act to allow the bodies of all murderers to be made available for anatomising, 'in no case whatsoever the Body of any Murderer shall be suffered to be buried'. In a time when crimes as varied as theft and murder had the same punishment – hanging until dead – some felt there should be a greater punishment for the greater crime of murder. Hanging until dead followed by public dissection was quite literally considered a fate worse than death.

The situation in the eighteenth century was beautifully illustrated by William Hogarth in his satirical cartoon *The Reward of Cruelty* (the last in the series, *The Four Stages of Cruelty*). The illustration shows Tom Nero in a courtroom, having been tried for robbery and murder, and hanged. His body is cut down and anatomised in front of the court. In a dual role, the judge is also the anatomy professor, pointing out interesting parts of Tom Nero's innards to the crowd (who represent both lawyers and the public, as well as anatomy students), as his assistants carry out the more unpleasant and riskier task of the actual dissection. Each organ is removed from the body, the bones are boiled and the dog in the foreground gets the heart. In the background a figure points to a skeleton showing the ultimate fate of Tom Nero's body, displayed for examination by anatomy students.

The burgeoning industry of private anatomy schools was needed to meet the needs of increasing numbers of medical students. This brought with it a greater demand for materials for dissection, especially when some schools promoted themselves by offering anatomy taught in the 'French manner',

Figure 5 The Fourth Stage of Cruelty: The Reward of Cruelty *by William Hogarth, 1751.*

a discreet way of saying that every student got a corpse. Demand for fresh corpses soon outstripped supply and dead bodies acquired monetary value. Over the course of the eighteenth century a lucrative trade developed in selling dead bodies. Anatomists would barter with hangmen and even offered money to convicted criminals as they awaited execution. Some criminals managed to sell their soon-to-be dead bodies several times over. Undignified scenes of people trying to snatch corpses from the scaffold occurred, but still it wasn't enough.

This was the era of bodysnatchers, resurrectionists or the 'sack-'em-up men'. Groups of men would enter graveyards, dig up the recently interred and sell the cadavers to anatomy schools at fantastic prices. It was a lucrative career; open to anyone willing to get their hands dirty. Such was the demand, some anatomy schools in Edinburgh even accepted payment for tuition in corpses rather than cash.

The practice of bodysnatching was an almost exclusively British problem; the horror of the resurrectionists was virtually unknown in continental Europe. That's not to say that anatomy was less popular abroad. Laws varied from region to region, but whatever form they took, they generally allowed for more bodies to be legally available for dissection. In Germany, for example, where the character of Victor Frankenstein studied anatomy, the law allowed for the body of anyone who died in prison, and those of suicides, to be available for dissection, unless friends or family were willing to pay a fee to the anatomy schools to have the body returned to them for burial. In addition, anyone who died leaving inadequate finances for their burial, or the poor who had been supported at public cost, could also be dissected. There would have been no shortage of material for Victor to choose from in German dissection rooms.

For British anatomy professors it was much more difficult, and the morally and legally dubious practice of grave robbing meant they were understandably reluctant to talk about how they obtained their materials. As a Mr Guthrie pointed out, 'A surgeon might be punished in one court for want of skill, and in another court the same individual might also be punished for trying to obtain that skill.' It was all very different on the Continent, especially in Italy where anatomists were at the forefront of anatomical knowledge. In Bologna, for example, there was an annual public dissection carried out during the carnival period, which was a festive event attended by students, local authorities and the general public. Luigi Galvani, who we will meet in Chapter 11, had the honour of conducting the dissections at these popular events on several occasions.

In Britain, by contrast, anatomy was often taught on small, private premises that tried to attract the minimum of attention from the general public, who were understandably very hostile to the practice of grave robbing. Much of the detail of what we know about the 'sack-'em-up men' comes from a diary kept by the resurrectionist James Blake Bailey between 1811–12. In addition to noting down how many bodies were obtained and from where, the prices they fetched, and rivalries with other gangs, there was also a lunar calendar written out at the back, so the gang could avoid the full moon and work on the darkest nights.

The general population may have been disgusted and outraged at the practice, but as we have seen it was extremely lucrative, and the gangs became highly skilled in their art. A resurrectionist could earn five to 10 times the average wage of a manual labourer at that time and they had summers off. In London in 1826 it is estimated that 600 bodies were dissected. By 1828 there were estimated to be only 10 full-time resurrectionists but around 200 part-timers working in London. When bodies were in short supply, resurrectionists moved beyond the cities to raid more rural graveyards and even imported bodies from Ireland.

The gangs would go out in the dead of night to scout for fresh graves. Often, they had an arrangement with the warden in a churchyard who would conveniently turn a blind eye, or even collude with gangs to tip the wink when a new burial had taken place. The gang would dig out the soil from the top third of the grave down to the coffin lid using wooden shovels to avoid noisy chinks if the blade hit a stone in the process. Using the weight of the soil on the bottom two-thirds of the grave as a counterbalance, they would then pull back the coffin lid until the thin wood snapped, having covered the lid with blankets to muffle the noise. One of the members would then climb down into the grave to inspect the corpse. Sometimes the bodies were too decayed or diseased to be of any use, but fresh occupants had a rope put under the arms so they could be hoisted out of the coffin. The body was then stripped and any clothes returned to the grave. Taking the clothes would be theft, but taking the body itself was not, since technically it was not real property. Finally, the lid and soil were replaced and carefully smoothed over.

Fearful of grave robbers, many relatives put markers or mementoes on the grave so they would notice any disturbances. However, the resurrectionists were well aware of the practice and carefully noted the position of any such markers and, equally carefully, replaced them after they were finished. Those that could afford it went to greater lengths to protect their loved ones. The rich invested in triple coffins and heavy 'dead' locks to make it more difficult to reach the body. More elaborate defences were also contrived: pistols were buried just beneath the surface with trip wires that would shoot any potential grave robbers, and in Glasgow and Edinburgh you can still find cages over graves. These haven't been built to keep zombies or vampires in – they were put in place to keep the resurrectionists out. These and other more effective deterrents cost money and consequently it was mostly the poor who ended up on the dissecting room table.

Choosing their targets carefully, a practiced gang of six or seven men could remove a corpse from a grave in 15 minutes and could acquire 10 corpses in a night. The bodies would then have any teeth removed to be sold to dentists, who used them to make sets of false teeth. Consequently, the teeth were almost as valuable as the rest of the corpse. More money could be obtained by selling the body fat, which was sometimes prescribed as a remedy for wounds and disease as well as being used to make candles and soap. The body was then placed in a sack and taken to an anatomy school. These clandestine operations carried out in the middle of the night sometimes resulted in mistakes. Crates containing corpses shipped from Ireland would not have been marked, or given false labels to avoid detection. One anatomy school opened its door to find a crate containing 'a very fine ham, a large cheese, a basket of eggs, and a huge ball of yarn'.

Digging up the corpse may not have been illegal but being found in possession of one knowing it to have been disinterred *was*. This put both resurrectionists and anatomists in a legally, as well as morally, dubious position.

Many anatomy schools had carefully negotiated arrangements with specific gangs. They relied on them to maintain a supply of fresh bodies, paid well for what they received, asked no questions, and financially supported any individuals who fell foul of the law. By 1826 the body of an adult could fetch the handsome price of £10*, interesting

---

* More than £800 in today's money.

medical cases commanded a premium and children, referred to as 'smalls', were sold by the inch.

Things took an even more sinister turn in 1828 when two men sold a body to Dr Robert Knox's anatomy school in Edinburgh. As usual, no one asked any questions, but when the body showed no signs of having been buried, perhaps someone should have been a little concerned. Regardless, the pair, named William Burke and William Hare, were handed their money, £7.10s – nearly £700 in today's money, a staggering sum from the pair's point of view.

Hare ran a boarding house with his wife. When one of their tenants had died before paying the rent, Hare, and his friend Burke, decided to sell the body to cover the debt. They opted to take the corpse to Dr Monro's anatomy school, but had to stop a student to ask directions. The student instead directed them to Dr Robert Knox's school, where he was studying.

The pair hadn't realised how easy it was to sell a corpse and the fantastic sums they commanded. When another lodger became ill, Burke and Hare administered whisky until he fell unconscious and then smothered him. This time they received £10 for the body.

Over the next 10 months Burke and Hare killed 15 more people, 12 women, two handicapped youths and an old man, and sold their bodies to Knox's anatomy school. Knox had agreed a contract with the pair – £10 a body in winter and £8 in summer*. Burke and Hare would lure their victims, usually poor, with promises of drink and hospitality, only to suffocate them when they fell unconscious.

No questions were ever asked at Knox's school, even when the corpses were delivered still warm. However, it may have unnerved a few students when they recognised one of the corpses they were given to dissect – one victim, Mary Patterson, was well known on the streets of Edinburgh. Knox

---

* Around £900 and £700 today.

decided to keep the young pretty body preserved in alcohol for three months before she was dissected.

Suspicions began to arise when 18-year-old 'Daft Jamie', a popular figure on the Edinburgh streets, disappeared. Jamie was mentally disabled, and he was described as 'entirely simple and inoffensive'. Though physically large he refused to fight even when taunted, for 'it was only bad boys who fought'. Burke and Hare lured Jamie to Hare's lodgings where they plied him with drink until he fell asleep. Jamie was roused by Burke's attempts to suffocate him and fought back. It took the strength of both Burke and Hare to subdue then eventually kill Jamie and both were left battered and bruised by the encounter. It seems too incredible that those who anatomised Jamie's body didn't notice any signs of the struggle, and yet, still no one challenged Burke or Hare.

The pair were eventually brought to justice after a body was discovered in Hare's boarding house by one of the other lodgers. Even though the alarm had been raised, Burke and Hare had quickly moved the body to the anatomy school. By the time the authorities arrived at the anatomy school there was no evidence left, since the body had been swiftly anatomised. Regardless, the pair were arrested.

Hare turned King's evidence and testified against Burke so that he would be released without charge after the trial. Burke was found guilty of murder and hanged in front of a huge crowd that screamed 'Burke him' – his crimes were now so notorious that Burke's name had become a byword for strangulation or suffocation.

Burke's body, in accordance with the law, was anatomised, just like his victims, but this time there was a much bigger audience. Indeed, there was a near riot when people tried to gain admittance to the anatomy theatre and the following day 25,000 people filed past Burke's displayed body. Finally, his skeleton was preserved and articulated to form part of the anatomical collection at Edinburgh's Medical School, along with sections of his skin that were tanned and turned into wallets. They are still there.

After the trial, Hare had to flee Scotland in fear of his life – anger against him was so intense that he changed his name in an effort to hide. The only person who apparently came under no legal scrutiny was Knox, who didn't even appear as a witness at the trial let alone be accused of any crime. Knox himself was surprised at the public hostility towards him and eventually moved to New Zealand where his association with Burke and Hare was unknown.

The Burke and Hare case was a sensation at the time and galvanised debate in Parliament about regulating access to bodies for dissection and improving what everyone agreed was an appalling situation. Sadly, though, it was not the last case of murdering for dissection. Several cases of 'Burkers' in London may not have had the same notoriety as the Burke and Hare case, but they contributed to the general clamour that 'something should be done'. The proximity of the London cases to Parliament may have been the final prompt that led to the passing of the 1832 Anatomy Act, which made any unclaimed bodies from workhouses available for dissections. This brought an end to the resurrectionist gangs but it was still the poorest in the community who ended up on the dissecting table.

The Burke and Hare case lives on in popular culture even today. Though the murders occurred after Mary's publication of *Frankenstein* in 1818, it would have been very firmly in the public consciousness when the 1831 edition appeared. The taint of resurrectionists, and murderers such as Burke and Hare, meant that anything connected with anatomy schools and dissection would have been considered by the majority as suspicious and abhorrent. Any hints at these kinds of practices would have induced a real and tangible fear in Mary's British readers.

Among the many anatomists who came to prominence in the eighteenth and early nineteenth centuries, a few stand out as possible influences on *Frankenstein*, quite apart from their association with grave robbing. The first we shall look at is John Hunter, perhaps the most famous anatomist and surgeon of the period, and a possible model for Victor Frankenstein.

Hunter was particularly tenacious in his acquisition of interesting specimens for his dissecting table. He had himself taken part in grave robbing in his early days as an anatomy assistant to his brother William, another eminent surgeon and professor of anatomy. However, when John Hunter opened his own private anatomy school, in what is now London's West End, he managed the supply of corpses through resurrectionist gangs.

His most famous acquisition, which went on to take pride of place in Hunter's anatomical specimen collection, was the skeleton of Charles Byrne. Byrne was also known as the 'Irish Giant' and had come to London from his native Ireland in the 1780s to seek his fortune. Byrne had decided to exhibit himself as a freak, a horrible idea by today's standards, but at the time he could profit from his exceptional height by charging people for the privilege of looking at him. Contemporary accounts claim he was between 8ft 2in and 8ft 4in (2.5–2.6m) tall, a similar height to Frankenstein's creature.

Byrne was soon making money from London's curious public, but he turned to drink and rumours started to circulate that he was unwell. Hunter heard these rumours and kept careful watch on Byrne in case he should take a turn for the worse. Byrne knew he was of interest to anatomists and had a terrible fear of being dissected after his death. He wanted to be buried at sea so that no resurrectionist gang could get hold of his corpse and he begged his friends to protect his body if he died. Unfortunately for Byrne, things did not work out that way.

Byrne died in 1783 when he was only 22 years old. A group of men were paid to guard his coffin before the burial, but the guards were bribed and the body ended up in Hunter's dissecting rooms. It is rumoured he paid £130 for the cadaver*, an exceptional price at the time. Hunter reduced the body to a skeleton as quickly and as secretively as he could. Discretion was important, as being found with the body of such a well-known figure as the Irish Giant would have been a direct acknowledgement of consorting with grave robbers, and would not have done Hunter's reputation

---

* More than £16,000 purchasing power today.

any good. Everyone knew that was how he obtained his vast collection, but it was quite a risky thing to openly acknowledge it. Despite this, Hunter was enormously proud of his acquisition and when his portrait was painted by Sir Joshua Reynolds in 1786, Byrne's skeletal feet can be clearly seen in the top right corner. Not long after that Byrne's skeleton became the centrepiece for Hunter's collection, which was available for public viewing from 1787. Charles Byrne's remains are still on display in the Hunterian Museum at London's Royal College of Surgeons.

Analysis of the skeleton suggests that Byrne was a mere 7ft 7in (2.3m) tall rather than the more than 8ft (2.4m) that he claimed, but still impressive. Analysis of the bones and DNA indicate the cause of his great height (Byrne's parents were of average height) was due to a tumour of the pituitary gland, a condition that will be discussed more in Chapter 12.

There are many other similarities between John Hunter and the character of Victor Frankenstein. Both worked with a frightening intensity and were dedicated to detailed yet broad studies in anatomy and physiology. Hunter spent long, intense hours teaching, dissecting, treating patients and dictating his findings to dedicated but long-suffering assistants.

Hunter is said to have dissected a thousand bodies during his career and didn't restrict himself to humans, either; he dissected any animal he could, from whales to insects*. He also maintained a large collection of live animal specimens at his home in Earls Court, which included an unchained lion, buffalos and a wolf. The exotic creatures that could be found in the grounds of his home led to his being the inspiration for Hugh Lofting's Dr Dolittle character.

Hunter also carried out experiments in resuscitation by attempting to revive fish and other animals after they had been frozen. He was able to extend the knowledge he gained from animal experiments to propose suitable methods for resuscitating humans. In the case of a drowning, Hunter

---

* Hunter's descriptions of whales are said to have inspired Herman Melville's *Moby Dick*.

recommended using bellows to artificially respirate the victim, warming the limbs and using electric shocks, delivered from a Leyden jar, to restart the heart.

Hunter was even given the opportunity to personally test his theories of resuscitation on a human subject. In London, in 1777, Reverend William Dodd was convicted of forgery and sentenced to hang for his crimes. Dodd was a popular figure and there was a huge public campaign for his pardon. All attempts to save Dodd from the scaffold were, however, unsuccessful so John Hunter assembled a team to attempt to revive him after the hanging. Once Dodd's body had been cut down from the scaffold, it was taken to a room on Goodge Street, London, which we know that Hunter had prepared with a warm fire, medicines and a pair of bellows. There is no record of the exact methods Hunter and his team used to try and revive Dodd, but they were all unsuccessful. There had been a long delay before the body arrived at Goodge Street meaning they had little hope no matter what methods they tried.

The attempts to resuscitate Dodd were not as hare-brained as they may appear. Others had famously appeared to be resurrected after being hanged at the gallows. The first recorded case is from 1587 when a man sprang up from the dissecting table just as the knife began to cut into his chest, but unfortunately he died three days later. In 1740, William Duell woke up on the dissecting table and survived. As a result of his miraculous recovery he had his sentence commuted to transportation. However, the most famous example of sudden reanimation occurred in 1650 in Oxford after Anne Greene was sentenced to be hanged for murder.

The case was a tragic one: Greene was a servant to Sir Thomas Reade and was seduced by his grandson. Four months later, Greene was overcome by pain and, to her great surprise, she gave birth. The child was dead and Greene, horrified and distressed, hid the tiny body in an attic in the Reade house. The body was soon discovered and Greene was brought to trial for murder.

Greene declared her innocence even as she stood on the scaffold, and protested against the licentious behaviour she had been the victim of in the Reade household. Regardless, the hangman put the noose round her neck and pushed her from the ladder. She was hanging for almost half an hour with friends and bystanders hanging on to her legs and thumping her chest. One soldier was seen to give her several blows to the chest with the butt of his rifle.

Once she had been cut down Greene was placed in a coffin, which had been sent to the gallows by local anatomists and surgeons William Petty and Thomas Willis. Willis had opened his doors to the public during his dissections and they had become popular events. When Greene's body arrived at Willis's house in its coffin, the rooms were already packed with friends and relatives, as well as those who had just come along for the spectacle. However, when the coffin was opened, Greene made a rattling sound, so a bystander quickly stamped hard on her chest and stomach until Petty and Willis arrived to take over resuscitation efforts.

The pair prised open her mouth, even though her teeth had become set, so they could force 'strong waters' down her throat. They then rubbed her hands and feet for 15 minutes, bled her, rubbed turpentine on the rope burns on her neck and gave her medications containing rhubarb, spermaceti and ground-up mummies. Eventually Greene was placed in a bed and a woman climbed in beside her to rub her gently. Incredibly, Greene survived all these further abuses and opened her eyes.

During this time, more and more people had packed into Willis's house to watch the proceedings. So, Petty and Willis had Greene moved to a smaller room so she could sleep. When she woke the next morning, she asked for beer and a few days later she was up and tucking into chicken dinners, apparently fully recovered from her ordeal.

The courts were keen to hang Greene again but Petty and Willis intervened. They explained that the baby born to Greene was dead already and was so small that it would not have survived in any case. In fact, they argued, Greene deserved compensation from the man who had brought her to this situation, not further punishment. Her survival was clearly a sign of her innocence. The doctors' protestations were successful and Greene was allowed to stay on at Willis's house for a while, earning money by charging the public to see her lying in her coffin in the room where she had been about to be dissected. When she finally moved out she is said to have taken her coffin with her 'as a Trophy of her wonderful preservation'.

Cases of survival after hanging may sound strange, but all these cases occurred during the time of short-drop hangings whereby individuals died as a result of slow strangulation as the rope crushed the windpipe. Victims would lose consciousness after three or four minutes and died after an average of 10, but it could take far longer.

Diagnosing death is surprisingly difficult, even today – when definitions of what constitutes death have been discussed and generally agreed upon – with most countries defining it as when the brain dies. In the eighteenth century, though, brain function simply couldn't be measured and so the point of death would have been defined as being when the heart stopped beating. However, the first stethoscope was not invented until 1819 and even then was not as good as modern devices. Before the nineteenth century a faint heartbeat would have been very difficult to detect.

In the eighteenth and early nineteenth centuries, criminals were usually left hanging for an hour before they were cut down, presumably to make sure there were no sudden revivals. While they hanged, friends and family would pull on the legs of their loved ones to hurry their death and shorten their suffering. Nevertheless, several criminals were believed to have expired on the anatomists table rather than at the gallows.

It wasn't until 1875 that William Marwood realised there was a better way of carrying out the grisly task of hanging. By tying the rope tightly around the neck, with the knot arranged at the point where the jaw meets the left ear, and using a longer drop, the rope tightens and breaks the neck, crushing the spinal cord. Unconsciousness is instant and brain death occurs within seconds. As Marwood said, 'They hanged 'em; I execute 'em.'

John Hunter died in 1792, before Mary Shelley was born. He was no hypocrite when it came to dissection. He was well aware that he had a heart condition that would probably kill him and specifically requested that an autopsy should be carried out on his body. He wanted his preserved heart to become the centrepiece for his anatomical collection – a request that was notably different to those of other anatomists of the time, who often went to extraordinary lengths to protect their bodies from their colleagues and rivals after death. It was, though, entirely in keeping with Hunter's ethos of learning and research.

During his great career, Hunter had sought out the bodies of his own patients after death so he could analyse the results of his earlier surgical ministrations. This may seem macabre but it provided a means of evaluating and following up the efficacy of surgical procedures – something that was rare among other surgeons who thought little more about the fate of their patients after they had completed their operations.

Hunter was very popular with his students and commanded huge respect, and it must have been emotionally devastating to dissect his body. It was Hunter's own brother-in-law who opened his chest, with students craning their necks to watch. The autopsy confirmed Hunter had been suffering from angina, but no one could bring themselves to preserve his heart, as he had requested, and it was buried with him.

Hunter's reputation as a surgeon and anatomist lived on long after his death thanks in part to the incredible collection of anatomical specimens he left behind. Hunter's collection was acquired by the Royal College of Surgeons in 1799. Only a fraction survives today, because of damage suffered during bombing raids during the Second World War, but it is still breathtaking to see the number and diversity of specimens on display in the Hunterian Museum, which are still available as teaching and research tools. For any potential Victor Frankensteins wandering among the bottles and bones, it must feel like being a kid in a sweetshop.

John Hunter also has a significant literary legacy. Apart from inspiring Dr Dolittle, and possibly *Moby Dick*, Hunter is also cited as the model for *Dr Jekyll and Mr Hyde* (published in 1886).

Hunter's house in Leicester Square was in fact two houses that were connected by the dissecting rooms in the middle. Fashionable society members would arrive through the front door facing on to Leicester Square, and dead bodies would be delivered to a smaller, more discreet entrance at the back.

How much of Hunter's life and work influenced Mary is not clear. Her father, William Godwin, probably met Hunter at least once in 1791, but he may have met him more often. Percy Bysshe Shelley might have heard stories about John Hunter and his work when he briefly considered medicine as a career. We know he attended anatomy lectures given by John Abernethy, who we met in Chapter 3 during the vitalism debate, and who was one of Hunter's devoted students. Abernethy was interested in all aspects of medicine and was known to be very proficient in chemistry. He also repeated some of Galvani's electrical experiments on frogs. Shelley's interest in a medical career was, however, very short lived and probably didn't give him much opportunity to learn about Abernethy's work from him directly.

Another of Hunter's students, Antony Carlisle, was a good friend of Godwin's and a frequent visitor to the Godwin household during Mary's childhood. Carlisle was a respected surgeon and anatomist in his own right and was made surgeon extraordinary to King George IV. In 1815 Carlisle was made professor of anatomy and appointed to the council of the College of Surgeons. One of his roles at the college, in addition to his surgical work at Westminster Hospital, was as curator of the Hunterian Museum.

When Carlisle was asked to deliver the 1804 Croonian Lecture at the Royal Society, he chose the topic of muscular motion and speculated on the cause, citing his mentor's belief in the *materia vitae* (stuff of life), and followed this with a discussion of the electrical organs of the torpedo fish. He had broad interests in science and would have been a fount of knowledge and amazing stories in the Godwin home.

Carlisle was also an early experimenter with the galvanic pile and, within weeks of reading about Volta's invention, he was conducting experiments with it that decomposed water into its constituent elements: hydrogen and oxygen. He and his colleague William Nicholson, the friend of Godwin who read Mary's physiognomy when she was a newborn, were the first to use electricity to isolate chemical elements. Their work led on to the experiments of Davy at the Royal Institution that isolated a host of new elements.

There were thus many opportunities for Mary to learn about how to obtain body parts, and she poured her knowledge into her creation of the character of Victor. But this was only the first step towards building a creature.

CHAPTER EIGHT

Preservation

'My cheek had grown pale with study, and my person had become emaciated with confinement.'

Mary Shelley, *Frankenstein*

Collecting the materials would have been the easiest part of Victor Frankenstein's project to build a creature. From this point on, the practical side of his work got significantly more difficult. One of the problems faced by any Victor Frankenstein, real or fictional, is that after death, bodies begin to decay very quickly. Mary's character, as we have seen, took a particular interest in the process of decay. Indeed, his realisation of the secret of life came from his study of decaying bodies. It was the initial processes of decomposition, the stage described as 'fresh', which would have concerned Victor when he was acquiring the materials for his creature.

Techniques for preserving human remains after death have been in existence for millennia. However, it has only been very recently that technology has become sophisticated enough to maintain a cadaver in a state suitable for future reanimation[*]. Victor would have had a constant battle to prevent the spread of decay through his acquired specimens, and the creature he made showed signs that he was not always successful.

By the late eighteenth century a huge range of techniques had already been developed for the preservation of anatomical specimens. Increasing numbers of anatomy students, and shortages of bodies to dissect, meant that preserving specimens to use as teaching aids had a real advantage. Unusual ones could be embalmed and studied at leisure rather than in the

---

[*] However, none of these bodies has yet been reanimated so we will have to wait and see how successful modern techniques really are.

hasty few days before an unpreserved body became too putrid to work on. As collections grew, comparisons could be made between individuals and healthy and diseased organs and studies could be made of comparative anatomy between species – studies that were of such importance in developing theories of evolution and adaptation.

Nevertheless, it would have been virtually impossible to keep anything Victor acquired for his monster in a suitable state for reanimation. The processes of decomposition, beginning very soon after death, are difficult to halt and almost impossible to reverse. Although eighteenth-century anatomists knew the importance of keeping specimens dust-free to prevent moulds and decay occurring, they knew nothing of germ theory and were working in conditions very far from sterile. Some degradation would have been inevitable.

When a human dies there is no more oxygen being introduced via the lungs to enable respiration and generation of energy within the cells. Without energy, cells cannot carry out even the most basic functions within the body, and any damage incurred cannot be repaired. Whatever oxygen is drawn into the body in the last breath is quickly metabolised and there is no energy available to expel the carbon dioxide that has been produced. Carbon dioxide dissolves in water to form a weak acid (carbonic acid) and the lower pH this creates within the body causes the weakening of cell membranes, which can rupture and release their contents into the surroundings.

Certain elements and molecules are held in high concentrations at specific sites within the body so they can function normally. For example, nerve cells have a high concentration of potassium inside the cell and sodium outside the cell when at rest. Molecular pumps maintain the segregation, but this requires energy. Without a supply of energy to keep molecules in their right place, diffusion takes over and chemicals will leach out of their concentrated pockets to spread into an even distribution*. Without energy for the molecular pumps to return everything to its proper place, nerves no longer function. Without a supply of oxygen, brain death occurs within six to 10 minutes and is irreversible, even with today's medical advances.

When the body is alive, enzymes are used to break down the body's own structures, an important process in recycling material within the body that has gone beyond its usefulness. An example of this is red blood cells. The cells that carry oxygen around the body are effective for approximately three months before they are broken down and components are recycled. New red blood cells are constantly being produced to maintain a healthy stock, which is why we can donate blood regularly without running out.

In a living human the enzymes involved in the processes of breaking up molecules are held in check so that they don't destroy healthy structures. After the body dies there are no such checks. Enzymes begin to digest the body from the inside out in a process called autolysis. These enzymes break up proteins and cell membranes, and the process of decay accelerates. As more and more cells rupture, their contents leak and penetrate further through the body. Eventually the gut walls will be breached and the partly digested fluids leak into the intestines.

The intestines are host to rich and diverse colonies of bacteria. Enzymes and chemicals produced by the bacteria break down compounds from their surroundings into useful units. These units are reorganised by other enzymes and tweaked into structures the bacteria needs to stay alive and replicate. The by-products of these reactions are in some cases beneficial to humans and so we have a symbiotic relationship with bacteria. For example, there are many bacteria that help us break down certain foods we would

---

* Potassium levels in the vitreous humour of the eye steadily increase post mortem and this has been suggested as a way of determining the time of death.

otherwise be unable to digest. When a human being dies, the billions of bacteria cells (the human body contains more bacteria cells than human cells) don't die with us. These colonies of microbes will continue to metabolise, grow and multiply as long as conditions are favourable.

After death, when the bacteria run out of food we have introduced into our gut from eating, they will begin to feed on us: protein is protein and the bacteria doesn't distinguish between human, animal or vegetable varieties. When the gut lining is breached, partly digested material produced by the autolysis process is introduced into the bacteria's environment. The sudden abundance of food means a rapid increase in numbers. One of the main by-products of the bacterial feast is gas. This can be expelled when alive, but in death the body enters the second stage of decomposition: bloat.

Early signs of decay could have been seen even with the simple microscopes available in Victor Frankenstein's day. The breakdown of tissues would be visible as cells ruptured, but the earliest stages of damage to small numbers of cells would have been more difficult to observe. Victor would have had to choose the freshest samples to have any hope of being able to reanimate his creature. One assumes Victor would have instantly dismissed any samples he had acquired if they had reached the bloat stage of decay.

◄ ►

If the cells, as part of a large group forming tissue or even a whole organ, are to be brought back to life, the decay process must be halted as quickly as possible before too much damage has occurred. One way of slowing down the decay process is by reducing the temperature. Despite their incredible efficiency, enzymes are extremely picky about the conditions under which they will work. The optimum working temperature is around 35°C (90°F). Much above 40°C (104°F) and the enzyme is denatured, effectively cooked, and permanently disabled. At cooler temperatures activity slows dramatically but the enzyme is not permanently damaged by cold, and activity should resume with subsequent warming.

There have been miraculous tales of individuals reviving after having been trapped under frozen lakes and streams for an hour or more. Despite the lack of oxygen to the brain, a few people have recovered from their icy ordeal because of their body being cooled rapidly, slowing metabolic processes. The successful outcomes in these cases have been used as inspiration for cooling bodies during surgery, giving surgeons vital extra time to carry out their work. However, these individuals were alive when their bodies were cooled.

Reducing temperatures further, below the freezing point of water, effectively stops any chemical reactions within the body. Water is the medium for the majority of interactions within the body and every human is approximately two-thirds water. If the water is frozen, molecules become locked in place as they cannot move around and interact with each other.

Freezing the body would solve the problem of immediate chemical decomposition but it would introduce other problems. Water expands when it freezes, so freezing the water inside individual cells causes the cell to swell and break. This is why fingers are blackened by frostbite and food doesn't have quite the same texture after it has been frozen and thawed.

Cooling and freezing of biological specimens is possible using modern techniques. Organs donated for transplants are cooled to give extra time to reach the recipient and for the surgeons to implant it. Smaller structures, such as eggs, sperm and embryos are frozen indefinitely for later use. However, in the cases of small biological structures, cell damage is avoided by the use of antifreeze agents such as glycerol. In addition, rapidly freezing the biological material using liquid nitrogen at -196°C (-321° F) prevents the water ice expanding as it forms.

Preserving larger specimens long term is much more difficult and is the subject of ongoing research. Some individuals have elected to have their heads, or even their entire bodies, frozen at the point of death, in the hope that future generations will have the knowledge and technology to revive them. The process of freezing has to be started as soon after the point of death as possible. Water in the body is replaced, via the circulatory system, with chemicals that act as antifreeze to prevent damage from ice. The body is then cooled and stored. Recent research suggests the optimum temperature for storage in order to prevent damage is -140°C (-220° F), a temperature that is not easy to maintain even with modern technology.

Victor would have been working at a time when refrigeration was practically unheard of, let alone antifreeze and cryogenics, which weren't successfully applied to human tissue until more than a century later. Though it was known that keeping perishable things cold preserved them for longer, there were very few practical means of cold storage in the late eighteenth century, and almost nothing that could be done within the confines of Victor's chosen laboratory – a small room at the top of a staircase in a rented apartment.

The anatomy schools suffered from the same problems that Victor would have faced in terms of preserving specimens. Corpses were dissected over a number of days until they became too putrid to continue with. The exact amount of time available depended on the condition of the cadaver when it arrived, as well as the season in which the dissection was being carried out. The organs most susceptible to decay were dissected first – the intestines, lungs and the brain – and then the anatomist would move on to other parts. Even so, some method of preserving tissue had to be devised to allow even this relatively short length of scrutiny. Victor Frankenstein, by comparison, was depicted working on his creature for months, even through the heat of the summer.

Mary Shelley goes into few details about the construction phase of Victor's project. We don't know exactly what the component pieces were that he was trying to stitch back together, but there are some clues in the text. On a purely practical note, he decided to give his creature a gigantic structure, knowing that the intricacies of the human body would be easier to work on if they were scaled up. The enormous height, 8ft (2.4 m), could only be achieved if Victor chanced upon a particularly tall specimen in one of the anatomy rooms or crypts he frequented. It seems more likely that he used long bones from another species and grafted muscles, nerves and connective tissues on to them. The creature was certainly a composite of several individuals and it seems from the text that Victor carefully chose each piece for its beauty. Given that the source of much of his material was the dissection room, it seems he would have been collecting relatively small items. These would also have the advantage of being easier to store.

Methods for preserving human tissue have existed for millennia in terms of embalming. Beautifully preserved bodies have been found in South America. These remarkable examples of mummification have resulted in individuals who look as though they are merely asleep even though they last took a breath more than 500 years ago. Even further back in history, the ancient Egyptians were experts in preventing decay after death, though their knowledge was lost for many centuries. Alternative methods of preservation were developed in the intervening period, though the goal of ancient embalmers was not the same as Victor Frankenstein's need to preserve biological material.

Egyptian practices of mummification were for empowering the soul after death. The ancient Egyptians therefore saw no need to preserve everything in the body. Most of the internal organs were thus removed with only the heart being returned to the body. The brain was probably allowed to liquefy so it could be drained out of the skull. Quite apart from the missing organs, however successful these techniques were for preserving other parts of the body, they significantly altered the materials themselves. Bodies were desiccated using salts, left exposed to the elements, or dried out in ovens. Such techniques would not have been appropriate for Victor's requirements.

The increase in interest in human anatomy in Europe from the time of the Renaissance brought with it a need to preserve certain specimens beyond the dissection process. After dissection, some samples would be permanently preserved to be used as teaching aids or form part of a collection of anatomical specimens and curiosities. By the eighteenth century several methods of preservation had been developed, which could be broadly categorised into five groups: drying, storing in fluid, injecting, corroding and articulating. These techniques were designed for displaying specimens to their best advantage and their effectiveness was judged based on how well they conserved the texture, colour and size of the living part.

Not all of these methods were directly applicable for someone like Victor, who merely wanted to preserve his acquired bits and pieces in as near perfect state as possible until they were reanimated. From that point of view not all of the techniques would have been useful to Victor, or he would have had to adapt them considerably to suit his needs.

The oldest available technique was drying and was used for a wide range of tissue types. The tissue in question, such as skin, blood vessels or nerves, would be stretched out on clean drying boards to allow the sample to desiccate. Sometimes blood was left in the vessels to add colour but at other times colour was painted on afterwards. Alcohol could be added to speed up the rate of evaporation. Cartilage, for example, could be dried, although this caused it to shrink. However, re-immersion in water would restore it to its original condition. Other tissue could not be restored so easily. Moreover, though it was cheap and easy to do, drying was the least satisfactory method available.

The most successful technique, storing in fluids, was developed in the seventeenth century and became the preferred method of preservation. William Croone was the first to demonstrate the process to the Royal Society and showed that puppies, soft parts and all, could be preserved in 'spirit of wine'. In 1663 Robert Boyle was the first to publish the recipe.

The method was not as simple as dunking prepared specimens in a bottle of pinot grigio and securing a lid. The concentration of alcohol was important. Too much water and the specimen spoils because mould and bacteria are still able to survive and cause damage. Higher concentrations of alcohol can distort the shape of proteins and enzymes (which is why alcohol gels are effective at killing germs) and it will halt any enzymes that might be involved in decaying the sample. However, if the alcohol concentration is too high it will damage the proteins within the sample itself, not just the bacteria. This could give the specimen a corrugated appearance. As it turned out, distilled liquor was about the right concentration*.

Even then the method was not straightforward; the specimen had to be carefully prepared. Any blood in the sample would discolour the liquid and so initially it had to be replaced at regular intervals until all the blood had seeped out and the liquid remained clear. For larger specimens, careful incisions or injections had to be made to ensure the fluid penetrated throughout the structure. When the specimen was in a stable condition, the container had to be sealed carefully to prevent the alcohol evaporating. Unfortunately the seals were rarely perfect and much time was spent by anatomists and museum curators in topping up and maintaining wet specimens.

The main drawback to preservation in spirits was the expense: both the cost of the glass vessel as well as the spirits themselves had to be taken into account. The city of Edinburgh allocated 12 gallons of whisky per year to the University of Edinburgh anatomy museum for use in the preservation of anatomical specimens. It is probable that not all of this would have made it into the specimen jars – many working in the dissecting room were known to take a tipple or two. They could hardly be blamed given the conditions they were working under, but more than one technician was

---

* Admiral Nelson's body was placed in a cask of brandy to preserve it during its return voyage to England after his death at the Battle of Trafalgar. It led to the phrase used in the Royal Navy of 'tapping the admiral', referring to when liquor was drunk directly from the cask through a straw. Lord Byron's body was also returned to England from Greece in a cask of spirits.

dismissed for being repeatedly drunk on the job. Less tempting and safer alternatives, such as methylated spirits and formaldehyde, were discovered decades after *Frankenstein* was published.

Done well, preservation in spirits is very effective. For example, the brain without any preservation has the texture of butter, making detailed dissection nearly impossible. It is not surprising that until the seventeenth century the brain was not considered the centre of thought. How could this soft, mushy organ, full of holes, be the seat of reason and rational thought? When it was realised that immersing the brain in alcohol solidified the texture and preserved its material, it allowed for more detailed study. The complexity of the organ and its potential as the hub for all nerves, and perhaps even the organ of thought, emerged as a consequence of improved methods of preservation.

Specimens prepared in alcohol during the eighteenth and nineteenth centuries are still intact today. What is left of John Hunter's collection can still be seen in the excellent Hunterian museum. The specimens have a bleached appearance, because the blood has been drained as well as due to the effects of the alcohol, but they are structurally intact.

The third category of preservation available to eighteenth-century anatomists, injections, served several purposes. A range of fluids could be introduced into specimens via blood or other vessels. Turpentine could be used and, as well as being effective at preserving tissue, it also made it transparent – an advantage for anatomy professors who could use it to reveal structures within a large specimen. In *Frankenstein*, the creature's parchment-like skin, so transparent that the workings of the muscles underneath could clearly be seen, suggests that turpentine or drying are techniques that Mary may have been aware of.

Molten, coloured wax could be injected into the vessels of the body and allowed to solidify to reveal the paths of the veins and arteries. Solutions of mercury salts were also used. These would kill any bacteria that were present and slowly infiltrate the surrounding tissue to preserve it. Mercury metal was sometimes used to stop the vessels themselves from collapsing, preserving the three-dimensional structure of the material so it could be dissected more accurately. The liquid metal had the advantages of being able to infiltrate into the narrowest vessels, highlighting the delicate structures within a specimen, and its toxicity would kill any bacteria. However, the weight of the metal increased the risk of tearing and damaging the structure, and the slightest nick to any vessel meant all the mercury would spill out.

The toxicity that kills bacteria that would normally decay the specimen would also have potentially toxic effects on the creature itself when it was brought to life. Mercury, and the salts of mercury especially, are particularly damaging to nerve cells but they can also cause problems with the kidneys. Either Victor had discovered less toxic alternatives to preserving his tissue or he had a way of repairing the damage caused after removing the mercury and before bringing his creature to life.

Corrosion was another important method used in anatomical preparations, especially for obtaining bones free from flesh, a process called maceration. Other methods were available but they all had the same aim: removing all the surrounding tissue without damaging the bones themselves. Vesalius, the sixteenth-century anatomist from the previous chapter, used lime and boiling water to remove the flesh. Others buried the bones and let the flesh rot away in the soil, or utilised insects to devour the flesh and pick the bones clean. Some simply immersed the parts in water and left them for months in sealed vessels (called macerators) until the tissue was completely destroyed. Emphasis was put on making a tight seal for these containers, to keep rats out and the stench in. In the first few weeks the water had to be changed regularly to remove the blood and skin. After this stage the parts could be left for weeks until the destruction of all the soft tissue was complete.

Care was needed to choose the optimum moment to retrieve the bones from the macerator. Pieces had to be left until all the tissue had disintegrated, but not so long that small bones or softer structures such as cartilage had been destroyed. Anatomists then had the unenviable task of sifting through the mess to retrieve all the bones. And this was by no means the end of the process. To gain access to the interior of the skull, dried peas were used to fill the internal cavity and the whole immersed in water. The peas swelled and the pressure exerted evenly on the skull separated it along the suture lines. The whole process of maceration was relatively easy, but it left the bones greasy and in need of further cleaning before they were suitable for articulating them for display. Cycles of rinsing and washing with alum water or pearl ash were needed to whiten the bones before they could be dried.

As anatomy schools proliferated so did the techniques available for preserving anatomical specimens. Anatomists and museum curators developed their own recipes or variations on established methods. The preparation and preservation of tissues and bones was intensive, laborious and skilled work carried out by experts, or the anatomists themselves, since such delicate and important work was not trusted to unskilled technicians. Techniques were learned face to face, often as part of an apprenticeship. Anatomists and museum curators from Dublin were prepared to travel to London and Edinburgh regularly to learn new techniques.

As collections and museums grew in number and size, maintaining a collection became a full-time job. In Edinburgh Frederick Knox was employed by his brother Robert Knox (the eminent anatomists we met during the Burke and Hare case – see page 132) to prepare and maintain anatomical specimens. Frederick was a qualified physician in his own right and maintained a small medical practice as well as being elected fellow of the College of Surgeons. Though Robert was the renowned professor of anatomy, the university paid Frederick more than his brother for his work. Preservation was specialist knowledge, but a number of books and papers were published outlining techniques for new students and this is perhaps where Mary's character Victor could have learned much of what he needed to know.

The skill of those working to preserve and present these specimens is beyond doubt: the delicacy and beauty of the models prepared, in such awful surroundings, during the eighteenth century can still be seen in museums today.

◆ ➤

Working conditions for Victor must have been nearly unbearable and it is no surprise that Mary glossed over the gory details. Victor's own description of the work as 'filthy' must be something of an understatement. Victor worked through the heat of the summer months. His lab was described as a simple room at the top of his lodgings, 'my workshop of filthy creation', hardly the ideal location for sophisticated and delicate anatomical work. During the drying process plenty of space was required for stretching out samples; at the university in Dublin they used the roof for lack of a better alternative. Those who worked in preserving specimens from the dissection rooms located their macerators and drying boards in rooms as far away from others as possible – some even resorting to sheds. This gave them more space in which to work but it also kept the worst of the smell away.

It wasn't only humans who noticed the smell. Several anatomists in the eighteenth century complained of problems with rats. Mary had Victor living in lodgings and it would have been difficult to keep the smell and vermin from giving away what he was up to. And this wasn't even the worst of his problems.

Working in a tiny room lit only by candles would not have been easy. It was also considerably hazardous: naked flames and alcohol vapours do not mix well. Apart from the very real risk of fire, Victor would have also had to cope with the headaches frequently complained of by those who worked in the preparation rooms.

Anatomical curators in the nineteenth century were described as prematurely aged, emaciated and plagued with fits of coughing. It wasn't just the alcohol fumes impairing their performance: the chemicals they used did direct damage to curators' health. Experienced curators warned against letting novices try out methods involving mercury salts due to their associated dangers. Mercury salts are highly toxic; elemental mercury, used to distend vessels, will vaporise and end up in the curator's lungs; and turpentine can cause lung and skin irritation. Yet even these are mild inconveniences compared with the hazards associated with the anatomical material itself.

The most serious risk to Victor's health would have been infection. The slightest slip of the knife or an open cut on the hand could very easily have introduced bacteria from a cadaver into Victor's body. In a time before antibiotics this would very likely be fatal. Several young medical students died because of a little carelessness in the dissecting room. In April 1778, Erasmus Darwin's own son, Charles – who had followed in his father's footsteps and was studying medicine in Edinburgh – cut himself when dissecting the body of a child. He fell ill from the cut almost immediately, complaining of severe headaches. The following day he was in convulsions and haemorrhaging. He died on 15 May, just days before his 20th birthday.

It is extremely unlikely that Mary ever had first-hand experience of dissection or preservation facilities, but she may have heard anecdotes from John Polidori, Byron's doctor who was staying at Villa Diodati, or William Lawrence, the Shelleys' physician from Chapter 3. This perhaps explains the paucity of detail in her description of Victor Frankenstein's work and the implausibility of carrying it out in his tiny attic room.

◆ ▶

Despite the hazards, anatomical collections grew. Anatomy professors built up huge personal collections, providing an invaluable resource for future surgeons and medical students. John Hunter, Britain's most famous surgeon and anatomist who was introduced in the previous chapter, along with his brother William, had what was probably the largest collection of specimens in Britain. Since they ran private anatomy schools, all of these specimens would have been obtained through bodysnatchers and grim negotiations at the scaffold.

The Hunterian collection in London was open to visitors from the 1780s. And even if Mary had not been to the museum as a regular visitor, she may have had access to the collection through family connections, as we heard in the previous chapter.

Mary had plenty of other opportunities to see delicate and captivating anatomical specimens for herself. The high number of anatomy schools in London meant that the number of medical collections proliferated. Collections were bought and sold, and some formed part of anatomical shows that opened their doors to anyone prepared to pay the entrance fee. The division between medical education and anatomical showmanship was far from clear cut in the eighteenth century. The audiences these displays attracted would have included surgical apprentices, fairground-goers and the nobility. Mary would not have been out of place peering into bottles and jars at the pale tissues inside. The collections themselves were hugely varied in content and did not confine themselves to purely medical, or even human, items.

Galen's work on animal dissection had shown the value of comparative anatomy even if he stretched the link between humans and animals further than perhaps he should have. John Hunter and William Lawrence both put huge emphasis on the study of animal anatomy – Hunter's collection includes specimens from lions, elephants, octopuses and much more besides. Medical curiosities or 'monsters' would also form an integral part of any anatomical collection.

Some showmen took things even further. Benjamin Rackstrow opened a museum of anatomical figures at 197 Fleet Street, London, in the middle of the eighteenth century. This comprised an odd assortment of stuffed animals, foetuses preserved in jars, an articulated skeleton of a sperm whale, as well as anatomical figures made of wax. One figure of a woman eight months pregnant showed the blood circulating through veins and arteries as well as the motion of the heart and lungs. It must have been a spectacular sight. He also had an electrical crown for his visitors to wear, from which 'a continual stream of fire would appear'. Although Rackstrow died in 1772, his museum and collection, in various forms, was still in existence in the nineteenth century.

So, although Victor would have potentially had plenty of access to information about preservation techniques, as well as the opportunity to study examples in anatomical collections, he would still have had to use all his ingenuity to adapt existing knowledge to his needs. Overcoming the many challenges of storage and preservation of the materials for his project was only the beginning of Victor's difficulties. Having separated and preserved all of the component pieces, and with perhaps a few spare, Victor would have been ready to start the next phase: assembling his creature.

CHAPTER NINE
Construction

'... *perhaps the component parts of a creature might be manufactured, brought together, and endued with vital warmth.*'
Mary Shelley, *Frankenstein*

Sourcing, preserving and storing the materials for Victor Frankenstein's creature may have been the most unpleasant task he faced, but the technical challenges did not end there. Assembling the pieces into something that could potentially function as a living being would test even today's scientists and surgeons. It is interesting that Victor does not decide to reanimate an existing, complete corpse. In fact, Mary's text shows that he doesn't know how to do this. He speculated that he may progress to reanimating the dead but the first step is to build a creature from parts, before bestowing life on it.

Mary had Victor only briefly contemplate attempting to build something smaller and simpler than a human, but her character was carried away by his enthusiasm. His energy and passion for his new project sustained him through the inevitable problems he faced during his work. Acquiring the materials had taken months, but the construction phase was even longer, stretching through the winter, spring and summer.

The practicality of stitching together tissues and organs into a functioning whole is no easy thing. The majority of surgical history has involved removing parts of the body rather than reattaching them. Nevertheless, the idea of surgical repair has a very long history. Accounts of nose-reconstruction surgery go back to 1000 BC in an Egyptian papyrus known as *Sushruta Samhita*, written by the surgeon Sushruta. The practice had originated in India at a time when cutting off the nose was a common form of punishment and many were keen to disguise their loss and hide evidence of their previous misdemeanours.

A flap of skin from the forehead or the cheek was separated from the face leaving only a small connecting thread of tissue to maintain the blood supply. The flap was then twisted and stitched in place over the missing nose. The same procedure was applied to missing earlobes.

Interest in surgical techniques and skin grafts was revived in Renaissance Europe after Arabic and Greek texts had been reintroduced through Arabic documents that were then translated into Latin. A new need for nasal-reconstruction surgery in particular appeared at this time because duels and other swordplay occasionally resulted in the loss of a nose. In 1557, Gaspare Tagliacozzi, a professor of surgery in Bologna, expanded and developed Sushruta's technique to repair defects of the nose, lip and ear, using a flap of skin from the upper arm.

Tagliacozzi is credited with writing the first book devoted to reconstructive surgery, *De Curtorum Chirurgia per Insitionem* (*On the Surgery of Mutilation by Grafting*). In it, he described how a flap of skin from the upper arm, with a small bridging piece of tissue remaining, could be attached to the wound where the nose once was. The arm had to be held in place with a scaffold-like structure until the flap of skin had grafted on to the wound. The flap, now fixed in place over the damaged feature, could only then be completely separated from the arm.

When the number of noses lost in duels increased, surgeons diversified. The noses of slaves began to be utilised and transplanted on to the gap on their masters' faces. Contemporary accounts claim these nose transplants were successful but only for the lifetime of the donor. When the slave died, his nose, now on the face of his master, would turn gangrenous and fall off. The subject became a rich source of comedy for contemporary satirists.

A century later, members of the Royal Society experimented with skin grafts in general, not just to replace lost noses. Dr Walter Charleton, who was physician to Charles I as well as a member of the Royal College of Physicians, together with Robert Hooke, made their first attempt on a dog. A piece of

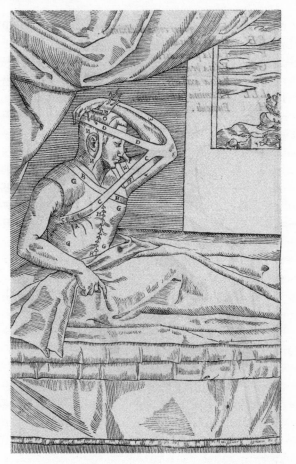

Figure 6 Gaspare Tagliacozzi, De curtorum chirurgia per insitionem, libri duo. *Gasparem Bindonum juniorem, 1597. Plastic surgery of the nose. Wellcome Library, London.*

skin was removed from one part of the animal before being transplaned to another site on the dog's body. However, the animal managed to remove the graft after it had been carefully attached to his skin. The Royal Society requested that Hooke make a second attempt and attach the graft more securely this time, but the dog had other ideas and ran away. Hooke's interest in the project disappeared with the dog.

It was during the Enlightenment period that evidence began to appear of the biggest problem faced in transplant surgery:

tissue rejection. Guiseppe Baronio, a physician from Milan
with broad scientific interests – including bone regeneration,
the treatment of rabies and electricity (he was a good friend of
Alessandro Volta) – made his most significant contributions in
the field of skin grafts. He noted that skin transfers made
between sites on the same host were mostly successful.
However, transfers from one individual to another were
generally not successful, especially if the donor and recipient
were of different species. Few people seem to have taken notice
of Baronio. His book, *Degli Innesti Animali* (*On Grafting in
Animals*), published in 1804, in which he details his skin-graft
experiments, found few followers. Attempts at skin grafts both
between individuals of the same and different species continued
and were largely, and unsurprisingly, unsuccessful.

Despite many failures, skin grafts were increasingly carried
out in the nineteenth century. In April 1817 the prominent
London surgeon Astley Cooper covered an open area on a
man's hand using part of his own skin. Further skin grafts
were made by British and French surgeons throughout the
century usually using skin from the patient's thigh. With
patches held in place with bandages or stitched on with crude
stitches, scarring must have been considerable. The modern
images of Frankenstein's monster with heavy stitching and
deep scarring may not have been so far from the reality of
piecing together such a creature.

All of these surgical procedures on the skin would have been
highly visible and therefore the progress and success of such
techniques was easy to monitor. However, surgeons were not
brave enough to carry out procedures on the internal organs, let
alone attempt to transplant organs between individuals.

The idea of transferring biological structures other than skin
between individuals also has a long history. According to the
ancient Chinese, the surgeon Tsin Yue-Jen performed the
first double heart transplant in the fourth century BC.
Presented with two soldiers, one of whom was strong in spirit
but physically weak, and the second with opposite qualities,

Tsin Yue-Jen anaesthetised the pair and exchanged their hearts to correct the imbalance in their temperaments.

Some 700 years later, in the fourth century AD, brothers Saints Cosmos and Damian are credited with the first successful limb transplant. Little is known about their lives, but the twins are thought to have been born in Arabia and were said to have been accomplished physicians. When they refused to recant their faith, even under torture, they were sentenced to death, but proved remarkably resistant to attempts to kill them. The twin brothers survived stoning, arrows, flames and were finally beheaded. After death the brothers are supposed to have reappeared to substitute the gangrenous, or possibly cancerous, leg of the custodian of a Roman basilica with the lower limb of an Ethiopian gladiator who had recently been buried in the Church of St Peter in Chains. They are therefore the patron saints of modern transplantation.

The eighteenth-century surgeon and anatomist John Hunter was also interested in transplants. When he served as an army doctor in Spain he observed lizards and became intrigued by how they could regrow their tails, which led to experiments in transplants. He transferred human teeth into the combs of cockerels and was surprised and pleased to observe that both the tooth and the cockerel appeared to flourish. From animals he moved on to transplanting teeth between human subjects, from both living and dead donors. In Hunter's book, *The Natural History of Teeth*, he wrote about the potential effectiveness of tooth transplants.

Hunter's fame and recognised expertise meant that tooth transplants became a popular but expensive way of preserving a complete set of teeth when one was lost. The results looked considerably better than the alternative of ill-fitting dentures but were not without their own problems.

Hunter recommended young women be chosen as donors, since their teeth were smaller and fit better in the gaps left by the missing tooth in another's mouth. Their young age would also mean that hopefully they had not been infected with any sexually transmitted disease, but it was no guarantee. Before an understanding of germ theory, eighteenth-century doctors and dentists saw no need for working in sterile environments; the best a recipient could hope for was that the donor tooth would be rinsed in warm water before being implanted in the jaws of the recipient. These rather inadequate precautions certainly resulted in fatalities. It must also have caused a few awkward conversations when individuals had to explain how they had acquired syphilis or similar diseases while remaining faithful to their spouses. Incredibly, the practice of teeth transplants continued into the twentieth century.

Yet Hunter didn't restrict himself to transplanting teeth. As part of a larger programme of animal experiments, he transplanted the testes of a cockerel into the abdomen of a hen and the spurs from the foot to the comb. All donors and recipients appeared to thrive but, aside from the teeth, these transplant experiments were never attempted on human subjects. Surgeons at the time were happy to amputate limbs, even when there were no effective anaesthetics available and the chance of dying from shock, blood loss or subsequent infection, was high. The skull might be trepanned (a hole drilled directly through the skull bone) to relieve pressure on the brain. Tumours might be removed from the chest, but no one even considered operating on the vital organs within. The thoracic cavity remained almost a complete no-go area for surgery until the first half of the twentieth century.

The closest surgeons came was operations on the abdomen, such as lithotomies: removing stones from the bladder. The best surgeons could complete the procedure within a few minutes, while others, less well versed in human anatomy, prodded and poked their victims for much longer. Caesarean sections were also performed but were seen as a last resort to save a child when the mother had died or where the case was considered beyond hope. Before anaesthetics, germ theory and modern surgical procedures, the mortality rate for mothers in caesarean sections was approximately 85 per cent.

One of the initial stumbling blocks faced by early potential transplant surgeons, and any Victor Frankenstein-like characters, was the very basic, practical aspect of stitching things together. With relatively simple skin grafts, the patch of skin was sutured in place and small blood vessels would form through natural growth and repair processes within the body. This was simply not possible with whole organs, as the vessels supplying blood to the organ are large and the patient would bleed to death long before the vessels grew and healed naturally. Saints Cosmos and Damian had divine intervention to aid them, but surgeons up until the nineteenth century had to make do with very simple stitches: haemorrhage and thrombosis would have been common.

Victor would have had to drain the blood from his stored specimens to prevent decomposition, and would have needed to reintroduce it at a later stage, probably the final step before animating his creature. The crude stitching techniques that would have been available to Victor in the later eighteenth century suggest his creature is likely to have sprung a few leaks when blood was infused back into the body. However, there would have been a range of methods available to Victor for stemming the flow.

Damage to small blood vessels could be stopped by cauterising with red-hot metal, a method used by early Arabic surgeons who were forbidden to cut flesh for religious reasons. In an emergency, fingers could also be plunged into the wound and the vessel compressed. Vessels could also be sealed shut with the twist of a hook and the flow of blood could be cut off by applying a tourniquet of thread wound round the affected vessel in a figure of eight. In this method, used in the Renaissance, the threads were left long so that the affected area could be easily reached when the inevitable infection and sepsis occurred.

Improvements in techniques for stitching together structures such as blood vessels had to wait until long after the publication of *Frankenstein**. The most significant development

---

* Advances were also made in connecting other structures. During the nineteenth century, a few innovative surgeons developed techniques for connecting sections of bowel by means of a button that would be passed naturally after the wound had healed.

happened, as many surgical advances do, because of a particularly violent episode in history. France in the late nineteenth century was in turmoil, with riots, bombings and social unrest. The president of France, Marie François Sadi Carnot, was still popular and toured the country despite the risks. On 24 June 1894, as he was getting into his open-topped carriage, he was stabbed in the abdomen by Italian anarchist Santo Caserio. Despite the best efforts of local doctors, they could not repair the damage to Carnot's liver and, in particular, the main vein carrying blood to the organ, which had been cut. He haemorrhaged badly and died shortly before midnight the following day.

Alexis Carrel, a young surgeon at the time of the assassination, was spurred to improve suturing techniques and decided to take lessons from an embroideress, Mme Leroudier. Using silk thread and practising on animal subjects, he developed the technique of 'triangulation', which is still in use today. He learned to separate the edges of the vessels to give a clear view of the sutures. The sutures themselves were made with fine oiled silk thread, using sharp needles and with as little suture material as possible presented to the vascular lining in order to prevent clotting. Carrel's success with connecting veins and arteries using his new triangulation technique meant that organ transplantation was now a theoretical possibility and he was awarded the Nobel Prize in 1912 for his contributions.

Carrel himself chose to look into the possibility of transplanting kidneys. There were a number of reasons for selecting this organ above others: kidneys usually have only one major vein and one artery joining it to the rest of the circulatory system, meaning it should be relatively simple to graft to a number of sites around the body. Humans have two kidneys but can live perfectly healthy lives with only one, so donation should be much easier than for other organs such as the heart. Also, the outcome of any transplant could be monitored in some detail by analysing urine output.

The first human-to-human kidney transplant was made in 1933 by Russian surgeon Yuriy Voroniy but the patient died just two days later when the organ was rejected. The first successful transplant occurred in 1950 and the patient survived a remarkable 10 months in a time before immuno-suppressant drugs. The most successful transplant of this early period was between identical twins Ronald and Richard Merrick. Richard lived a further eight years with his brother's donated kidney. Success in kidney transplants, although limited, encouraged interest in transplanting other organs.

Despite the apparent success of Tsin Yue-Jen, for a long time no one even considered operating on the heart. This was in part because for centuries, the heart has held a special elevated status in human culture. Until only recently it was the failure of this organ in particular that marked the point of death. Something so obviously central to life gave the heart an almost unique position within the minds of the populace and tampering with it in any way was thought to be a death sentence for the patient. Things changed slowly.

A few cases showed that the heart was not as vulnerable as everyone had assumed. In the sixteenth century, French surgeon Ambrose Paré told the tale of a man wounded in the heart during a duel who ran 230 yards to chase down his opponent before collapsing. Dissections of hanged criminals had revealed scarring on some hearts, evidence that it had healed from some previous injury.

As anaesthetics and antiseptics improved, surgeons became braver. In the early twentieth century, some congenital defects were being repaired and with the advent of the Second World War, surgeons were required to removed shrapnel and debris from around, and sometimes within, the heart and major vessels. However, it was only with the increased availability of antibiotics after the Second World War that heart surgery could really be tackled.

The first human heart transplant was carried out by Christiaan Barnard in South Africa in 1967. The donated heart functioned quickly in its new host and the patient's heart failure disappeared within two days. The operation was hailed as a huge success and created a media furore. Several more heart transplants were performed within days. It was a major medical advance but it was not all plain sailing from there on. The recipient of the new heart, Louis Washkansky, died just 18 days after the operation, from pneumonia. Of these early heart transplants only a handful of patients survived beyond six months.

Similar levels of success were obtained with lung transplants carried out in the 1960s, with one exception that kept the surgeons motivated to find solutions to the difficulties they faced. A 23-year-old sand blaster had received a single lung transplant in 1968. The operation was performed in Ghent, Belgium, by Fritz Derom and the patient survived a remarkable 10 months before succumbing to pneumonia. Surprisingly, an autopsy revealed relatively little damage to the donated organ.

One of the additional problems of lung transplantation, as well as for replacement sections of bowel, is that they are constantly exposed to the external environment, unlike truly internal organs such as the heart. Although they are located within the torso, breathing and eating continuously introduces pathogens to the new organs.

Significant progress has been made in organ transplantation since the procedures carried out in the mid-twentieth century. By 1990, 785 heart and lung transplants had been carried out with a one-year survival rate of 60 per cent. Today, lungs, livers and sections of bowel are transplanted comparatively regularly. Livers are particularly useful in transplants because the whole organ is not needed. The liver grows and repairs itself extremely rapidly, perhaps something the ancient Greeks were aware of when they wrote of Prometheus's liver being repeatedly eaten and regenerating. This means liver donations can now be taken from living donors and one cadaveric liver can be given to two recipients.

Every month seems to mark another milestone in transplant surgery. Recently successful face, hand and womb transplants show the incredible opportunities and advances in this aspect of medicine. However, huge problems are still faced. At the time of writing, certain organs and procedures are still beyond the abilities of modern surgery but many are optimistic of developments just around the corner.

One of the most sensational and controversial transplants, that of a whole human head, has been promised in the next few years. The incredible complexity of such a feat might sound like the stuff of science fiction, but such transplants have already been carried out on animals with considerable success.

The fact that the brain can continue to function for a brief period after the heart has stopped supplying it with oxygen has been known for centuries. For example, Mary Queen of Scots was said to have continued praying after her head had been cut off by her executioner. If the heart was considered so important to life, how could a head appear to be alive after it had been separated from this vital organ? In a macabre experiment worthy of Victor Frankenstein himself, the French physician Dr Beaurieux decided to find out if these stories could be true and how long the head might remain conscious after the heart had stopped supplying oxygen.

In 1905, Beaurieux witnessed the execution of the prisoner Languille by guillotine. In the five or six seconds immediately after decapitation the lips and eyelids showed 'irregular rhythmic contractions'. When the eyelids had closed and the face was still, Beaurieux called out 'Languille' in a strong voice. The eyelids opened, as if Languille had been distracted from his thoughts, and his eyes focused on Beaurieux. Again the eyelids closed and again the doctor called out. The eyes opened and focused a second time, with a more penetrating look than before. The third call from Beaurieux was apparently not heard and Languille's eyes took on the glazed look of the dead. The whole period of activity was estimated to have lasted 25–30 seconds.

If the head could continue to function without a body, even for a brief period, perhaps it could be transferred successfully if it could be reconnected to a blood supply in time. In the 1950s, Russian scientist Vladimir Demikhov transplanted the head of a dog on to the neck of a second dog. The resulting two-headed beast appeared to thrive for a day or so before tissue rejection resulted in death.

In 1971, the American surgeon Robert White successfully transferred the head of a rhesus monkey on to the body of a recently decapitated second monkey. The monkeys in his experiments survived between six hours and three days. White saw the operation as a whole-body transplant rather than a head transplant. Such experiments might recall fictional stories of crazed scientists manipulating animal bodies, such as in H. G. Wells' *The Island of Doctor Moreau*, but White had different aims. Head or body transplants have the potential to benefit quadriplegics whose organs often fail at a much younger age. Rather than transplanting one or two organs at a time, using the whole body has the potential to extend life.

In 2015, Italian surgeon Sergio Canavero announced that he intended to carry out the first human head transplant in 2017. For a long time the major stumbling block in such a procedure was reconnecting the nerves of the spinal cord. In 1970 no such option was available and White's monkeys had to be artificially supported in their breathing because signals from the brain could not reach the lungs once the spinal cord had been severed. Today, chemicals such as polyethylene glycol, electrical stimulation and other techniques have shown promise in encouraging nerve repair. Canavero predicts his first head-transplant patient, with physiotherapy, will be walking within a year. The reality of Victor Frankenstein's ambition may seem to be getting closer but with one significant difference: the recipients of the donor organs in all these cases have been living.

The major barrier to any form of organ transplant, even today, is tissue rejection, although it had been noted that autografts (transplants from one site to another on the same body) fared better than allografts (transplant from a genetically different donor within the same species), and xenografts (transplants between different species) performed worst of all.

The reasons behind the different outcomes remained obscure for a long time.

Different organs are rejected at different rates but the pattern of acute tissue rejection is the same regardless of the type of tissue involved. Even if the tissue appears to function well initially, there will soon be inflammation. Blood vessels dilate to increase blood flow, giving the area a red and swollen appearance. This has been recognised as an indication of infection or damage for a long time, but John Hunter was the first to propose that the blood rushing towards the site might be the body's attempt to restore the tissue to its natural state. As microscopes improved, scientists could see the flood of host white blood cells surging into the area, but what their role could be was not clear.

The human body's immune system operates, very broadly speaking, by dividing everything into two categories – self and non-self. Cells within the body have tiny identifiers in the form of proteins, called antigens, presented on the cell surface. White blood cells (leukocytes) roam around the body chemically examining everything they encounter and the antigens it expresses. If the object under scrutiny displays antigens it knows to be self, it is ignored. If it is not recognised, or is recognised from a previous infection as non-self, an immune response is launched and the object, be it a bacteria, virus or donated organ, is attacked and destroyed.

The most well-known example of these identifying antigens is in blood typing. In 1901 Dr Karl Landsteiner discovered the A, B, O system of blood typing. On red blood cells two types of antigen can be expressed, resulting in blood groups A (one type of antigen), B (a second type of antigen), AB (both antigens present) and O (no antigens present). If someone with type A blood were to be given type B blood in a transfusion, the recipient's white blood cells would examine the B antigens on the surface of the introduced red blood cells and, not recognising them as self, would launch an immune response. Hence, people with type O blood are known as universal donors. Anyone can receive this type of blood because it has no A or B antigens to identify it as self or non-self and won't be attacked by white blood cells. Since 1901 more antigens have been identified. By the 1950s, 25 red blood cell antigens were known. Today, there are now over 300 identified.

Although not always considered in the same way as solid organ transplants, blood transfusion is arguably the most successful form of transplant. Ideas of blood transfusion had originated in ancient Rome with Ovid's tale of Medusa giving youth to an old man by draining his blood and replacing it with a magical fluid. However, it wasn't until the sixteenth century that anyone looked into such a procedure in practical rather than mythological terms.

Robert Boyle's experiments on preserving tissues, which we encountered in Chapter 8, had extended beyond dunking organs in jars of spirits. Boyle had tried to find a way of preventing the veins and arteries from collapsing after they had been drained of blood, including injecting various substances that would travel into the extremities of the vessels and then harden to preserve the shape. The substance could be almost anything; it was the process of injecting that offered new possibilities. Could this new technology be used to inject blood from one animal to another?

Blood was known to be vital to life so perhaps blood could be injected to prevent a patient from bleeding to death. Robert Boyle, with Richard Lower, one of Oxford's finest physicians, made their first attempt at blood transfusion using dogs. The jugular vein of one dog was opened and a pipe used to connect it to the jugular vein of a second dog. However, the blood clotted in the pipe and both dogs died.

In 1666, Lower took up the experiments again, but this time he paid closer attention to Harvey's theory of the circulation of the blood. This time he connected the pipe between an artery in the first dog and a vein in the second dog. The higher pressure in the artery forced the blood through the pipe and into the second dog without clotting. Lower almost bled the dog to death before transfusing it with a fresh supply. At the end of the experiments the dog apparently leapt off the table, licked Lower enthusiastically, and rolled on the grass to clean its fur.

The Royal Society, hearing of Lower's success, took up the baton and drained calves' blood into sheep and lambs' blood into foxes. Remarkably the sheep survived, but the foxes died. Undeterred, when Lower took over the transfusion experiments at the Royal Society, he decided to take the bold step of transfusing blood into a man. The subject chosen was Arthur Coga, a Cambridge-educated tramp who was found in a church congregation. Coga was said to suffer from a harmless form of insanity. If the choice of experimental subject seems unusual you would be right. Lower had tried to persuade Bethlem Royal Hospital, London's foremost hospital for the insane at the time – and the origin of the word 'bedlam' – to surrender one of its patients, but the hospital refused to let any of their patients take part in such a ridiculous experiment.

Lower hoped that the injection of blood would calm the insanity of the subject and 'improve his mental condition', and therefore the source of blood that was chosen for the experiment was a lamb. Silver pipes were used to connect an artery in the lamb's neck with a vein in Coga's arm. Miraculously, Coga survived two such transfusions. It would have been hailed as a tremendous success if Coga's subsequent behaviour had not taken the shine off things. Instead of the transformation into the calm, sane man they had hoped for, Coga used the money he had been given for taking part in the experiment to get drunk and raved about his experiences.

The experiment was still a considerable success and led others to speculate about the therapeutic possibilities of blood transfusions, from calming madmen to rejuvenating the old. The excitement was soon curbed, however, when experiments resulted in the deaths of their human volunteers.

Similar experiments had been conducted in France around the same time as Coga's transfusion, by Jean-Baptiste Denys. In 1667 Denys also transferred blood from animals to human subjects and his first two volunteers survived, probably because so little blood was actually transferred and the body could manage the immune response. This was not the case for Denys's third and fourth volunteers, Gustaf Bonde and Antoine Mauroy, both of whom died. Blood transfusions were promptly banned across Europe and research effectively came to a complete halt for the next 150 years.

In 1818, the year of *Frankenstein*'s publication, James Blundell, an English obstetrician, carried out a successful blood transfusion by injecting blood into a woman haemorrhaging after giving birth. The donor was her husband. Both survived. Blundell carried out 10 more transfusions during his career, five of which were beneficial. Blundell wrote up his findings, developed apparatus for transfusions and made a huge profit from them. However, transfusions remained highly controversial in medical practice because of the very real dangers to the patient. Why some patients died and others survived wasn't understood until Landsteiner's discovery of blood types. Early experiments with dogs had been potentially misleading because dogs' blood does not express the same antigens as human blood and can be transferred safely between different breeds.

All these instances of transfusion required a live donor because there was no effective method of storing blood, which quickly clots on exposure to the air. Even within the body, if the heart stops beating, blood will quickly settle at the lowest points in the body due to gravity and there it will begin to coagulate. Restarting the heart after any length of time therefore risks introducing blood clots into the circulation. Victor would have been wise to drain his creature's body of blood while he was working on its construction to prevent this as well as the decay that often occurs when blood remains in the tissues.

It wasn't until 1914–15 that sodium citrate was shown to prevent clotting in stored blood and that this citrated blood was safe to transfuse into patients. This opened the way to blood banks and more radical surgeries that would involve the loss of a lot of blood. In the 1930s heparin, an injectable anti-clotting agent, was discovered and this could be used during operations and allowed open-heart surgery to be conducted without the risk of thrombosis.

Blood would have to be reintroduced into Frankenstein's creature before it could be brought to life and Victor should have been wary of injecting just any blood into his newly built creature. But he may or may not have taken heed of previous transfusion disasters. Whatever the source, Victor would have had to use live donors but no one at the time *Frankenstein* is set would have felt the need to restrict himself to human blood. Mary Shelley's text refers to the torture of 'the living animal to animate the lifeless clay', but this may or may not have been specifically for blood transfusion.

Blood transfusions would have been relatively easy for a character like Victor compared with the complexity of transplanting solid organs. As well as red blood cells, other cells in the body also express antigens and so tissue matching for organ transplantation is not as straightforward as matching basic blood types. Human cells introduced into a body in the form of a transplant will undergo the same scrutiny from the immune system, and if the markers on the outside of the cells aren't similar enough to the markers used by the self, the organ will be attacked. This is organ or tissue rejection and the reason that medical teams go to great lengths to find a match as close as possible between recipient and donor of the organs before the transplant.

In the 1950s, French haematologist Jean Dausset defined the system of human leukocyte antigens (designated HLA). By 1970, 11 HLAs had been identified. In 2003, the number had risen to 70; now, there are more than 1,000 variants known to be expressed by humans. White blood cells known as 'killer T' cells are especially sensitive to non-self antigens and will quickly attack anything that appears foreign. Killer T cells seem to favour attacking cells that line blood vessels, destroying the vessel and thereby cutting off the blood supply to the transplanted tissue. The tissue turns white as it is starved of blood and perhaps this is one of the reasons for the creature's pale, parchment-like skin in *Frankenstein*.

An understanding of how antigens are used by the body to form part of its immune response, and how the immune response itself is triggered and carried out, has developed, in part, because of the interest in organ transplant. A direct need for improvements in human health has led to a greater understanding of fundamental processes that allow humans, and other animals, to protect themselves from invading organisms, and the development of a new discipline: immunogenetics. Alongside these developments has been progress in methods of tissue-matching techniques, meaning donor organs are more likely to find a suitable recipient, and resulting in much better outcomes.

As the significance of the immune response to donor tissue began to be appreciated, surgeons looked for ways to suppress the immune response and 'fool' the host body into accepting donor organs. Although in the early twentieth century, some chemicals were known to affect white blood cell production in rabbits, no immuno-suppressant drugs were used in humans until 1960. Instead, surgeons tried alternative methods.

Radiation had been shown to destroy rapidly dividing cells such as white blood cells. Many of the victims of the Hiroshima and Nagasaki bombs in the Second World War died of very ordinary infections that could not be defended against by their compromised immune systems, rather than the immediate radiation from the bombs. After successful studies with animals, humans awaiting transplants underwent whole body irradiation to effectively destroy their immune system.

Initially patients lay on a mattress within the beam of radiation, but greater amounts of control were introduced as the technique progressed. The new organs fared better than in patients with a normal immune response, but these new patients were very susceptible to any infection with such compromised immune systems. Transplant of organs along with bone marrow (the source of white blood cells) from the donor improved things further but many died despite strict sterile conditions being observed during the recovery period. It was found that the source of infection was often the patients themselves. Low levels of infection that were already present in the body at the time of irradiation were too much for the severely weakened immune system.

The discovery of chemical methods of immune suppression was a major turning point in the success of organ transplant.

The combination of immune suppression, steroids and anti-inflammatory drugs enabled many successful transplants, but these treatments also carry side-effects and risks. Treatment after organ transplantation continues to improve as new drugs are discovered to counter any immune response from the recipient.

In Mary Shelley's novel, Victor Frankenstein pushes tissue matching to its absolute limit by including parts not just from different human bodies but from animals, too. As well as the references to tortured animals, there are other clues to the use of animal parts in the construction of Victor's creature. The extreme height of the creature, 8ft (2.4m), means that Victor would probably have to resort to using animal bones. As we have seen from the experiments on blood transfusions, and the transplants carried out by John Hunter, little consideration was given by Frankenstein's scientific predecessors to human and animal compatibility.

There has been a long historical tradition of chimeras (human–animal composite creatures) stretching back to ancient times. Several Egyptian gods sported human bodies and animal heads, but these human–animal hybrids were not confined to Egyptian traditions. The Indian god of wisdom, Ganesha, for instance, has an elephant's head placed on a human body by another god, Shiva. Centaurs, the Minotaur and Medusa in Greek mythology combine both human and animal components. Mermaids and other fantastic creatures such as the manticore (lion's body, human head and scorpion's tail) were commonly depicted in medieval times. However, by the eighteenth century, no one truly believed that any of these creatures existed.

What was known was that closely related animals could be successfully bred to produce hybrid species, such as mules born from horses and donkeys. Horticulture had also shown the benefits of grafting one type of tree or plant on to the rootstock of another to produce a greater abundance of fruit. However, horticulturalists had known for a long time the importance of using closely related species for successful grafts. Even so, it would not have been a stretch to consider using animal parts as necessary in the construction of a human-like creature. The early experiments in blood transfusion illustrate how contemporary natural philosophers saw using lamb's blood as a positive advantage in calming the temperament of a recipient suffering from insanity.

However, the immune system guards particularly well against the invasion of tissue from other species. For example, the innate immune system, and specifically the compliment system, has a default setting of rapidly attacking almost everything. Highly reactive proteins called C3b bind to amine and hydroxyl chemical groups, which are found on pretty much every cell surface. This triggers further proteins to bind and results in a hole being cut in the cell membrane, like a can opener, spilling the contents and killing the cell. Our cells are constantly under attack, and the only reason our own cells are not destroyed in the process is that we have a defence mechanism that is equal to the task of protecting these surfaces.

When surgeons first speculated about using pig organs for human transplantation, they first experimented by giving a pig's heart to a baboon. Within minutes of the heart being put into the baboon's body it came under attack from the baboon's innate immune system and because the pig's heart did not have a suitable primate defence mechanism, the heart was soon reduced to a pulpy mush.

The possibility, as well as the ethics, of xenotransplants has resurfaced in modern times. Today, many people walk around with heart valves that originated in pigs. These valves are carefully treated to remove the cellular antigens that would trigger an immune response, leaving only extracellular material (the material that provides structure for the cells to organise themselves around). The structural components of bodies, such as bone, cartilage and collagen, stripped of their antigen-bearing cells can thus be safely transplanted between individuals and even species.

Recent experiments carried out in animals have removed cells from portions of a body as complex as legs, leaving only the inert scaffold behind that can be repopulated with cells from the recipient animal. Other proposed solutions to the dearth of donor organs is to breed human-animal chimeras that can be farmed for organs. Pigs are strong candidates for such experiments as they are very cheap and easy to breed, and their organs are of a similar size to humans'. Concerns over the ethics of such processes, as well as the safety aspects, must be thoroughly examined before these procedures become a reality. This may be the future of organ transplantation, but they are by no means straightforward and would certainly have been well beyond the technical capabilities of Victor Frankenstein and his contemporaries.

Given the complexity and effectiveness of the immune response within humans it is surprising that some organs and cells are unaffected by this process: a few organs have what is known as 'immune privilege'. Eyes, testicles, hair follicles and the brain, for instance, can be transplanted between any two individuals and no immune response will be triggered whatsoever. Why these organs should be different to others is difficult to say but it is of limited help to any Victor Frankensteins trying to build a complete creature from assorted parts.

The importance of matching tissue would simply not have been known to the likes of Victor Frankenstein. Victor should have been well aware that transferring organic matter between individuals, be they human to human or animal to human, was not always successful but the reasons for the failures would not have been obvious. This evidently did not discourage him and Victor apparently made no efforts to tissue match. Any success he achieved would have been purely down to chance. Alternatively, his creature would have needed a severely compromised immune system to accept the range of material it was constructed from. This would have made the creature incredibly vulnerable to infection and unlikely to live beyond a few days even if Victor had really succeeded in bringing it to life.

In some respects it might have been easier for Victor to construct mechanical parts for his creature. The stories of mechanical men in connection with the occult sciences stretch back into antiquity, as we saw in Chapter 5. In the Renaissance, Leonardo da Vinci designed mechanical men, and astrologer, occult philosopher and adviser to Queen Elizabeth I, John Dee, created a giant beetle that flew into the air, to the astonishment of the Oxford audience who witnessed it. The sight of the mechanical creature was undoubtedly linked to accusations of sorcery and magic that Dee was said to be a master of.

At a time when the universe and everything in it was being viewed in mechanical terms, it is no surprise that many attempted to create machines that mimicked living creatures. In 1737, Jacques de Vaucanson made a mechanical digesting duck with a glass vessel for chemically digesting the food it swallowed. Later in the eighteenth century, some remarkably lifelike humanoid automata were built. In the small Swiss town of Neuchâtel the Jaquet-Droz family constructed 'the musician', 'the draftsman' and 'the writer', among other mechanical devices. The musician is a female organ player who has several tunes within her repertoire. Her fingers press keys on a specially constructed organ to create the sound, rather than music being played from a music box. Her eyes and head follow the movements of her fingers, her chest moves in the appearance of breathing and her whole torso moves to balance her actions. She is wonderfully and, perhaps a little creepily, lifelike. The three mechanical people created by this Swiss family are remarkable feats of engineering that still work today, though apparently the musician doesn't always behave herself perfectly.

The three automata, as well as other mechanical curiosities, were on display in the town of Neuchâtel when Mary and Percy Shelley eloped and travelled through Europe in 1814. The couple spent several days in the town, though their accounts of the trip make no reference to the automata. However, in Mary's Introduction to the 1831 edition of *Frankenstein*, she does suggest the possibility of using artificial parts: 'perhaps the component parts of a creature might be manufactured'.

Artificial joints, mechanical heart valves and other devices are all part of regular medical treatment today. Dialysis machines and artificial respirators can perform the functions of kidneys and lungs. Attempts have even been made to make an entirely mechanical heart that can be implanted into a human, though sadly without success. Other synthetic components, such as artificial blood, are current areas of research that, if successful, would bring an end to shortages of donor blood. It would also bring the possibility of producing a living creature similar to Frankenstein's monster closer to reality.

However Victor managed to overcome issues of rejection, the assortment of parts he used in his construction presents an interesting question as to the identity of the resulting creature: was it part machine, human, hybrid or an entirely new species?

CHAPTER TEN

Electrification

*'He constructed a small electrical machine, and exhibited a few
experiments; he made also a kite, with a wire and string, which drew
down that fluid from the clouds.'*

Mary Shelley, *Frankenstein*

After months of toil under the most unpleasant and
dangerous working conditions, Mary Shelley's character
Victor finally stood before his completed creature ready to
'animate the lifeless clay'. Exactly how Victor achieved this
final momentous step is unclear. From the Frankenstein films
we remember a laboratory situated in a castle, cluttered with
electrical equipment, bubbling flasks and spiralling glassware.
Outside a storm crashes and thunders and in a dramatic
moment, a bolt of lightning appears to be the necessary 'spark
of life' that animates the creature. The book is a little different.

Mary Shelley is frustratingly vague on the details of how
Victor's creature is brought to life: 'I collected the instruments
of life around me, that I might infuse a spark of being into the
lifeless thing that lay at my feet.' The 'spark' is generally
interpreted as an electrical spark from a machine, or more
commonly from a bolt of lightning, but at least one film-
maker saw it as a spark from a fire. The 1910 Edison film
Frankenstein shows something resembling a melted clown
slowly emerging from a steaming cauldron. Presumably
advances in special effects, bigger budgets and a desire to
impress their audience pushed film-makers to depict dramatic
lightning storms and sparking electrical equipment.

Yet Mary makes no mention of electrical storms on the
night of creation. Stormy nights are reserved for a later
episode when Victor and his creature first confront each
other. On the night of reanimation, the only pieces of
equipment mentioned are 'the instruments of life', 'some

powerful engine' and 'chemical apparatus', which could be almost anything.

Nevertheless, it is fairly safe to assume Mary was hinting at an electrical source for her spark. Mentions of galvanism in the Introduction to the 1831 edition of *Frankenstein*, and Victor's interest in electricity as a result of seeing a tree blasted by a bolt of lightning when he was a child, would be evidence to support the use of an electrical spark. Another reason to suppose that Mary was talking about using electricity to bring her creature to life is the eighteenth- and early nineteenth-century obsession with all things electrical.

The fascination with electricity in the Enlightenment period can be attributed to several factors. Until the 1720s electrical phenomena were scarcely known and still less understood. In a period of around 30 years, however, a tremendous amount of research was conducted, with staggering results. Discovery followed discovery at a fantastic rate over the following century. The power and potential of electricity seemed unlimited.

Electrical experiments also lent themselves particularly well to impressive and inventive demonstrations that could entertain broad audiences, as well as giving philosophers something to puzzle over. Discovery and demonstration went hand in hand. There was little distinction between serious scientific research and experiments designed to entertain, meaning the field of electrical innovation was open to a wide range of practitioners as well as an even bigger demographic in terms of its audience. Electricity became the most popular area of scientific investigation and was the talk of every scientific society and social gathering.

A few electrical phenomena had been known to the ancient Greeks. They marvelled when a piece of amber was rubbed, causing it to attract feathers, straw and other light objects. A few other materials were found to possess similar properties, but no one seemed to be interested in investigating this further or even thought to try and explain how it happened.

Virtually no progress was made in electrical knowledge until the early eighteenth century, but then progress was rapid.

The explosion of interest in electricity was started by an observation made by Francis Hauksbee, who worked as curator, instrument-maker and experimentalist to the Royal Society. Around 1705 he found that when he introduced a small amount of mercury into the glass globe of an air pump, evacuated some of the air, and rubbed the glass with a cloth, a purple glowing light was produced. The light was strong enough to read by and it was the starting point for the later development of mercury discharge lamps and neon lights. The glow that Hauksbee had produced was due to a plasma, a state of matter where atoms or molecules of a gas have been stripped of their electrons. The modern incarnation of this experiment is the plasma ball novelty lamp that has streams of purple lightning that dart towards a hand placed on the exterior of the globe. Hauksbee's remarkable and beautiful discovery led him to carry out more experiments on static electricity, as we now call it, and he developed a number of electrical machines for generating and demonstrating static charge.

Hauksbee's electrical machine consisted of a glass sphere with a cloth or pad of leather held against it, while the globe was turned by a handle. This would have been the basis for the 'electrical machine' Percy Shelley kept in his university rooms at Oxford. Variations and improvements on the basic set-up appeared across Europe as more and more people became interested in conducting their own electrical experiments.

Despite this, for a few decades after Hauksbee, electrical phenomena remained a curiosity. The first systematic investigations into electrical phenomena were made by Dr Stephen Gray, who was primarily known as a chemist and astronomer. Towards the end of his life he was living at Charterhouse in London, an establishment that gave a home to destitute gentlemen who had served their country. Gray occupied his retirement years by conducting experiments in his rooms.

For his experiments with static electricity Gray used a glass tube, rather than a globe or sphere, rubbed with cloth or leather to generate a charge. He observed the glow described by Hauksbee but found other effects. When experimenting with his glass tube, Gray had stopped the ends with a cork to prevent dust and moisture from getting inside. He noticed that when he rubbed the tube, feathers and light particles were attracted to the cork rather than the tube. Electrical effects were not necessarily static; they could travel from the tube to the cork. Gray wondered just how far the effects would go.

Using an ivory ball instead of a cork (it attracted light objects better than the cork) attached to one end of a thread, with the other attached to the glass tube, he found that the effects could travel a considerable distance, more than 800m in one experiment. The electricity was not just restricted to travelling in straight lines – it could turn corners, and by lowering the ivory ball over his balcony into the courtyard below, Gray found it was unaffected by gravity. Electricity appeared to have some of the characteristics of a fluid, in that it could flow, through a suitable conductor, from one place to another.

As the length of his threads got longer, Gray tried to suspend them from the ceiling. However, he found that the metal wire he had used to form loops supporting the thread prevented the electrical effects from being transmitted from the glass tube to the ivory ball at the other end. Essentially he had discovered earthing and Gray realised it was the material itself that prevented the transmission of the electric fluid rather than the configuration or shape of the loops. By using silk loops, instead of metal wire to support the thread, the transmission of electricity was unaffected.

Importantly, Gray had discovered that some materials conducted the electric effects better than others. Experimenting with different materials for the thread itself, he found that silk was a poor choice for conducting the electric effects and that rough hempen fibre was much better. Most surprising at the time was that metal was particularly good at conduction. Previously, metal had been considered as a non-electric because a static charge could not be generated on a metal object no matter how vigorously it was rubbed. Later designs of Hauksbee's electrical machine incorporated a prime conductor, a length of metal, often a gun barrel or similar, held very close to the glass to allow the electric substance to be siphoned away from the globe.

Gray tried to electrolyse anything and everything from kettles to table cloths and even a live chicken (apparently its breast became particularly strongly electrolysed). While the ancient Greeks had known a handful of objects that had electric properties, Gray had begun to divide every known substance into two categories, conductors and insulators, and even extended his investigation to humans.

In his most spectacular experiment Gray electrolysed a boy resting on a platform suspended from the ceiling. Gray's Charterhouse home was also home to a boys' school and no one seems to have minded him using one of the pupils for his experiments. The electrically insulated boy was charged using one of Gray's electrical machines. Feathers were drawn up to the boy's face and fingers, and sparks could be drawn from his nose using a metal rod. Images of a boy suspended on a platform with sparks flying and a scientist in the foreground enthusiastically waving his arms is not so far removed from the silver-screen scenes of Frankenstein's creature being raised to the ceiling on a platform to receive bolts of lightning.

Gray demonstrated the experiments on the suspended boy when French scientists visited him in 1732. The Frenchmen returned home full of excitement over Dr Gray's 'fluid theory' of electricity and repeated his experiments, the most famous of which came to be known as 'the flying boy'. Scientific demonstrators and electrical showmen took the demonstration a step further and created the 'electrified Venus' whereby a woman standing in glass slippers was electrified before members of the audience were invited to come and give her a kiss. Anyone bold enough to take up the offer was rewarded with a stinging electric shock to the lips.

Figure 7 Experiment known as 'The Flying Boy' recreated in a French salon after Nollet witnessed it performed by Stephen Gray in England. Essai sur l'électricité des corps by Jean-Antoine Nollet, 1746. Wellcome Library, London.

More and more demonstrations were added to the stock of itinerant lecturers giving public courses on electricity, and others brought them to fashionable salons or dinner parties. Glass spheres were made to glow with purple light, sparks crackled from the tips of conductors and more. Alcohol was set on fire by electric sparks directed at metal spoons filled with brandy. Guests at dinner parties were surprised by electrified cutlery.

The French scientist, Jean-Antoine Nollet, in particular did much to popularise electricity, and though he saw himself very much as a serious experimentalist, he could put on a spectacular show when required. Nollet set up demonstrations of chains of soldiers or monks linked by holding hands, and would send electrical shocks along the line, making them all jump simultaneously. Though the experiment showed that humans were capable of conducting electricity, the scale and spectacle of these demonstrations were primarily aimed at impressing his royal witnesses rather than making some deep scientific discovery.

The scene described by Thomas Jefferson Hogg of Percy Shelley in his university rooms, standing on a glass-footed chair and hooked up to an electrical machine, hair and sparks flying, is no longer so surprising. It is also easy to see where film-makers may have found their inspiration for Victor Frankenstein's laboratory.

Despite the diversity of electrical experiments there were considerable limits on what could be achieved at this time due to the fact that electricity could not be stored or transported easily. Electrical charge had to be generated as required by turning the handles on electrical machines, a laborious process usually carried out by assistants or servants so that the experimenter was left free to manipulate the prime conductor and carry out the experiment in question.

Another landmark discovery was needed. This came along in 1745 in Poland when Ewald von Kleist used an old medicine bottle and a nail to collect the electric fluid. He claimed he could produce shocks that would knock children off their feet, but kept the details of his design so secret that no one else could replicate his results. It was only when Pieter van Musschenbroek, a professor at the university of Leyden, decided to try and bottle electricity that the experiment became widely known.

Musschenbroek's bottle was half-filled with water and charged using the static electricity generated by a derivative of Hauksbee's machine. When he accidentally completed the circuit between the inside and outside of the bottle by touching the wires protruding from it, he was given a powerful shock. He was terrified, and the experience spurred him to warn others about the dangers of his invention.

Few people seem to have heeded Musschenbroek's warnings and soon everyone was using old bottles and wires to construct their own Leyden jar. It was probably a home-made Leyden jar that Percy Shelley terrified his sisters with when he was a boy. Variations were made to the original design and the final configuration had a jar lined inside and out with metal – water was found not to be necessary. Wires in contact with the metal linings were used to 'fill' or 'charge' (a word borrowed from military terminology), the bottle from an electrical machine. This store of electric fluid remained in the bottle for days. It could be moved from one site to another without lessening the electric charge so long as the wires did not come into contact with another conductor. The bottles could even be connected up in huge arrays or 'batteries' (another word borrowed from military terminology) to give a more powerful shock. However, the amount of electricity delivered to the bottle could only be managed very crudely by limiting the number of turns of the handle of the electric machine. The only way to determine the quantity of electricity that had accumulated in the bottle was thus to discharge it and feel how powerful the shock was or measure the length of the sparks it gave off.

Nevertheless, the Leyden jar evidently worked, and improvements to the design increased the jar's capacity to dangerous levels. One experimenter, accidentally brushing against the wires of a charged Leyden jar, was thrown across the room and knocked unconscious. When he woke up there was a powerful smell of sulphur in the room and the experimenter was convinced he had summoned the Devil. He swore off Leyden jars for the rest of his life and advised others to do the same. However, enthusiasm for the new device wasn't dimmed, and the ease of construction meant many people had the opportunity to experience the effects for themselves. Several experimenters described some of the lesser effects of accidently discharging the Leyden jar through their body, which included nosebleeds, chest pain, temporary paralysis and dizziness.

Leyden jars were powerful enough to fuse metal and blast holes through reams of paper. How such tremendous forces could be generated by electricity, a substance that appeared to have no material presence, baffled natural philosophers of the day. Leyden jars 'filled' with the electric fluid weighed no more than an empty Leyden jar. And though electricity behaved in many respects just like a fluid, experimenters were puzzled at how this fluid could travel so quickly. Shocks could be transmitted over long distances, several miles through the ground and across rivers, apparently instantaneously. Some electrically charged objects attracted each other whereas others repelled. How could electricity distinguish between these objects and show such contrary behaviour?

Since Gray's first electrical experiments in 1729, knowledge of electrical phenomena had progressed from a curiosity to knowledge of conduction, induction and the invention of the first capacitor in just 16 years. Discoveries continued at a bewildering pace. What had gone almost unnoticed for more than a thousand years was suddenly everywhere scientists looked for it. But the more experimenters looked into electrical phenomena, the more questions arose.

The electricity being investigated so enthusiastically across Europe and America was what we refer to now as static electricity. Using friction, negatively charged electrons were being scraped from one surface to another, leaving one surface negatively charged (because of an excess of negative charge) and the other positively charged (due to a deficit of negative charge). Which surface becomes positive and which becomes negative depends on the relative properties of each surface, a fact that caused much confusion for eighteenth-century experimenters when they found one surface could be made positive or negative depending on what they used to rub against it. Today, young children can be entertained by rubbing balloons and sticking them to walls or using static electricity to make their hair stand on end. In the eighteenth century such things were cutting-edge scientific research. Serious men of science spent hours making their stockings spark in the dark. They watched their legwear stick to mirrors and walls, or wondered why a pair of black stockings repelled each other, but a black and a white stocking would fly towards each other and stick fast.

The French scientists who, after witnessing Gray's electrical demonstrations, had taken up the baton of electrical research, developed a new theory of electricity. Charles François de Cisternay du Fay explained attraction or repulsion by expanding Gray's fluid theory into a 'two fluids' theory. One electric fluid became known as 'vitreous', because it was formed on substances such as glass and wool. The other was known as 'resinous', because it was formed on materials such as amber and paper. Longer and longer lists of resinous substances and vitreous substances were compiled.

Du Fay's two-fluids theory only explained attraction and repulsion and could not explain one of the biggest puzzles of the time: how the Leyden jar worked. Though the jar clearly stored electricity and delivered shocks, no one could explain how. What was needed was a fresh mind to apply itself to the problem and that came in the form of Benjamin Franklin.

Benjamin Franklin, printer, writer and statesman, became one of the foremost authorities on electricity thanks to a gift from his friend, Peter Collinson. Franklin was geographically isolated from the frenzy of electrical experiments being carried out in Europe in the first half of the eighteenth century. Nevertheless, news of electrical phenomena made its way to the continent. In 1743, Archibald Spencer toured the British colonies in America with a series of lectures on natural philosophy, which included electrical demonstrations. Benjamin Franklin attended the lectures and was much taken with the new science. He duly wrote to Collinson in London requesting more information.

Collinson was a botanist and fellow of the Royal Society. He maintained a large correspondence with a range of scientists across the world, introducing their ideas and findings to the Society. He also maintained close connections with fellow botanists in America with whom he exchanged seeds, plants and ideas about crops and cultivation in the colonies.

When he was living in Philadelphia in the summer of 1745, Franklin received a glass tube from Collinson. In the same parcel was an essay entitled *An historical account of the wonderful discoveries made in Germany etc., concerning electricity*. The essay declared that electricity had been in vogue since 1743 and enthusiastically listed some of the discoveries made: 'Electricity accelerates the motion of water in a pipe, and that it quickens the pulse. There are hopes of finding in it a remedy for the sciatica or palsy.' Moreover, the article also described some of the spectacular demonstrations that had been devised to show the wonder of this marvellous substance. 'Could one believe that a lady's finger, that her whalebone petticoat, should send forth flashes of true lightning, and that such charming lips could set on fire a house?' Franklin was immediately taken with his new toy and was soon entertaining friends and family with demonstrations of electrical phenomena using the glass tube as well as devices and experiments of his own design.

Franklin learned of the Leyden jar in 1746, a year after its invention, and his interest in electricity moved from entertainment to more serious scientific experimentation. By the winter of that year Franklin had acquired his own Leyden jar and found that the effects it could produce were far more impressive than anything he had achieved with the glass tube. An interesting hobby morphed into an obsession.

Many of Franklin's discoveries in electricity were made after experimenters in Europe had hit upon the same thing, but correspondence between Europe and America was slow and infrequent. The isolation perhaps gave Franklin the freedom to think about electricity in new ways without following conventions rapidly being established among the scientific community in Europe. He brought a clarity to the subject that had been severely lacking and established some of the basic principles of electricity.

Franklin had a radical new interpretation of the fluid theory of electricity. Instead of the two fluids, he proposed that there was only one and that it pervaded all materials. It was the accumulation of excess fluid or the loss of the same that produced electric effects. All the time the electric fluid was in equilibrium nothing would be observed, but a positive or negative amount explained many of the observations that had been made by experimenters. The Leyden jar worked because one side of the bottle accumulated an excess of electric fluid while the other side suffered a loss. When the two sides were connected the shock felt was caused by the fluid moving to restore the electrical equilibrium.

Furthermore, the shape of the Leyden jar was unimportant. Though it had been originally conceived as a receptacle for a fluid, there was no need for a specific shape since it was only the separation of the two metal surfaces that was important. To demonstrate this, Franklin covered both sides of a flat piece of glass with metal and successfully charged it in the same way as a Leyden jar. His invention became known as a 'Franklin square' or 'magic square' and was another electrical instrument to add to the growing stock for experimenters across Europe and the American colonies.

For these contributions alone Franklin would be considered a great scientist, but he went further. Franklin's most famous experiment is described in Mary's 1818 edition of *Frankenstein*: 'He made also a kite, with wire and string, which drew down that fluid from the clouds.' The reference was edited out of the 1831 edition but in its place is an explicit reference to galvanism, a method of using electricity to animate dead material, which we will discuss in full in the next chapter.

Franklin's kite experiment has gone down in history as a classic, simple experiment to prove that lightning was in fact just a grander, natural form of the electricity that could be produced in laboratories. A few others had noticed similarities between the phenomenon of lightning and electric sparks produced by electrical machines, but Franklin detailed a dozen ways in which lightning resembled electricity and vice versa. Most importantly, he was the first to propose an experiment that would confirm his theories.

What is slightly disappointing is the fact that Franklin probably did not carry out the experiment himself. He would have been well aware of the dangers involved: lightning was known to kill animals and humans. Moreover, Franklin had personally experienced the terrifying effects of electric shocks when he accidentally discharged a Leyden jar through his body. The charged jar was apparently intended to be used to kill a turkey for thanksgiving (he obviously already knew of the jar's lethal possibilities). Franklin was physically and mentally shaken by the experience and this may have been enough to put him off personally carrying out his great lightning experiment.

Franklin had described his proposed experiment in a letter that was written to the Royal Society in London in 1749. He had been the first person to notice that electricity seemed to be attracted to points and suggested that a tall rod be raised up, with a sharp point at the top, could be used to attract lightning. Another conducting material could then be brought close to this rod to see if it would draw sparks. The suggestion was taken up by French experimenters in 1752.

In Marly-la-Ville in northern France, Thomas-François Dalibard erected a 12m (40ft) metal pole, resting on a three-legged stool supported by three wine bottles, and waited for a storm. When one was not forthcoming, and perhaps bored with waiting, Dalibard left the experiment in charge of Coiffier, an old dragoon, with clear instructions of what to do if a storm should appear.

At 2.20 p.m. on the afternoon of 10 May 1752, lightning struck. Coiffier immediately raced to the pole and managed to draw off sparks. He then sent for the local priest, who would be seen as a credible witness to such an incredible experiment, and a small crowd started to gather around. When lightning had been seen, along with the priest rushing towards the site of the experiment, several people thought Coiffier had been killed and the priest was going to give the last rites. The crowd thus grew significantly, unperturbed by the hailstorm that developed. When he arrived, the priest successfully drew sparks from the pole until the storm ceased.

Thankfully no one was hurt during the experiment and it encouraged others across Europe to repeat it.

Franklin, unaware of what had happened in France, made his own attempt at the experiment a month later. For himself he chose a different method to the one he had proposed in his letter to the Royal Society and it is this version that has gone down in history rather than the earlier successes of Dalibard and Coiffier in France. The most detailed account of Franklin's experiment we have is from Priestley's book *The History and Present State of Electricity* (more on this work later). Franklin himself did not leave a first-hand account of his most famous experiment, leading some to think that he had something to hide.

Given the obvious dangers of such an experiment, it has been suggested that Franklin found someone else to hold the kite string. One possibility is that one of Franklin's slaves was given the task. According to the account by Priestley, in June 1752 Franklin and his son alone decided to fly a kite into a thunderstorm. Made out of a handkerchief and a couple of sticks, Franklin attached a metal spike to the top of the kite and a long hempen thread, at the bottom of which he suspended a key. The line of the kite was made of insulating silk thread.

Despite promising-looking clouds passing overhead, the pair were growing disappointed by their apparent failure. As they were about to give up on the experiment, however, Franklin noticed that the fine hairs on the hempen thread were raised, indicating that they were electrolysed. The rain had probably soaked the thread sufficiently to allow some current to flow through it. Franklin brought his knuckle towards the key and felt a series of satisfying shocks. Lightning had been proved to be an electrical phenomenon.

His experiments with the kite and with metallic points led Franklin to propose the use of metal rods, raised above the highest point of a building and sunk into the ground or nearby water, as a method of protecting buildings from lightning strikes. His invention of lightning conductors was initially viewed with scepticism and even sparked a row about

whether round tops (promoted by the British) over pointed
tops (promoted by Franklin) were the best. John Hunter, the
anatomist from Chapter 7 and friend of Franklin, was one of
the first people in Britain to add lightning conductors to a
property, his Earls Court home.

People in the eighteenth century would have been well aware
that lightning could kill. In May 1666, Thomas Willis, one of
the Oxford surgeons from Chapter 7, had the opportunity to
dissect a man who had been killed by lightning while out in
his boat on the river. Willis could put his fist through the hole
made in the man's hat by the lightning and his doublet had
been ripped open and the buttons knocked off.

It was only the following evening that Willis and his
friends could proceed with the dissection itself, by which
time the body was in a fairly putrid state. Realising they
might never be presented with such an opportunity again
they carried on regardless of the stench. The skin of the
victim was remarkable: spots and streaks could be seen on the
torso and in places it seemed 'like leather burnt with the fire'.
Yet the burns did not reach below the skin. What the surgeons
found most surprising of all was that they could find no
damage to the internal organs. How the lightning had killed
its victim remained a mystery.

Following Franklin's experiments there was a surge in
interest in atmospheric electricity and an increased chance
that anatomists would have more opportunities to learn how
lightning killed. Electricians across Europe put themselves at
extraordinary risk to find out more about lightning and
atmospheric electricity – metal spikes were raised in gardens
and wires strung across lawns and into peoples' homes to try
and capture this enigmatic phenomenon.

Professor George Wilhelm Richman of Petersburgh had
set up an elaborate system of glass globes and wires in his
laboratory that led outside to be exposed to the weather. On
6 August 1753 he was standing in front of the apparatus and
examining it when a lightning bolt struck. He collapsed

immediately and attempts to revive him failed. Examination of his body showed a mark on his forehead where it was assumed the bolt had entered. His shoe had been torn apart where the bolt had apparently exited, but the stockings he wore underneath remained intact. Along his back his skin had the appearance of burnt leather and streaks of burning were found on his jacket. However, his internal organs showed no signs of damage.

Lightning is tremendously powerful: it can carry 150,000 amps, tens of millions of volts, and incredible heat (28,000°C or 50,400° F – hotter than the surface of the sun). However, human beings are not very good conductors of electricity and an individual is far more likely to survive a lightning strike than some other forms of electrocution. Pulses of lightning are incredibly short lived, existing for only milliseconds, so there is less time for damage to occur than from, for example, touching high-voltage railway lines.

There are three ways that lightning can cause harm: as a direct result of the electrical energy passing through the body; the heat of the lightning stroke causing burns; and mechanical damage caused by the shock wave from the lightning bolt or the rapid expansion of gases in the lungs that have been heated by the lightning. Two particularly vulnerable parts of the body are the heart, which can be stopped by tiny electrical currents passing across it, and the medullary respiratory centre of the brain, which controls breathing.

The damage to the bodies of lightning victims in the seventeenth and eighteenth centuries are typical, with burns to the skin but little damage to internal organs. Perspiration on the skin is a better conductor of electricity than the skin itself and the rapid heating of water in sweat causes the burns. It was probably sweaty socks, rapidly heated by the lightning current passing down the body, which caused the water to vaporise in the confines of a tightly fitting shoe, and ripped apart Professor Richman's footwear.

Even if only a tiny fraction of the electrical energy penetrates the body, it can stop the heart or breathing. Before effective methods of cardiopulmonary resuscitation had been developed, these individuals had little chance of recovering from the lightning strike. They were unlucky. For every person killed by lightning there are 10 or 20 more who survive a strike. Some emerge from the experience relatively unscathed but for others it can cause serious injury and lasting health problems, from deteriorating sight to tinnitus, depression, dizziness and fatigue. Why individuals have such different outcomes is not known. On the whole, using lightning seems an unreliable and risky way of bringing life to Victor's creature.

Lightning is caused by electrical discharges formed in clouds, as positively charged ice crystals rise and become separated from negatively charged water droplets and ice pellets that sink to the bottom of the cloud. It is the same separation of charge found on balloons rubbed against jumpers or the electrostatic machines used in the eighteenth century, but on a massive scale. The negative base of the cloud induces a positive charge in the ground, separated by the insulating air in between (the same principle as Franklin's squares, with opposite charges separated by a sheet of glass). When the charge difference becomes too great for the air to keep them apart (around 100 million volts), bolts of lightning travel to the ground at a speed of around 96,000km (59,650 miles per second) per second, to correct the imbalance, carrying with them enough energy to light a small city for several weeks.

The bolt of lightning will follow the path of least resistance towards the ground and often strikes tall buildings or trees. The enormous power focused into such a small area can rip apart buildings and shred trees as moisture in the bark is turned into superheated steam. It's little wonder that a young Victor Frankenstein would be so impressed by the sight of a tree destroyed by lightning.

Proof that lightning was just another form of electricity only seems to have increased its fascination for natural philosophers and electricians of the eighteenth and nineteenth centuries. With around 800 lightning storms occurring at any one time across the globe, discharging four million lightning strikes per day, it may seem like an obvious source of electrical energy. However, the unpredictability of when and where lightning will strike, as well as difficulties in storing the energy until it is required, makes such ideas impractical.

If electricity could explain lightning what else might it account for? The fact that electrical energy could be detected in the atmosphere even when there was no storm directly overhead led people to speculate it might be the cause of other atmospheric phenomena, such as the aurora borealis. Some even tried to explain the occurrence of earthquakes as being due to electrical processes such as lightning strikes.

That electrical phenomena and lightning are wonderful spectacles is of no doubt, but towards the end of the eighteenth century some were becoming frustrated with the lack of applications found for this source of power. Shelley was fascinated by lightning and talked enthusiastically about it to his friend Thomas Jefferson Hogg when they were at university together. He predicted a day when the immense power of lightning would be drawn down from the clouds for some purpose, all for the betterment of society, but at that time no one had managed to turn electricity from any source into something useful.

One possible exception to the lack of utility of electricity was medicine. Almost as soon as electricity came under investigation in the first half of the eighteenth century its potential use in medicine was explored. The sensations felt from electric shocks clearly demonstrated an effect on the body and perhaps this could be put to good use. What almost certainly started off as experiments with the best of intentions, soon descended into quackery and outright fraud. French and Italian physicians claimed the most astonishing cures of cases of palsy and headaches, but no one else seemed to be able to replicate the outcomes outside of the laboratories of these few individuals. When Nollet set out for Italy to witness these cures for himself, nothing appeared to work in his presence.

Electrical therapy was tried on almost every conceivable ailment, from colds to tuberculosis. Most successes were claimed for paraplegics but even here results varied. Benjamin Franklin himself treated palsy patients with electricity but failed to produce a cure. Therapies usually consisted of electrifying the patient and drawing sparks from the afflicted area or applying shocks directly to the paralysed limb. Therapies were repeated daily and many claimed improvement but only for the duration of the treatment, relapsing when treatment was discontinued. Others claimed more miraculous cures.

As with many other medical treatments at the time, electricity would have been virtually ineffective in the form it was administered. Patients who showed improvement got better in spite of their treatment rather than because of it. Many of these therapies seem ridiculous at best and frightening at worst. However, there is always one person who takes things to ludicrous extremes and in the case of electric therapy it was Scotsman James Graham, an acquaintance of Percy Shelley's father.

Graham was involved in a series of health fads, such as earth baths that involved being buried in the ground up to the neck, but his 'Temple of Health' was his crowning glory. In its heyday, the Temple of Health had drawn 200 patients per day to be restored to their former virility. Located in London's fashionable Pall Mall, the premises opened its doors in 1781 and took paying customers through a series of richly decorated rooms adorned with scantily clad women. Those who were having marital difficulties, and could afford the exorbitant prices (£50 a night, around £7,000 in today's money), could enjoy the dubious benefits of the 'celestial bed'. The highly decorated bed was adorned with a canopy and lined with mirrors. Soft music, spicy aromas and white-robed vestal virgins enticed patients inside the room. Brass rods were charged with electricity from two giant Leyden jars and conducted the electricity to a fiery dragon. Despite aristocratic patrons backing the venture, Graham went bankrupt in 1784.

With little or no understanding of what electricity was and how it acted on the body, it is hardly surprising there was a lack of success of medical electricity at this time. What is remarkable is how long interest was maintained even when the results were so poor. Despite the doubtful medical results that some claimed, there was clearly some kind of effect on the body: muscles could be made to twitch in living and dead animals long after chemical and mechanical stimulants had stopped working. There was something special about electricity and its interaction with the body. Such experiments would have given Mary Shelley and her creation Victor Frankenstein plenty to think about while building his creature.

So rapid were the advances in the understanding of electrical phenomena, that Joseph Priestly was able to write a history of electricity in 1767, less than 40 years after the first true systematic experiments in the field. Priestley's seminal work on electricity, *The History and Present State of Electricity*, was enormously popular and ran to many editions. In his book, from the time of the ancient Greeks to the first modern experiments in electricity takes up only 14 pages of a book more than 700 pages long, showing how little interest had been shown in the subject prior to the eighteenth century.

Joseph Priestley, perhaps best known today for his discovery of oxygen (see Chapter 6), was a polymath living in the west of England and a prominent member of the Lunar Society. Born into a dissenting family, he held strongly radical views throughout his life and was a supporter of the French Revolution. Among Priestley's many interests were theology, philosophy, science and education, but he was also considered one of the first experts in electricity. He published more than 150 works on various topics, including politics and religion, as well as scientific subjects. He only took up work in electricity in 1766, just a year before publishing his *History*, and his enthusiasm for and dedication to the subject, meant that he was soon acknowledged as an expert in the field. Many of his contemporaries described him as an electrician, a word first coined by Benjamin Franklin in 1751.

His written works were hugely popular but his political views were considered more controversial and at one point prompted an angry mob to destroy his laboratory. Priestley was pilloried in the British press but the French offered him citizenship when life in England became intolerable for him. With such similar views, it is unsurprising that Priestley and William Godwin were friends. Mary never met Priestley since he had emigrated to America in 1794, where he remained until his death in 1804, but it is likely she heard of his many and varied ideas from her father.

Priestley, true to his radical Enlightenment principles, wanted as many people as possible to benefit from new discoveries and scientific advances. His books were written to encourage his audience to take part in the process of discovery. *The History and Present State of Electricity* stressed the ease of conducting experiments and gave precise details about the construction of equipment as well as where to buy the best or most cost-effective materials. Priestley encouraged the performance aspect of electrical demonstrations and wrote enthusiastically about the joy of electrical phenomena. What may have attracted Priestley to this specific aspect of science is the ability to carry out experiments at minimal cost, meaning it was open to almost everyone to be part of this great experience.

In his book, Priestley clearly outlined electrical phenomena that had no current explanation and encouraged his readers to contact him with new discoveries and theories. There was still a lot to be discovered. Even when the differences between resinous and vitreous electricity had been resolved into a single electrical fluid that could be in abundance (positive) or deficit (negative), there was still no consensus over what the electric substance actually was. Further, distinctions were still made between natural and artificial electricity. Electricity generated by machines or by rubbing a piece of amber, was considered artificial. The electricity seen in lightning was clearly a natural phenomenon and even static electricity generated by stroking a cat was considered to be natural because it had originated on a living thing. Although they all gave the appearance of electrical phenomena, no one was completely sure that natural and artificial electricity were one and the same thing. The existence of certain animals that appeared to give electric shocks only added to the confusion.

The ancient Greeks knew that certain fish, named 'torpedoes' after the Latin for 'numb' or 'paralysed', could produce a stinging shock that left limbs painfully numb afterwards. Catfish from Africa that gave shocks were also known and South American 'trembling eels' were introduced to Europeans when the continent was colonised in the sixteenth century. However, it wasn't until the eighteenth century that a connection was made between the shocks received from these fish and electricity.

Experiments conducted by John Walsh in 1772 showed that the shocks produced by the torpedo fish really were electrical in nature. However, Walsh was not able to produce a spark from the torpedo fish, which left doubt in some minds. It wasn't until 1776 when Walsh was able to experiment on the trembling eels (so called because of the effects they could produce on the human body) imported from Guyana. Under the right conditions, these eels could produce a spark, a fact accounted for by the much higher voltage produced by the eels (around 600 volts) compared with the torpedo (around 50 volts).

Specimens of the torpedo, sent to England preserved in brandy, allowed John Hunter to dissect the creatures in an attempt to discover their secrets. What he found inside the fish were what appeared to be columns made up of disk-like units heavily connected by a mass of nerves. The dissections highlighted the importance of nerves in electrical conduction within living bodies. The physical appearance of the electric organs in the eel and torpedo, now named Hunter organs, was to be a strong influence on the later design of Alessandro Volta's famous electrical device – the pile.

In a few examples, electricity could evidently play a role 'in animal economy' but this simply presented more problems. How could the fish generate the electricity in the first place? How could the fish generate a shock capable of stunning and killing animals without being shocked itself?

This would have been approximately the state of electrical knowledge when Victor Frankenstein was depicted leaving his family home to study natural philosophy at the University of Ingolstadt – there were far more questions than answers and a staggering opportunity for anybody and everybody to make valuable contributions to the field.

The final decades of the eighteenth century thus saw an intense amount of activity in electrical investigations that led to another great scientific advance, seismic in its scope and implications: the battery. What started off as a curiosity into the effects of electricity on muscle contractions brought about one of the biggest scientific conflicts in history and incidentally led to the possibility of Frankenstein-like reanimation of the dead.

CHAPTER ELEVEN

Reanimation

'I collected the instruments of life around me.'
Mary Shelley, *Frankenstein*

The development of electrical theory and devices over the course of the eighteenth century would have been of interest to characters like Victor Frankenstein in terms of building devices he could use in his experiments. However, it was work carried out in the last two decades of that century that, to its contemporary readers, made *Frankenstein* appear to be a little too close to reality.

The explosion of interest in electricity in the eighteenth century had produced a vast number of experiments and observations. The diversity, almost randomness, of the investigative paths taken by experimentalists had raised more questions than answers. Slowly, more systematic research was carried out as philosophers focused on exploring specific facets of electrical phenomena.

Experiments carried out on humans and animals had shown astonishing results – involuntary motion of muscles, apparent cures for deafness and even death. It was the biological aspect of electricity that interested the anatomy professor Luigi Galvani and spurred him to devise his own detailed programme of research into this area. These extensive investigations led him to develop the controversial theory of 'animal electricity', sparking an argument with another Italian professor, Alessandro Volta.

The significance of the debate over animal electricity between Galvani and Volta cannot be understated. The impact of the discoveries made by the two scientists has been enormous and though the controversy is settled, the influence of their work is still very much present today.

From the moment the debate erupted in 1791, it was the hot topic of conversation in every philosophical and fashionable gathering and it was still being discussed by the Shelleys, Byron and John Polidori at Villa Diodati decades later during the critical summer of 1816.

It all began in 1780 when Galvani, a professor of anatomy at the University of Bologna, embarked on a series of electrical experiments on frogs. What started as an attempt to understand the effects of electricity on muscle contraction eventually produced the new scientific discipline of bioelectricity. Volta's opposition to Galvani's theory resulted in the invention of the battery and the formation of a whole new branch of science: electrochemistry. In its darkest moments, the debate spurred individuals to conduct macabre electrical experiments on the bodies of executed criminals.

T

Luigi Aloisio Galvani was born to a prosperous but not aristocratic family in Bologna, Italy. He was the only child the family could afford to send to university and, in 1755, Galvani enrolled at the University of Bologna to study medicine. This was a time when medical education would have been based on the works of Galen and other similarly outdated ideas, although more modern attitudes to human biology were creeping into the course. He also studied surgical techniques, which would have been of undoubted use in his later frog studies.

After completing his degree, the bookish Galvani became a lecturer in anatomy at the same university and married Lucia Galeazzi, daughter of one of the university's most eminent professors, Domenico Gusmano Galeazzi. In 1776 he obtained an appointment to the Academy of Sciences in Bologna, as a lecturer of surgery and theoretical anatomy. His appointment required him to present a paper to the Academy every year and it was around this time that he began to become interested in medical electricity, the topic that was then all the rage in Europe.

Although the effects of electricity on the muscles had been demonstrated, Galvani's planned experiments were more detailed and thorough than those that had gone before. He hoped to discover more about how muscles contract and if electrical fluid was the cause. At the time there was considerable debate over the mechanics of exactly how muscles contracted. The traditional view was that animal spirits were transmitted along fine canals throughout the body. The nature of these spirits was open to debate and electricity appeared to fit the bill: it could travel at astonishing speed, seemed to be weightless and had been shown to be conducted by biological material such as humans holding hands in a chain, although the theory lacked details.

In order to address the problem, Galvani had equipped his home laboratory with state-of-the-art apparatus, including electrical machines for generating static electricity, as well as Leyden jars that could store the accumulated charge. There were also Franklin, or magic, squares to condense the electric fluid alongside all the equipment necessary for dissection. Such an ambitious project would require Galvani to devote a considerable amount of time and effort to his experiments, and so he also had a series of assistants to help him, most prominent of whom was his beloved wife Lucia.

Lucia Galeazzi was a well-educated Bolognese woman, but education for women in the eighteenth century was mostly confined to historical and religious topics. In addition to her normal studies, Lucia learned Italian and Latin to assist her husband in his writings. She was also well enough versed in scientific matters to work in the laboratory alongside Galvani. Lucia was an active participant in her husband's scientific research, as well as assisting him in his medical work in obstetrics and editing his medical texts. She was also known to participate in, and animate the scientific discussion at, the 'conversazioni' that were held in the salons of all of Bologna's notable families. Galvani was devastated by her death from asthma in 1788.

Luigi and Lucia were aided in the laboratory by Galvani's nephews Camillo Galvani and Giovanni Aldini (Aldini would become Galvani's biggest promoter in later years). In addition to family members, some of Galvani's university students also worked in the laboratory.

For his investigations into muscle contractions, Galvani had elected to work with frogs, an animal that has since been described as the 'martyr of science' for reasons that will become obvious. Frogs were a natural choice for such experiments since they were relatively easy to obtain in large quantities, their nerves could be easily isolated from the body and they remained responsive to electrical stimulation for a long time after death. Galvani noted that frogs could still be responsive to electrical stimuli up to an astonishing 44 hours after they had been killed, as long as they had been properly prepared.

Galvani began his diary entries on electrical experiments on frogs on 6 November 1780. In his first set of experiments he prepared frogs 'in the usual manner', suggesting he had already begun the experiments at an earlier date or was well read in similar experiments conducted by other scientists. He dissected away the top half of the frog to leave just the legs attached to the spinal column and exposing the crural nerves that led directly to muscles in the leg.

Initially Galvani used wires, and other conducting materials, attached to Leyden jars and other electrical devices, inserted into the body of the frog to directly stimulate different parts. He observed contractions in the leg muscles of the frog when he stimulated the nerves attached to them. This was not new or remarkable in itself – similar results had been obtained with both live and dead animals before – although those outside of the scientific community might have been surprised to see what was evidently a dead frog move as though it were alive. What made Galvani's experiments different is the level of planning, experimental detail, the sheer amount of time he dedicated to the research and the conclusions he drew from his findings.

The experiments continued much as Galvani would have expected until one day he made a surprising discovery. The frog's legs could be made to twitch even if they were not in contact with an electrical device. This twitching occurred if one experimenter touched the crural nerve with the dissecting knife at the same time as a second experimenter, possibly Galvani's wife, and completely unconnected to the first experimenter, drew sparks from an electrical machine some distance away.

This 'contractions at a distance' was new and initially Galvani could not explain it. He thus set about conducting a huge number of experiments, altering tiny details and changing every conceivable variable in the experimental set-up. For instance, he placed the frog near the machine, far away, in a separate room, isolated under a glass jar, yet frustratingly he still found variability in his results, even when working on the same frog. Even with the variations he observed, however, the contractions triggered by the sparking of a remote electrical machine was not a 'one-off' – it was the intensity and duration of the effect that varied. He struggled to find an explanation for his results.

The fact that he obtained variable results is not a comment on his abilities as a researcher but instead highlights the difficulties of working with the natural variabilities in complex biological organisms, something modern scientists are well aware of. The phenomena of contractions at a distance were explained by Galvani's rival Volta and other contemporaries as 'the action of electric atmospheres'. The static electricity that accumulated on the electrical machine created an electric atmosphere that the frog's nerves were sensitive to. Eighteenth-century electric machines could produce more than 10,000 volts and would have been easily capable of inducing enough charge in the frog's nerve to cause contractions even when they were separated by several metres. This is the same principle by which lightning can induce a charge in the ground even though it is separated by a huge volume of air, as discussed in Chapter 10 (see page 199).

After several years of experimenting on the phenomenon of contractions at a distance in his laboratory, Galvani moved his experiments outside, to see if 'natural' electricity would produce the same effects as the 'artificial' electricity he had been using in the laboratory. When the weather was favourable, several frogs were prepared with metal hooks piercing the spinal column allowing them to be hung from the railings on the balcony at Galvani's home. As a thunderstorm approached over the horizon, the frogs' legs began to twitch.

Although these results could be interpreted as further evidence of the unity of atmospheric and artificial electricity, for Galvani this only confused matters. Even more surprising to him was the fact that no thunderstorm was required to produce the same effect. All Galvani or one of his assistants had to do was press the metal hook piercing the spinal cord against the railings and the legs would twitch exactly as before. He could not decide if the contractions were caused by external electrical effects, from a thunderstorm or a machine, or from the frog itself. Galvani started to wonder if there was yet another type of electricity, one that was inherent to the frog.

Galvani moved his experiments back indoors to his laboratory and another round of experiments was begun. With no other source of electricity nearby, he found he could produce the same effects on the muscles with just hooks and metal surfaces. The conditions were varied in every permutation he could think of: he changed the metal used for the hook and placed the frog on different surfaces (both metals and non-metals) before he connected the new surface to the metal hook by pressing on it. Importantly, contractions were only observed when conducting metals were used, something Galvani saw as evidence that the metals were merely allowing the movement of the electricity inherent within the frog.

As his experiments with different materials advanced, Galvani found he could make frogs' legs twitch just by placing an arc, made of metal, with one end touching an exposed nerve and the other end touching the leg of the frog.

At the end of 10 years of research, variation and repetition, Galvani concluded that there was something he called 'animal electricity' inherent within the body of the frog and in all animals. It was the movement of this intrinsic electrical fluid, through the conducting metals, or triggered by sparks, that caused the muscle contractions. Animal electricity was perhaps the 'vital fluid' that Victor Frankenstein could have potentially tapped into to animate his creature.

Benjamin Franklin had explained the cause of shocks and sparks of electricity by the movement of the electrical fluid to restore an imbalance. Galvani therefore concluded that there must be an imbalance in electrical fluid in the frog. He placed this imbalance within the muscles, stating that the inside and outside of the muscles contained different amounts of the electric fluid and that nerves were merely conductors. Franklin had used the unbalanced fluids theory to explain how the Leyden jar worked. Now Galvani likened muscles in the frog (and other animals) to Leyden jars with their excess and deficit of electrical fluid on the inside and outside of the muscle, rather than a jar. The metals used to form the arc in his experiments formed an alternative path for the electric fluid to flow through.

Galvani wrote up his findings in *De Viribus Electricitatis in Motu Musculari Commentarius* (*Commentary on the Effect of Electricity on Muscular Motion*) and in 1791 presented the world with the concept of 'animal electricity'. Experimenters across Europe scrabbled to recreate Galvani's experiment – leading to shortages in frogs. Among the first to take a detailed interest in Galvani's work was Volta who began his experiments within weeks of reading *De Viribus*.

T

Alessandro Volta was then 47, professor of physics at the University of Pavia and had recently been elected a fellow of the Royal Society in London. His contemporaries referred to him as the 'Newton of electricity'. His research interests at the time were in low levels of electricity that could not be detected by contemporary techniques. The best that was on offer were electrometers, which were only sensitive enough to detect around one volt. However, exposed nerves can be stimulated by a tiny fraction of this voltage. Galvani's results seemed to indicate that frogs might be a particularly sensitive detector for electrical atmospheres. Volta was therefore interested in using the frog as a tool to measure low levels of electricity.

Volta's initial enthusiasm for Galvani's work soon gave way to doubts. Regarding Galvani's experiments with hooks placed through the frog's spinal cord, and the metal arcs used to connect muscle and nerves, he thought the contractions might be caused by the metals themselves rather than animal electricity within the frog. When he replicated Galvani's experiments he noted strong contractions when dissimilar metals were used. He believed the electricity was being generated or moved by the metals and the frog was merely a conductor. He therefore described metals as 'electrical motors' rather than passive conductors.

Volta's initial response was to write a commentary on Galvani's work. It was the beginning of a long epistolary argument between the two. Although they remained polite, each became increasingly entrenched in his own view. Volta discredited Galvani's knowledge of electricity by stating that he clearly knew nothing about atmospheric electricity, a phenomena that would easily explain his observations of the frogs twitching in a thunderstorm. However, he evidently respected Galvani's research enough to reproduce his experiments and counter each argument Galvani presented specifically and in detail. Indeed, both Galvani and Volta developed new experiments that were devised to prove conclusively, in their minds, one argument or the other.

Others were drawn into the debate from across Europe and beyond. Experimenters, natural philosophers and the simply curious replicated the experiments, conducted their own variations, formed opinions of their own and chose their side in the debate. Battle lines were drawn along scientific as well as national boundaries. The scale of the debate was described by Emil du Bois-Reymond thus, '… wherever there were frogs, and wherever two dissimilar metals could be fastened together, people could convince themselves with their own eyes of the marvellous revival of severed limbs. Physiologists thought they grasped in their hands their old dream of a vital force … no person was in danger of being buried if he had been previously galvanised.'

To counter Volta's theory that electricity was being generated by dissimilar metals, Galvani showed that an arc made of only *one* metal was necessary to produce contractions. However, he conceded that these contractions were not as strong as those observed when two metals were used. Volta shot back that there was no way of proving that the metal was pure and an undetectable amount of a second metal would be the cause of Galvani's observations. Volta's assertion was impossible to prove and not therefore helpful for either side of the argument. So, instead, Galvani eliminated metals from his experiments completely.

Aldini, Galvani's nephew, had shown that carbon (not a metal) could act as an arc between the nerve and muscle to produce contractions*. In his laboratory, Galvani also found that humans holding hands could provide the necessary conducting path. There was not even a need for an external arc. When Galvani placed the dissected nerve of a frog on its own leg muscle he found it produced contractions. The frog had acted as source of electricity *and* conductor. 'All scientists predicted imminent defeat for Volta, and total triumph for Galvani.'

In return, Volta brought into question Galvani's experimental technique and suggested that no matter how carefully the nerve was placed on the frog's own muscle, the experimenter could never completely discount accidentally knocking the point of contact. This mechanical force acting on the nerve would be enough to trigger contractions. The fact that Galvani's experiment was difficult to reproduce only supported his argument. Neither side had advanced and neither side would concede defeat.

T

---

* Carbon, in the form of graphite (the stuff that makes pencil leads) is unusual among the non-metals in that it is able to conduct electricity because of the way the atomic bonds are arranged within its structure.

In spite of all his contradictory arguments, however, Volta did admit that animal electricity existed: he acknowledged that the torpedo and electric eel possessed an electric fluid that could produce shocks. He even admitted that there was animal electricity within the nerves of all animals that depended on the soul for it to act, but it was constrained within the limits of the nerve. In Galvani's experiments, Volta conjectured, the electric fluid could no longer be moved by the soul as the animals were dead and so it was the metals that now provided the external cause.

In 1795 Galvani conducted experiments on the torpedo fish. He wanted to find out more about the fish's electrical properties and use it to bolster his theory of animal electricity. In his experiments, one fish had one of its two electric organs taken out. Galvani found that the electric organ, removed from the body of the torpedo, could not produce any discernible electrical effects. The organ that remained in the fish, by contrast, still connected to the rest of the body by a mass of nerves, continued to produce shocks and other electrical effects. Another fish had its brain removed, and the electric organs of this fish ceased to function – the brain, and its connection with the nerves, was therefore important. Yet another fish had its heart removed to ensure the experiments were being carried out on a dead animal. This time the electric organs continued to work for some time afterwards. The heart was not critical to the function of the electric organs and therefore there had to be some other property within the animal to cause these effects after death. In Galvani's opinion this property was 'animal electricity'.

Galvani didn't stop at frogs and torpedo fish. He also used metal arcs on birds and quadrupeds, especially lambs, achieving muscle contractions and proving, in his mind and to many others, the existence of a *universal* animal electricity.

Galvani's side of the argument came to an abrupt halt on 4 December 1798. The French had gained control of the northern states of Italy where Galvani lived but, a man of principle, he refused to swear allegiance to the new rulers and was stripped of his job and income. As a result he was living with his brother when he died a penniless and broken man. Many others continued the discussion in Galvani's absence, notably Giovanni Aldini, Galvani's nephew, as we shall see later.

Galvani's legacy was considerable. He had brought the notion of animal electricity, and electrical stimulation of muscles to produce movements after death (galvanism), firmly into the public consciousness. The idea of scientists exploring and manipulating what was potentially the very stuff of life must have been awe-inspiring and terrifying. It is understandable that many challenged his view and the debate rumbled on without Galvani.

⟙

Volta's investigations with metals and different conductors continued and eventually led to a brilliantly simple device that would demonstrate the same electrical effects that Galvani had observed, but without the need of a frog, or any other animal for that matter. Galvani had eliminated metals from his experiments, Volta now eliminated frogs. If it was the metals generating the electric effects then all Volta should need was two different metals.

This became Volta's biggest contribution to science – the invention of the pile: a stack of alternating silver and zinc disks, about an inch in diameter, with water-soaked pasteboard sandwiched in between. The pasteboard took the place of the frog. When wires were attached to the top and bottom of the pile, a shock was produced.

Volta announced his invention of the pile to the Royal Society in a letter written in French, which was immediately published in the *Philosophical Transactions* with the English title *On the Electricity Excited by the mere Contact of conducting Substances of different Kinds*. A translated version followed soon after in *The Philosophical Magazine*. Volta called his invention the '*organe électrique artificiel*' because of its deliberate similarity to the electric organs of the torpedo fish. The device acquired many other names, but today we would call it the first battery.

Although Volta hadn't exactly disproved Galvani (there could still be an animal electricity) the scientific community at the time saw it as a conclusive victory. It brought an end to the animal electricity debate but, more importantly, it heralded a new era in electrical, chemical and physiological science. It would transform our understanding of electricity, scientific investigations and society itself.

News of Volta's ideas and invention soon spread. It was first announced to the general public in the *Morning Chronicle* on 30 May 1800 and the same paper later published a complete description of how a voltaic pile could be constructed. Tiberio Cavallo, an Italian natural philosopher living in London and a great friend of Dr James Lind, Percy Shelley's teacher at Eton, also did much to promote the new device. Within weeks experimenters across Europe were constructing voltaic piles and conducting new experiments.

For the first time a continuous current of electricity could be produced, something that, initially, contemporary instruments could not measure. Although some of the effects produced by the pile were undoubtedly electrical in nature it was not exactly the same as the static electricity machines and Leyden jars that experimenters were familiar with. For example, it was difficult to produce a spark from the voltaic pile and it didn't easily attract light bodies in the way that the static machines did. This led experimenters at the time to consider the possibility that yet another form of electricity had been discovered and this one was named 'galvanic' electricity, undoubtedly much to the chagrin of Volta.

In fact, both Galvani and Volta were broadly correct in their theories of electricity. Yes, two dissimilar metals can be used to produce an electric current (this is the basis for most modern batteries). And, yes, there is an electricity inherent within animals, though in the nerves and not the muscles as Galvani had thought. With the benefit of hindsight, Volta and Galvani were arguing at cross purposes.

Although Volta's invention produced a continuous flow of electricity that has since enabled the development of electronic devices as we know them today, it is actually not very useful for stimulating nerves. What is needed is a rapid change in voltage, which is what is delivered by the sparks of the electrical machines and Leyden jars Galvani was using in his experiments. Muscle contractions were only observed when the wires from Volta's pile first made contact with a nerve or muscle and, sometimes, when they were removed.

Volta and Galvani's battle over the nature of electricity and its action on muscles and nerves was far from concluded by the invention of the voltaic pile. There was still a lot to be investigated in the science of both electricity and mechanisms of the animal body. Further contributions to animal electricity were made by Johann Wilhelm Ritter and Alexander von Humboldt, the German physiologists we met in Chapter 3.

Today, the role of the frog has been supplanted by squid. The nerves of squid are so large that tiny electrodes can be placed inside the nerve cell to directly measure the voltage across the cell membrane. This feat was only achieved in the twentieth century and proved, finally, that nerve signals are electrical in nature, as Galvani had suggested so many years before.

What Galvani nor Mary's Victor Frankenstein could have known was how an electric potential was generated in nerve cells. To them and their contemporaries electricity was a substance in itself, not the consequence of the properties of atoms and electrons.

T

In nerve cells it is two dissimilar metals in the form of sodium and potassium ions moving in and out of the cell that creates the electrical signal. So that the nerve cell is primed and ready to transmit its signal, a 'resting potential' is set up whereby the inside of the cell is more negative than the outside. This is similar to the accumulation of charge on one side of the Leyden jar, with the opposite charge located on the other surface. It is the disequilibrium that Galvani erroneously thought was located in the muscles, though he had no way of determining this with eighteenth-century technology.

To achieve the resting potential, or disequilibrium, the nerve cell does two things: potassium is accumulated inside the nerve cell and sodium is kept outside. To maintain this disequilibrium, molecular pumps use energy to sort potassium and sodium ions into their correct places. When an individual dies and the supply of energy stops, this sorting process also stops and sodium and potassium ions will start to drift away from the usual position by diffusion.

When at rest, the segregation of potassium and sodium ions results in a -70 millivolts difference between the inside and outside of the cell. When a small trigger, be it a chemical reaction occurring naturally in the body or an external source such as an electric spark, stimulates a nerve it changes the properties of the cell membrane. This allows sodium ions to flow into the cell and potassium to flow out to restore the balance. This initial stimulation can be much smaller than -70 millivolts as it only has to modify the cell membrane slightly to allow a much bigger change from the movement of ions. This initial signal is like using a remote control to switch on a TV. A small amount of electrical signal is used to trigger a much larger flow of electricity that powers the TV. The minimum requirement to switch on the TV (assuming it is plugged in and ready) is therefore what is available from the small batteries in the remote control rather than a much bigger supply that is needed to power the TV itself. The nerves have a similar system.

This minimum threshold that needs to be surmounted before the cell membrane is modified to allow the flow of ions, ensures that nerves are not firing at the slightest provocation. However, it is an all-or-nothing system for each individual nerve cell (a larger stimulus will not produce a bigger signal in an individual cell). When Galvani noted an increase in muscle response from an increase in electrical strength, he was in fact triggering different nerve cells with different threshold limits. Despite this, his experimental techniques were subtle and detailed enough to appreciate that an all-or-nothing system was in operation, although he had no idea how it worked.

When the sodium channels open, positive sodium ions rush into the cell, neutralising the negative charge that has accumulated there. Potassium ions are triggered to flow out of the cell and a wave of sodium and potassium ion channels opens along the length of the nerve cell to transmit the nerve signal – what is called the 'action potential'. After the nerve signal has been produced, the end of the process involves molecular pumps moving everything back to their start positions.

To ensure the signal along the axon of the nerve (the part of the cell that transmits the electrical signal) isn't lost to the surrounding tissues, the axon is insulated by the myelin sheath, just like insulation around a wire. Motor neurons (nerve cells that control movement) can be up to a metre in length and, to make sure the signal doesn't lose power as it travels along the nerve, there are stations along the way that can gently boost the signal.

When Galvani and others were stimulating the nerves of the frogs, they only needed a tiny voltage (around 20 millivolts) to trigger the changes in the nerve cell membrane that allows the nerve to send a signal. Even if the nerves had been cut during the dissection, the stations along the axon that boost the signal can also be points to stimulate and start the signal.

Given that Mary, and therefore her character Victor Frankenstein, could not have known any of this, could Victor have substituted a simpler system such as metal wires when he was constructing his creature? After all, metals are far better conductors of electricity than nerve fluid. However, because of the way metal wires conduct electricity, by the movement of electrons along its length, to be able to transmit the same information along a wire a metre long, without losing intensity, would require wires much thicker than nerve cells (not including the insulating layer that would be needed to prevent short circuits). Despite their complexity, nerve cells can transmit signals at a speed of up to 150m per second and the whole process from stimulus to signal and back to resting potential can take a total of only 400ths of a second.

Nerve cells are transmitting messages from one part of the body to another in a beautifully orchestrated series of systems that monitor and regulate fundamental process such as breathing and digestion as well as allowing us to move and think. It is staggering in its complexity. The nervous system does not just consist of individual nerve cells – they are highly interconnected. Most nerve cells have around 1,000 contacts, and specialised nerve cells known as Purkinje cells can have as many as 80,000. Victor would have faced a considerable technical challenge in connecting up the nervous system from the parts he used to assemble his creature, one that would be daunting, if not impossible, for even the best surgeons today.

Volta's invention of the pile in 1800 may have triumphed over the theory of animal electricity initially, but there were still some who were reluctant to give up on the theory altogether. Galvani's nephew, Giovanni Aldini, took up his uncle's cause and sought to convert as many people as possible to Galvani's theories of animal electricity. To this end he conducted public demonstration of the effects of electricity on animals, replicating his uncle's experiments. Ironically, he used Volta's invention as the source of electrical stimulus but insisted on calling it a 'galvanic' battery rather than 'voltaic'.

To begin with Aldini used the electrician's old friend the frog, but soon making frogs' legs twitch became tame and he decided to move on to something more impressive – bull's heads, fresh from the slaughterhouse. Wires from his galvanic battery were placed on the head of the bull, making the face muscles move: the tongue would loll, the lips would curl back and the eyes would roll. But the animals had to be fresh. Several experimenters noted that the muscles of mammals were much harder to excite and the effects wore off quickly (when molecular pumps could no longer return the ions back to their original positions). In cats and dogs, for example, the effects wore off after about 15 minutes. The fact that the dead bodies of warm-blooded animals soon become unresponsive to electrical stimuli would have been yet another obstacle in Victor Frankenstein's path to reviving his creature.

When Aldini's audiences became unimpressed even by gruesome demonstrations with slaughtered animals, he moved on to something even more dramatic – human subjects. Heads and bodies were taken from the executioner's scaffold to lecture theatres, where Aldini and others would apply wires from their batteries to the face and body of the recently dead criminal. Heads, completely separated from their bodies were seen to grimace, frown and contort as though they were still living.

These vivid and grotesque demonstrations were eventually outlawed in Germany, as it had become clear that these shows had developed into macabre entertainment rather than lectures on scientific principles or part of scientific research. There is only so much that can be learned from applying electrical wires to the face of a decapitated head in front of an audience. However, not everything Aldini did was merely for show – he had even bigger ambitions: bringing the dead back to life.

Electric shocks were already being used in the eighteenth century in attempts to revive those who had drowned. Aldini advocated the use of a small battery to resuscitate people in a 'state of suspended animation', as he termed it, or those who had suffocated, when other treatments had failed. What Aldini really needed was a whole body to prove his theory, preferably one that had recently died from suffocation, and just such a one became available in 1803 in London.

Aldini was in England at the invitation of the Royal Humane Society, an organisation concerned with the preservation of life from accidents with water that offered financial rewards and medals for anyone who attempted to save the lives of those who had drowned. During his visit to England Aldini lectured to packed halls and demonstrated his now-famous experiments on bulls' heads.

On 18 January 1803, however, it was a much more exclusive audience that witnessed his most famous experiment. Aldini's subject that day was George Forster. Forster had been found guilty of the murder of his wife and daughter and, as was the normal punishment for murder at the time, the law prescribed that Forster be sentenced to be hanged and anatomised. This time, though, there was an extra twist: Forster's dead body would be handed over to Aldini for him to conduct electrical experiments.

Though there are doubts over whether Forster was guilty of this crime, he made a full confession the day before he was hanged at Newgate. It was a freezing-cold January morning and his body was left for an hour before being cut down. Moreover, there were further delays before the body reached Aldini since it had to go through a formal dissection to satisfy the law. In practice this was little more than an incision into the chest, which was then stitched up before the body was delivered to Aldini. In attendance were a select group of surgeons and friends who had gathered at a nearby house to witness the experiments.

Aldini's battery consisted of three troughs, each containing 40 plates of zinc and 40 of copper. He applied the wires from the battery to Forster's jaw and ear, 'the jaw began to quiver, the adjoining muscles were horribly contorted, and the left eye actually opened'. When Aldini moved the wires to the ears the head moved from side to side. As the power of the battery was increased, 'a convulsive action of all the muscles

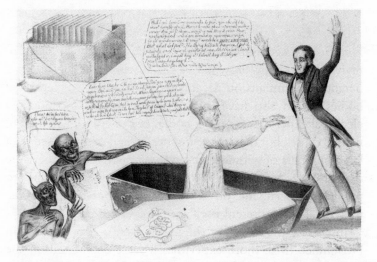

Figure 8 A galvanised corpse *satirising Giovanni Aldini's experiments on George Forster's body. Library of Congress prints and photographs online catalogue.*

of the face' occurred, and 'the lips and eyelids were also evidently affected'. In an attempt to restart the heart, Aldini cracked open Forster's ribs and applied the galvanic device directly to the organ but 'without the slightest visible action being induced'.

The experiments were too much for some of those present. 'Mr Pass, the Beadle of the Surgeon's Company, who was officially present during this experiment, was so alarmed that he died of fright soon after he had returned home.'

Aldini's experiments on the body of George Forster were reported widely, a detailed account appeared in *The Times* – so the young Mary Godwin may well have read about the strange goings-on at the Royal College of Surgeons in newspapers. Yet she could also have heard about the experiments from a first-hand witness, Anthony Carlisle, the eminent surgeon and friend of William Godwin. He may well have been present at Aldini's electrical experiments on the corpse of George Forster. Even if Carlisle wasn't a personal witness to Aldini's experiments, he was sure to have been interested in reading the reports of it and was very likely to have discussed the topic on a visit to Godwin's home.

T

Electric shocks continued to be used, off and on, in attempts to revive the recently drowned or those who had fallen from a height. Experiments on decapitated heads and their separated bodies would also have carried on. Aldini even conducted electrical experiments on the bodies of those who had died of natural causes, but these were not performed in the presence of large numbers of witnesses and weren't publicised in the same dramatic way as those on George Forster. The opportunity to publicly experiment on a recently deceased and whole individual didn't present itself again for some time.

Just a few months after the publication of *Frankenstein*, in November 1818, more experiments were conducted on the body of a dead criminal, but this time by Dr Andrew Ure. Could it be on this occasion that *Frankenstein* had influenced science rather than the other way around?

Ure obtained his medical degree from the University of Glasgow in his home town. He was made professor of natural philosophy at the Andersonian Institute (now the University of Strathclyde) in 1804, and was known for his skill and knowledge in chemistry. In 1818, Ure turned his attention to galvanism and conducted his experiments in front of a large audience rather than the select group who attended Aldini's 1803 attempts at reanimation. This time the subject of the electrical experiments was the convicted murderer Matthew Clydesdale. Dr Ure prepared his instruments and waited for the body to be delivered.

Ure was well aware of Aldini's experiments performed 15 years earlier in London and saw room for improvement. His criticisms were that previous experiments had transmitted the electricity directly through the muscles and that little attention had been paid to the positive and negative parts of the battery – both Galvani and Volta had noted that there was a different response from positive and negative electricity in biological systems. Although Ure acknowledged that galvanic electricity was capable of taking the place of the 'nervous influence' and acting in the same way, he was not convinced that electricity and the 'nervous influence' were one and the same thing.

Clydesdale had been convicted of murdering a 70-year-old man in a drunken rage. His was the first public execution in Glasgow for 10 years and it drew a huge crowd. Clydesdale's body had been left to hang for the customary hour before being cut down and was delivered to the anatomy theatre 10 minutes later. Just before the police arrived with the body, Ure charged his 270-plate battery with nitro-sulphuric acid. What happened next was reported by Ure in a paper he delivered to the Glasgow Literary Society the following month. More lurid descriptions appeared in Scottish newspapers much later.

Clydesdale's body was stretched out in front of Dr Ure and his assistants. Ure made an incision into the back of the neck to remove one of the vertebrae and expose the spinal cord. Further incisions were made to the heel, and the sciatic nerve through the buttock. At no point did blood flow. Clydesdale was dead.

Using his galvanic battery, Ure applied one wire to the freshly exposed spinal cord and the other to the sciatic nerve. Matthew Clydesdale's dead body shuddered as though from cold.

In a second experiment the wires were applied to the spinal cord and to a nerve on the heel. Clydesdale's leg kicked out, nearly knocking over one of the assistants. Next, the wires were applied to the phrenic nerve in the neck and through an incision at the bottom of the ribcage, where a wire could directly touch the diaphragm. Initially, nothing happened. Ure had to adjust the battery to increase the power. Then, 'Full, nay, laborious breathing commenced. The chest heaved and fell; the belly was protruded, and again collapsed. This process continued without interruption, as long as I continued the electric discharges.'

When Ure moved the wires to an incision above the eyebrow and to the heel, the whole face was thrown into a convulsion: 'Rage, horror, despair, anguish and ghastly smiles, united their hideous expression in the murderer's face. At this point several of the spectators were forced to leave the apartment from terror or sickness, and one gentleman fainted.'

In another experiment the wires were touched to the spinal cord and the ulnar nerve in the elbow. Clydesdale's fingers began to move 'nimbly, like those of a violin player'. With the wire touching an incision on the tip of one finger, Clydesdale's dead arm appeared to point to members of the audience, some of whom thought he had been brought back to life.

Importantly, all the effects on Clydesdale's body stopped as soon as the wires were removed. Clydesdale was dead. Ure had no intention or desire to revive a convicted murderer, but he did write about the potential benefits of reviving the dead in other circumstances. He acknowledged the main stumbling block in the process was restarting the heart – an organ that Galvani had noted was resistant to the effects of electricity.

Aldini had failed to restart the heart in his experiments on George Forster, despite cracking open the ribcage and applying an electric current directly to the organ in question.

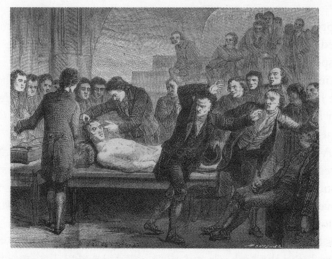

Figure 9 An illustration labelled 'Le docteur Ure galvanisant le corps de l'assassin Clydsdale' *from* Les merveilles de la science, ou Description populaire des inventions modernes, *1867, by Louis Figuier. Houghton Library, Harvard University.*

Ure, on the other hand, made no attempt to restart Clydesdale's heart. He thought it would have been useless to try because the body had been nearly drained of blood, known to be essential to its function. However, Ure had thought about this problem and proposed a solution.

Ure realised that electricity needed to be directed along the main nerves that led to the organ. He suggested that to restart a heart the points of the wires from a galvanic battery could be placed on the skin, rather than to the muscle of the heart itself, one above the phrenic nerve, and one in a position on the other side of the heart around the seventh rib. There might not even be a need to cut into the body. Instead, a cloth soaked in a solution of sal ammoniac could be wrapped around a brass knob at the end of the wires and applied to the skin to improve conduction to the underlying nerves. 'It may first be tried.'

Dr Ure's description of his proposed experiment may sound familiar. Unfortunately, he never carried it out. If he had, it is possible that he might have invented the defibrillator approximately 150 years before electronic devices were used to control heart rhythms for real. In the 1950s, in desperate attempts to save people from cardiac arrest, patients were literally plugged into the mains to stimulate the heart with the alternating current that normally powers our homes. This technique worked about 50 per cent of the time.

A few years later, in 1961, Bernard Lown developed a direct-current method of treating ventricular fibrillation using a specific waveform, now known as the Lown-waveform. A single jolt of electrical power (monophasic), following a particular pattern, was sent across the heart. It was hugely successful until further developments in the 1980s introduced the biphasic system that is still in use today.

The process of defibrillation is of course more complex than merely delivering a simple jolt of electricity to start the heart. In fact, defibrillators do not start the heart at all, contrary to what you might have seen on TV shows featuring patients flatlining and doctors administering shocks until a neat, regular heartbeat reappears on the monitor. Defibrillators stop the heart when it is in fibrillation (a rapid heartbeat that apparently makes the heart look as though it is fluttering). By stopping the heart, the natural pacemaker, found within the heart's own cells, are able to re-coordinate themselves and a normal rhythm is resumed. It's a bit like hitting the reset button. In this respect, a defibrillator, or similar device available to Victor Frankenstein, would have been of little use in restarting his creature's heart.

Whatever methods Mary's character Victor used to reanimate the collection of parts he had assembled to form his creature, he was successful. On that fateful night in November his creature was brought to life – the culmination of two years' intense work. The similarity of the scene with the experiments of Aldini and Ure on the bodies of George Forster and Matthew Clydesdale is unmistakeable.

In the early hours of the morning, when his candle was nearly burnt out after an exhausting night of work, 'I saw the dull yellow eye of the creature open; it breathed hard, and a convulsive motion agitated its limbs.' In an instant Victor's enthusiasm for his project turned to horror when he saw the thing he had created stir and move. The beautiful creature Victor had hoped to produce had become a living, breathing, terrifying monster.

PART THREE
BIRTH

Life

CHAPTER TWELVE

Life

'I am thy creature.'

Mary Shelley, *Frankenstein*

The culmination of Victor's ambitious science project was a collection of assorted parts stitched together and imbued with life. It's a staggering achievement by any standards. Victor's lofty ambitions for a beautiful creature that would worship him as his creator were brought sharply back down to earth when the creature opened its eyes and looked back at his creator. 'I had gazed upon him when unfinished; he was ugly then; but when those muscles and joints were rendered capable of motion, it became a thing such as even Dante could not have conceived.' Victor, swept along by his enthusiasm for his project had blinkered himself to the horrors of what he was constructing. Only at the moment of bringing life to his creature does he appreciate the reality of what he has achieved. His revulsion at his creation's appearance caused Victor to label this being 'monster', 'daemon', 'filthy creation'. But what was this living, breathing, thinking being?

Ϙ

The physical appearance of the creature has become part of modern culture. The image most of us have fixed in our minds is Boris Karloff in the 1931 film as the towering figure with a square head and a bolt through his neck. The enlarged forehead, green skin and lumbering gait have become part of the iconic image of horror. Mary Shelley's description is a little different.

How can I describe my emotions at this catastrophe, or how delineate the wretch whom with such infinite pains and care I had endeavoured to form? His limbs were in proportion, and I had selected his features as beautiful. Beautiful! His yellow

*skin scarcely covered the work of muscles and arteries beneath;
his hair was of a lustrous black, and flowing; his teeth of a pearly
whiteness; but these luxuriances only formed a more horrid
contrast with his watery eyes, that seem almost of the same colour
as the dun white sockets in which they were set, his shrivelled
complexion, and straight black lips.*

Victor Frankenstein's 8ft (2.4m) creature composed of bits
and pieces scavenged from dissection rooms, graves and
charnel houses would certainly have been a terrifying sight,
'The filthy mass that moved and talked.' The dull-yellow,
watery, clouded eyes, black lips, yellow skin and shrivelled
complexion is perhaps evidence of the dead materials he was
constructed from. Maybe the pale parchment-like appearance
of the skin and the watery dead eyes were something Mary
had seen in the bleached appearance of medical specimens
kept in jars in museums and at shows. However, there is no
mention in the novel of a square head, and other details of the
creature's appearance are frustratingly vague.

The first edition of *Frankenstein* was not illustrated so there
was no image by which to gauge the appearance of the creature.
Yet perhaps that is what makes him all the more terrifying, forcing
us to use our own imagination to fill in the blanks left in Mary's
text and shaping the monster to our own particular fears. The
1831 edition, however, has a frontispiece, which presumably had
to be approved by Mary. It depicts Victor's 'laboratory' in his
apartments, looking more like a study than a science lab, with
plenty of books but no scientific equipment. On the floor is the
creature, all 8ft (2.4m) of him. Apart from his gigantic size he
shows no apparent deformities or objectionable features. There
are no scars or bolts, but to emphasise the terror induced by the
creature Victor is shown fleeing the room in horror.

The attitude and position of the being on the floor of
Victor's apartment is not a million miles from another figure
with a striking resemblance to our modern ideas of
Frankenstein's monster. This being is found in an aquatint
titled *Los Chinchillas* created in 1799 by the Spanish artist
Francisco Goya. The 50th plate in the series of 80 shows two
straightjacketed figures being spoon-fed by a dark, sinister

person in the background and it appears to show Frankenstein's monster 17 years before the novel was conceived. The image is part of the *Los Caprichos* series Goya created as a comment on the follies, foolishness and absence of enlightened reason he saw in the Spanish life around him.

There is no mention of Mary having seen Goya's *Los Caprichos* series, let alone being inspired by it. Mary studied Spanish literature but there is no mention in her diaries of Goya. However, her illustrator, Theador von Holst, may have used Goya as inspiration. He was known for illustrating works of German Romantic fiction, such as Goethe's works, and was particularly interested in the supernatural and demonic. Moreover, even if

Figure 10 Frontispiece by Theodor von Holst to the 1831 edition of Frankenstein: Or, The Modern Prometheus.

Holst didn't take his inspiration from *Los Chinchillas* it is possible that the creators of the 1931 *Frankenstein* film did.

Goya's two figures in straightjackets are certainly closer to our modern ideas of Frankenstein's creature, with large features and an enlarged forehead, than Mary's description. The physical appearance of Goya's figures show characteristic signs of the medical condition acromegaly.

Acromegaly is caused by a benign tumour growing in the pituitary gland that causes the continued release of growth hormone after adults have normally stopped growing. Those affected can grow to a great height and it can result in large hands and feet, though a large forehead, chin and nose can also occur, as well as gapping of the teeth and a thickening of the skin. Swelling of the soft tissue can cause enlarged lips and ears and there are effects on internal organs such as the vocal cords, resulting in a deepening of the voice. In addition, more seriously, there can be damage to the heart and kidneys. If the condition occurs in childhood it results in gigantism – individuals of particularly high stature, such as Charles Byrne, the 'Irish Giant' we met in Chapter 8.

The effects of acromegaly would certainly explain some of the physical characteristics of Frankenstein's creature, particularly the modern film interpretations. The first *Frankenstein* film produced in 1910 by Edison Studios also has a creature with an enlarged forehead, huge feet and hands, but average height. Actors with acromegaly have sometimes been employed to play Frankenstein's creature-types on TV and in films. For example Ted Cassidy, who played Lurch in the 1960s TV series *The Addams Family*. The creature's stumbling gait is perhaps explained by the arthritis associated with acromegaly. In the films the creature is usually mute, but in Mary's novel he speaks eloquently with a voice described as 'harsh' but not deep.

The only other image of her creature that Mary saw was the interpretation by T. P. Cooke in a theatrical version of *Frankenstein* titled *Presumption: Or the Fate of Frankenstein*. The play was in its fourth week when Mary arrived back in London in 1823 and Mary went to see it within a few days of her return. Cooke took on the role of the unnamed monster who

Figure 11 Plate 50 from Los Caprichos: The Chinchillas (Los Chinchillas) *by Francisco Goya, 1799.*

burst out of Victor's laboratory and crashed down some stairs to create havoc and generally terrify the audience. Cooke was an established actor who had already made his name in another Romantic horror role, Lord Ruthven of *The Vampyre* by another of the guests at the Villa Diodati party, John Polidori.

Critics and theatre-goers were impressed with Cooke's performance as the monster and he revived the role several times as new productions were staged. His portrayal became the template for all those that followed and laid the foundations for the image we have of the creature in our mind's eye. Cooke's interpretation borrowed heavily from his previous role as Lord Ruthven, apparently both in characterisation as well as physical appearance. The look of the creature involved ragged clothes, which looked more like a toga than typical eighteenth- or nineteenth-century garb; heavy green, yellow and black make-up; and lank hair. Cooke's creature was described by one reviewer as being like one of the wax figures of a plague victim he had seen in a museum in Florence, but brought to life.

It was in this theatrical presentation of *Frankenstein* that the creature lost his voice along with his graceful movements. The name of the creature and his creator also began to be confused. This production also saw the introduction of another staple of the *Frankenstein* myth, the character of Fritz, the faithful assistant to Dr Frankenstein. By the time the 1931 film was made, Fritz had acquired a hump and the terrible behaviour of the monster was attributed to the use of a 'bad brain'.

The novel has a more complex explanation. Mary's text repeatedly asserts that the creature is fearfully ugly, tapping into contemporary theories of physiognomy and phrenology that were popular in the nineteenth century. It was believed that a person's character could be read in their features. Many tried to turn physiognomy into the subject of serious scientific investigation. From a physiognomy point of view, the creature's appearance is all that is needed to condemn him as a brutal monster in the eyes of those he meets.

Phrenology, developed in the late eighteenth century by Franz Joseph Gall, used measurements of the skull to determine mental characteristics. Because the brain was the organ of the mind, it was thought it should exert its influence in physical changes to itself and therefore the skull. Although now entirely debunked, it was an important step on the road to neuropsychology. However, it seems unlikely that anyone got close enough to the creature in *Frankenstein* to read the bumps on his head.

However much he asserted his kind nature, no one, not even his creator, could overcome their belief in this being's hideous nature based on his hideous appearance. Despite this, Mary's presentation of the creature challenges the view of an inherently evil monster. Her monster showed many acts of kindness, rescuing a drowning child and carrying out menial tasks on behalf of the family whose cottage he lived beside. He was driven to murder and destruction by the behaviour of others towards him. The book drew on Godwinian theories of duty and truth and other prevailing Enlightenment ideas at the time. It is for this reason that the book was seen as controversial, rather than the shock of any violent scenes or immoral goings on.

Later interpretations have Victor's creature as a bumbling simpleton whose violent rages are like the acts of a petulant child or caused by the misapplication of science. For example, in the 1910 Edison Studios film version, 'the evil of Victor's mind' somehow infiltrates the creature as he is being formed. Mary's original creation is intelligent, thoughtful, eloquent and graceful in his movements. The creature may not have had Victor's scientific knowledge, but he had a much better understanding of the ethical and social consequences of his creator's actions. The self-taught creature is able to outwit the university-educated Victor Frankenstein. Not bad for a two year old.

♀

Because of his appearance, the creature was rejected from the moment he was given life. When the creature first stirred, 'it breathed hard, and a convulsive motion agitated its limbs'. Victor rushed out of the room from sheer terror. He didn't even stay to witness the creature's first tentative steps in the world.

Within hours the being was walking and followed Victor into his bedroom. Victor watched as the creature's cheek wrinkled as though it appeared to smile, and sounds were articulated, but Victor was too terrified to tell if they were coherent words. When the creature stretched out his hand towards Victor it was too much for him and he fled.

For most of the night Victor paced and fretted in the courtyard of his lodgings, unable to face returning to see his creation. When morning arrived he walked out aimlessly into the streets of Ingolstadt. In his wanderings he stumbled upon his childhood friend from Geneva, Henry Clerval, who had just arrived to begin his own academic studies. Excited to meet his old friend again Victor invited Clerval back to his rooms, quite forgetting the creature he had left behind. He realised just in time and rushed to search the rooms after leaving his friend outside. To Victor's relief, the being was gone. He wouldn't see his creation again for two years.

The horrifying thought of Clerval meeting his hideous creation, coming after months of intense and exhausting labour, was too much. Victor collapsed with a 'nervous fever'. Selflessly, Clerval set aside his own studies to nurse Victor back to health. Victor had nightmares and raved incoherently, but when he regained his senses he was careful to conceal the cause of his trauma from everyone.

Eventually Victor regained enough strength to return home to Geneva. However, shortly before he was due to set off news arrived of a tragedy that had occurred at home: Victor's younger brother, William, had been found strangled.

Victor made haste to return home immediately, but arrived so late that the city gates of Geneva had been closed and he was forced to spend the night at nearby Sécheron. Frustrated by the delay he walked to the spot where his brother's body had been found. In the skies above Lake Geneva, a storm built. Bolts of lightning illuminated the surrounding mountains. In the distance, framed against the skyline by flashes of lightning, Victor saw the gigantic frame of his creature. In an instant he became certain this creature was responsible for his brother's death.

One death led to another when Justine, a servant in the Frankenstein household, was convicted of William's murder. Victor was fully aware of Justine's innocence but was unable to prove it. He wouldn't even speak out in her defence, terrified of not being believed.

Justine's death at the scaffold led Victor into another deep depression. He took to spending hours out on the lake at night, isolated from everyone. On one occasion he decided to take himself off on a journey to the valley of Chamonix.

His spirits lifted in the beautiful scenery familiar from his childhood. He set out to explore the vast ice wilderness of Montanvert, the glacier on Mont Blanc mentioned in Chapter 4, the spot Mary and Percy Shelley had visited in the summer of 1816.

When he reached the highest point on the glacier Victor looked back over the sea of ice and in the distance the creature appeared, bounding towards him with superhuman speed. It was the pair's first meeting since the creature's reanimation and Victor's reaction was to attack. The creature easily evaded him – his movements were swifter and more assured than Victor's. The creature was also more eloquent: he was able to persuade Victor to listen to his story before passing judgement on him.

The creature told Victor of his life over the past two years. After his reanimation and being abandoned to look after himself he had fled Victor's apartment, confused by all the sensations he was experiencing for the first time, and wandered through forests near Ingolstadt. His first sight of Victor had already demonstrated that he struck fear into people but this was only confirmed when he met a stranger. He was attacked, beaten and chased away. Spurned by everyone he met, he soon discovered it was best to avoid people. He thus hid himself in the forest and learnt to subsist on foraged food, discovering more and more about the environment around him so that when he came across a fire left by some others, he appreciated the warmth it gave off but could not understand how to create fire for himself.

Even these basic skills – walking, finding clothes to keep him warm and feeding himself – are huge achievements that are well beyond a human newborn. Perhaps the creature retained memories of these concepts and actions from the previous life of his borrowed brain. If so, his memory was very selective since he appears to have had no knowledge of any previous life lived by his brain or any other part of his assembled body.

Viewed scientifically, Victor's experiment was an incredible success. He had not just created a living being from dead parts but seems to have improved on the human race. The creature is strong, intelligent and does not feel the cold as humans do, and he is able to subsist on simple foodstuffs such as nuts and berries. The creature's life in the forest is very similar to the idealised life of the savage man exalted by Enlightenment philosophers such as Volney (who we will met again shortly) and Baron d'Holbach, whose work both Mary and Shelley read before the publication of *Frankenstein*.

Theories of the savage man were satirised by the Shelleys' friend Thomas Love Peacock in his 1815 novel *Headlong Hall*. In this book and again in *Melincourt*, Peacock discussed ideas of wild men in terms of human development. Some of the great apes that had been discovered in distant lands, such as the gorilla* and orangutan†, were seen in the eighteenth century as degenerative forms of human beings.

Peacock used the ideas of noble savages and wild primates to their absurd extreme for the purposes of satire. In *Melincourt* this is evident in the character Sir Oran Haut-Ton, a savage man who has been tamed, taught and at one point is put up for election to the British Parliament. The character shares many qualities with Mary's monster: he is very strong, very ugly, has a strong sense of right and wrong, and is clearly intelligent. However, like subsequent theatrical and film interpretations of the monster he is mute. *Melincourt* was published in 1817, when Mary was writing *Frankenstein*, and is a pastiche of the Shelleys and their friends as well as a satire on contemporary political and social issues. Around the time Peacock was writing *Headlong Hall*, the Shelleys and Peacock were spending a lot of time together and perhaps these books emerged out of conversations they were having in each other's company.

---

* Gorilla is derived from the ancient Greek word *gorillai* for 'tribe of hairy women' from when they were first described by Hanno the Navigator in the fifth century BC, though it is unknown if he was in fact describing what we know as modern gorillas or another species of ape or monkey.
† The name here derives from the Malay and Indonesian words *orang* meaning 'person' and *utan* meaning 'forest', so these primates are literally 'people of the forest'.

Peacock's novel *Melincourt* also draws on cases of 'wild men' – contemporary accounts of individuals, usually children, who appeared to have lived much of their young lives without human contact. Several of these individuals had been discovered in the eighteenth and early nineteenth centuries and some of their circumstances and characteristics are shared with Mary's creature.

Another source of information about wild men was the Shelleys' doctor, William Lawrence. Although Lawrence was part of the vitalism debate discussed in Chapter 3, he could also have supplied information about wild men and other 'monstrous' creatures.

Lawrence was particularly interested in wild men, or *homo feras* as he termed them. In his book, *Lectures on Physiology, Zoology, and the Natural History of Man*, he cited the case of Peter the Wild Boy who was found in 1724 near Hamelin (the town of the legendary pied piper). When Peter was discovered he was estimated to be 12 years old, couldn't speak, was said to have acute senses of hearing and smell and behaved 'rather brutish at first'. He initially shunned bread in preference for peeled green sticks or he chewed grass for the juice.

Peter adapted to living with humans, travelled to England to meet members of the royal family and lived to the ripe old age of 70, but never learned to speak. Peter's early feral life also has several parallels with Victor's creature's first years of existence subsisting on food foraged from the wood[*].

Peter is not the only case of a wild boy growing up separated from humans. Another one emerged in Aveyron, France, in 1800. The case is interesting both because it occurred during Mary's lifetime and for the child's name: Victor. When he was found, Victor was approximately 12 years old and, from his behaviour and scars on his body, had apparently spent

---

[*] Modern assessments of Peter's case have suggested he suffered from a rare genetic condition, Pitt-Hopkins syndrome, which manifests as certain facial characteristics and learning difficulties. It is rare for individuals with this condition to learn to speak more than a few words.

most of his life living wild. Although he appeared to understand what was said to him he only learnt to speak and write a handful of words and never fully integrated into human culture*.

Lawrence was possibly the source of further inspiration regarding the physical attributes of Mary's creature, as well as ideas of his identity as a species distinct from humans. Lawrence had a particular interest in medical monsters and formed his own collection. He even wrote the entry on monsters in *Rees's Cyclopaedia* – an encyclopaedia compiled by Abraham Rees – most of which focuses on descriptions of birth defects, such as conjoined twins, Cyclops or other physical defects.

Lawrence had a strong interest in how humans develop, as can be seen from his published lectures. He took this interest to an extreme when he studied a boy born without part of his brain, and had him cared for in his own house. Some of his findings were incorporated into his entry on 'Monsters' in *Ree's Cyclopaedia*. One short section even discusses cases of birth defects that produced resemblances to animals, which could have suggested the idea of human–animal hybrids. However, he commented that though there were several historical cases it was unlikely that they would be so described by his contemporaries, though it shows that human–animal hybrids were, at some point in history, not just reserved for gods or mythical creatures.

As to the cause of these defects, he cited the common misconception that defects occurred because of some incident during gestation or some injury to the pregnant mother. The implication was that the mother's mood or behaviour could influence the physical appearance of her child, although he had no alternative theory as to how such defects really happened. To the eighteenth-century way of thinking, Victor's creature may have been influenced by Victor's mood when he was under construction.

---

* It has been suggested that Victor was autistic and had perhaps been abused when young.

How both physical and mental characteristics could be passed on to younger generations was a considerable topic of debate in the eighteenth century. *Rees's Cyclopaedia* was published long before any concepts of genetics were around, before even Charles Darwin's theory of evolution, but the idea of species changing over time had started to take root and be developed.

In addition to his other work, Lawrence had translated several medical texts from Latin and was familiar with works by eminent German scientists, such as Johann Friedrich Blumenbach's *Comparative Anatomy* – a book highlighting the differences and similarities of a huge range of animals, from mammals to reptiles to insects. The book could easily have served as a catalogue of parts for Victor Frankenstein when he was constructing his creature. In his translation of the work Lawrence added considerable notes and he used Blumenbach's theory of races as a starting point to consider the origins of the human race, speculating whether different human races had emerged separately or if there was one common ancestor that had diversified over time. He also considered the relationship between humans and other animals.

The comparison of animals was an important step towards the theory of evolution but the classifying of human races, though accepted at the time, makes for very uncomfortable reading today.

It is these discussions around the nature of man, and whether mankind consisted of different races or different species, which were going on in the background when Mary was writing *Frankenstein* and describing her creature as 'a new species' and 'a new race'. She used the creature's physical appearance as signs of his distinctiveness from other humans.

♀

The creature's development is an accelerated version of the development of mankind from primitive hunter gatherers to communities of people working collectively to farm, support each other, govern and educate. Following his early days in the forest where he learnt the basics of survival, the creature progressed to living in a communal group. However, well aware of the effects of his appearance on humans he was careful to hide himself. He was fortunate to find a cottage with a shed attached in which he could shelter himself and observe the cottagers. The creature's independent life, living in the forest and learning to feed and clothe himself, his progression towards communal life and then learning follows C. F. Volney's account of the progress of man in his book *The Ruins of Empire*. Volney's work is fortuitously the creature's introduction to abstract learning.

The being's chosen abode was doubly fortunate because the occupants of the cottage epitomise many of the Enlightenment's radical ideals. The inhabitants were educated, kind, hard-working and with no interest in wealth or personal gain. The creature was astute and used his position to observe the inhabitants of the cottage, an elderly blind father and his two grown children, to learn more about human behaviour and language. When the son's Turkish fiancée, Safie, arrived and began to learn the family's native tongue, French, the creature takes full advantage of the language lessons and soon exceeds her.

Safie was taught French from a copy of Volney's *Ruins of Empire*. Published in 1791, it is one of the Enlightenment period's most revolutionary works arguing against the necessity of religion and government, and a particular favourite of William Godwin's and the Shelleys'. Volney was a friend of Benjamin Franklin and electricity makes a brief entry, showing how up to date Volney was on the latest scientific advances; the book was written before news of Galvani's frog experiments had been widely publicised, but the link between electricity and the motivating life force was already suspected and Volney clearly made the connection.

Moreover, it wasn't just spoken language that the creature learnt. Using books he found he also began to appreciate the signs found within them and became able to link them to language through Safie's lessons. He thus taught himself to read. The books he had found became intelligible to him and his learning increased. He was extremely lucky in the three works he had stumbled upon – John Milton's *Paradise Lost*, Plutarch's *Lives* and Goethe's *The Sorrows of Young Werter* – all of which provided an excellent introduction to Enlightenment ideals and provided almost exactly the kind of education William Godwin recommended in *Political Justice*.

In *Paradise Lost* the creature initially identified with Adam, a being manufactured, in a sense, by another and at first, alone in the world. However, as his education increased the creature found he associated more strongly with Milton's fallen angel, who is loathed and despised. But, he remarked, 'Satan had his companions, fellow-devils, to admire and encourage him; but I am solitary and abhorred.' Milton's Satan is supposed to be the most detested creature but in the end he is the more memorable one over Adam. We find ourselves sympathising with the brutal, ugly, violent monster.

The Sorrows of Young Werter is the book that shot Goethe to literary fame. The semi-autobiographical novel tells of a doomed love affair through a series of letters. Werter is in love with Charlotte but she is to be married to Albert. Feeling rejected by those he loved, Werter commits suicide and it is implied that Charlotte dies of a broken heart. The book was a sensation when it was published in 1774, creating 'Werter fever' – people dressed themselves as the book's fatal hero and it is said that there were even some copycat suicides. Its Romantic style was a huge influence on many European writers including Byron, Shelley and Mary. In *Frankenstein* the creature identified with Werter because he was rejected by those he loved and he was perhaps in search of his own Charlotte.

The third book in the creature's library was Plutarch's *Lives* – a series of biographies of influential men written in the second century AD. The accounts are paired to contrast their common moral virtues and failings, with each pair consisting of one Roman and one Greek historical figure. From this book the creature learnt his moral code. So in the space of just a year the creature has not only mastered language but he also has a thorough understanding of the content of his small library.

The implausibility of the creature learning so quickly by simply listening at a window and the luck of finding such an informative collection of books was remarked on by early reviewers of *Frankenstein*, even those who were generally favourable towards the book overall. If the creature's education lacked anything it was perhaps a scientific component, which was fortuitously provided by Victor Frankenstein's laboratory notes that he found in the pockets of the clothes he took from Victor's rooms when he fled.

In it, as well as the details of his own construction, the creature read about Victor's impressions of the work as he progressed. He fully understood the implications of remarks like 'filthy creation' and learnt to hate his creator. The murder of Victor's brother William and his shifting of the blame on to Justine were premeditated acts of revenge for Victor's maltreatment and neglect.

The creature's confrontation with Victor at Montanvert was a deliberate strategy. He had not come to the remote glacier to destroy Victor but to bargain with him. The creature promised not to harm Victor, or any other human, in return for a companion. He knew the fear and revulsion he generated in humans and so he demanded a fellow creature like himself.

As part of the deal Victor would create a second creature, a female, for companionship. The monster would be satisfied with this and promised to remove himself and his mate from all human contact and live peaceably in a remote location. The creature proposed to live in South America, a part of the world recently explored and described in hugely popular books by Alexander von Humboldt (whom we met in Chapter 3). This sparsely populated region would provide ample opportunity for the two creatures to escape human discovery. Victor consented to the plan.

☥

The construction of the second creature is interesting. Victor knew that science had progressed in his two-year absence from scientific and academic studies. The best physiologists were now to be found in England and so he travelled there to update his knowledge and collect materials before embarking on building a female companion for his creature*. This time the materials would almost certainly have come from the resurrectionists, there being no other practical source of body parts for Victor to rely on in Britain.

The location for the construction of the second creature, on a remote Scottish island in a refurbished two-room cottage, is even more basic than the apartment room used for the first one. Even fresh water is a scarce resource in this isolated location. It is a far cry from the elaborately furnished laboratories of the films. Yet despite this creature number two took considerably less time to construct – only a couple of months; clearly Victor had learnt from his first experiences as well as from the contacts he made in London. In a relatively short space of time Victor's second project was near completion, but he was no less horrified by the results of his work. Whatever advances Victor made in terms of constructing a creature, there was little progress in making it more visually appealing.

At the point of deciding on whether to abandon his work for the day or to push on and finish his awful task, he paused to reflect on what he was about to do. His agreement had been with his first creation. There was no guarantee that the second creature would concur. Although he had obtained promises from his first creature – that he would remove himself from the environs of humans – he had no such promises from the female. Perhaps learning from his previous mistakes, he thought about the possible results of producing a second creature.

Victor also had a moment of realisation and fear at the prospect of two powerful creatures and what they could achieve together. He acknowledged that his creature is stronger and better adapted to living in extreme conditions, qualities that might have given him a competitive edge in terms of evolution. What would happen if the creatures produced

---

* His journey to England follows the route taken by Mary and Shelley on their elopement trip along the Rhine. Again, Mary takes a moment to describe the scenery around Mannheim and the site of Castle Frankenstein, without ever mentioning the castle itself.

offspring? Would Victor then be the cause of a race of powerful creatures capable of threatening humankind? Victor appeared to have swung from hardly any contemplation of the implication of his work to wild speculation. Yet his theorising was not so far-fetched.

The fact that Victor fully expected the two creatures to be able to breed many generations indicates he considers them to be of the same species even though they have been composed from a variety of animal sources; the modern definition of a species is two animals that can produce fertile offspring.

In the late eighteenth century, knowledge of reproduction was poor, let alone the concept of genetic inheritance, which was non-existent. But ideas of changes in animal forms over long periods of time were starting to appear and the idea that some physical characteristics were inherited was well established even if the mechanism was far from understood.

Mary's discussion of her creatures breeding a race of superhumans perhaps shows her knowledge of Lamarck's theories of inheritance. The theory put forward in 1809 by Jean-Baptiste Lamarck was that changes made to an animal during its life, such as a giraffe stretching its neck a little further to reach more leaves, could be passed on to subsequent generations. This theory is entirely consistent with the idea of Victor's creatures passing on the characteristics he had given them in their construction.

Based on Lamarck's theory it was difficult to understand why some characteristics appeared to be passed on but others weren't. Animals that had lost a limb could give birth to animals with all their limbs intact. Other animals, apparently healthy, could give birth to deformed offspring, as discussed by Lawrence in his descriptions of 'monsters'. The idea of mutation and inheritance – established much later, beginning with the likes of Charles Darwin and Gregor Mendel but confirmed and elaborated on by many others – is that it is not characteristics acquired during life that are passed on. Instead every newborn is constructed from the genetic information contained within the egg and sperm that fused at the moment of conception. Unless Victor Frankenstein could alter the genetics within the sperm and eggs of his manufactured creatures, their offspring would resemble a product of the original donors of those parts.

But Victor would not have known this. It would thus not have been unreasonable for the late eighteenth-century natural philosopher to assume the offspring of his two creations would resemble them in stature and strength. From this point of view, Victor's fears were justified.

A recent thought experiment has attempted to model the progress of Victor's synthetic species if the pair really had successfully bred a race of superhumans. Had they gone to South America, a relatively sparsely populated region in the late eighteenth century, there would have been little competition for food. The creatures' superior strength and apparent adaptability has suggested that, from a single breeding pair, these creatures could have wiped out the human race in 4,000 years. The notion of competition for resources leading to species extinction is decades ahead of its time and shows an astonishing appreciation for the implications of the proto-evolutionary theory that was in existence when Mary was writing.

⚲

The terrifying prospect of a race of creatures terrorising humans and overwhelming the human race was too awful to contemplate. At the very last moment before bringing the female to life, Victor tore the body apart and dropped the pieces into the ocean. The creature was outraged and swore revenge. To bring the utmost misery on his creator, the monster destroyed everyone and everything that Victor cared about: his best friend Henry Clerval was the first victim in a new round of murders perpetrated by the monster; Victor's wife was later strangled by the monster on their wedding night; and Victor's father collapsed and died shortly after hearing the news.

Devastated by his loss, Victor swore to destroy his creature before it could kill again. This was apparently the reaction the creature was trying to provoke to enable a confrontation between the pair. Victor hunted his monster across Europe. When he was weakened by exhaustion and the deprivations of his journey, the creature waited, left food for his creator to maintain his strength and lured him ever onwards. The pursuit terminated in the Arctic, where the novel began.

When Victor finished recounting his tale to his rescuer Walton, the captain tried one last time to learn from Victor the secret of bestowing life, but he refused to tell. Although he acknowledged his 'enthusiasm exceeded moderation' and his work had brought death and misery, Victor was unrepentant. Science and acquiring new knowledge, he thought, was still a noble pursuit and he hoped that others would succeed where he had failed. His final disappointment was that he had not caught his creation and destroyed him and begged Walton to complete what he now knew he would not live to do. Victor died a short while later.

Walton returned to his cabin where Victor's body had been laid out and found the creature standing over the remains of his creator. In the final scene the monster promised the captain of the ship that he would take the body and construct a funeral pyre that would destroy both himself and his creator. The final moments see the creature carrying his creator and disappearing into the Arctic mists. However, in the last brilliant twist to the novel, we never see what becomes of the creature. His eventual fate is unknown.

CHAPTER THIRTEEN

Death

'Live and be happy, and make others so.'

Mary Shelley, *Frankenstein*

Victor Frankenstein and his iconic creature were unleashed on the world in 1818. Only 500 copies of the novel were printed for its first anonymous publication, a small run even for the time. Financially, it brought Mary just £28 14s (about £2,000 in today's money), but success can be measured in many different ways. Books were an expensive commodity in the early nineteenth century and copies would be shared and discussed. *Frankenstein* may not have been an overnight financial success, but soon after its somewhat subdued entrance into the world people started to take notice of it. Slowly and almost imperceptibly the novel crept into the public consciousness and Victor Frankenstein, his monster and Mary Shelley became famous.

Mary Shelley had received copies of her debut novel in late December 1817, but the book was first published by Lackington's on 11 March 1818. Just as Victor abandoned his creation, so did Mary. The day of publication was the same day the Shelley party travelled to Dover for their third trip abroad. Their numbers had swelled since their first elopement to France in 1814; on this occasion eight people made up the Shelley group: Shelley, Mary and their two children, William 'Willmouse' and Clara, as well as Claire Clairmont with Allegra, her daughter by Lord Byron. There were also the Shelley's servant Elise and the nursery maid Milly Shields. They were leaving England for Italy.

Shelley had been trying to gain custody of his children by his first wife Harriet after her suicide, but the courts rejected his claim because of his atheism. The scandal of abandoning his first wife and living with Mary probably didn't help his case. Another factor in their decision to leave England was that the damp environment at their house in Marlow was affecting Shelley's health. The group's finances were also still in a poor state and with a growing family it would be cheaper to live abroad.

This time their trip to Italy was to be 'for good' and they were happy at the prospect. Their prediction turned out to be true for many of them, but for all the worst reasons and Mary's return to Italy was marred by tragedies and scandal. Unknown to them when they left, only two of the party would ever return to live in England.

Frankenstein was left behind in England to fend for itself. News of the success or failure of Mary's debut novel, her 'hideous progeny', would follow them, weeks later, in letters and reviews posted out to them by friends.

❧

Reviews of the book were mixed but generally more favourable than reviews of Shelley's work. Many complimented the powerful imagination and boldness of ideas. The magazine *La Belle Assemblée*, thought the work 'original, audacious, and written in an excellent style'. Others hated it. For example, *The Quarterly Review*, which Mary read in October 1818, was particularly sarcastic and concluded the novel was 'a tissue of horrible and disgusting absurdity'. The same issue also contained an attack on Percy Shelley. However, aside from noting in her diary that she had read the magazine, there is no mention of what Mary made of its contents.

Some reviewers were more measured in their criticism, seeing *Frankenstein* as a poor imitation of William Godwin's *St. Leon* and nearly all of them picked up on the influence of Godwin's work. This was the reason most disliked the novel – not because of any horror or graphic violence, but because of the obvious influence of Godwinian ideas.

Some of the most favourable comments came from Sir Walter Scott writing in *Blackwood's Edinburgh Magazine*.

After some constructive criticisms of implausible aspects of the plot, he wrote, 'Upon the whole, the work impresses us with the high idea of the author's original genius and happy power of expression. We ... congratulate our readers upon a novel which excites new reflections and untried sources of emotion.'

Mary had sent a copy of the novel to Scott early on. He was a writer Mary hugely admired and the admiration, based on *Frankenstein*, became mutual. However, Scott initially believed it was Shelley who was the author and Mary had to politely correct him. He was not the only person who misattributed the work: speculation about who was the author of this daring novel started immediately. Though the nature of the work suggested William Godwin might be behind it, the fact that *Frankenstein* had been dedicated to him negated this. The next likely candidate was thought to be Shelley, a myth that persisted for a considerable time.

Regardless of whether the reviews were favourable or not, the book certainly generated interest and discussion. For instance, a letter from Shelley's friend Thomas Love Peacock in November 1818 told how he had been at Egham races and everyone was talking of *Frankenstein*. Peacock had been questioned about the novel and its author; 'It seems to be universally known and read' even if it wasn't universally praised.

The Shelley group arrived in Italy on 30 March and stayed initially in Milan. Mary had plenty to keep her occupied and the reception of *Frankenstein* doesn't get a mention in her diary.

One of the many reasons for travelling to Italy was to hand over custody of baby Allegra to Lord Byron who was then living in Venice. Byron had agreed to look after his child on the condition that Claire had nothing more to do with her. He didn't even want Claire to see her daughter again. The Shelleys were initially outraged at the proposition, but eventually reasoned that it would be more beneficial for Allegra to grow up in a wealthy aristocratic household with all the advantages that went with it. The 18-month-old child was therefore handed over to Byron's care.

Their duty done, Mary, Shelley, their children and Claire were free to start their new life. From Milan they travelled to Livorno (known to the English as Leghorn) and then on to Bagni di Lucca, which reminded them of Marlow. Shelley's health had improved markedly with the return to a warmer climate and Mary was looking around for a new plot for her next novel. Claire, however, missed her daughter terribly and pestered Byron for updates. Byron, initially delighted with his daughter, appears to have tired of her rapidly and gave her over to the Hoppner family to look after.

Both Mary and Shelley hoped Byron would relent his complete ban on Claire visiting her daughter and in August 1818 Claire travelled with Shelley to Venice. The plan was for Shelley to convince Byron to let Claire see Allegra. Byron agreed to this, although he was under the impression that the whole Shelley party was living nearby and accordingly offered them his house at Este to stay in. However, Mary was actually house-hunting in Florence, where they hoped to settle.

Shelley thus sent a note to Mary telling her to come to Este urgently before Byron noticed her absence and Mary and baby Clara travelled across Italy as quickly as they could in blistering heat. Clara, who had been ill, got worse as the long journey wore on and, when she arrived at Este on 14 September, she developed dysentery. On 24 September, the child was no better and Shelley made a doctor's appointment for 8 a.m. in Padua. This meant a 3.30 a.m. start for Mary and her sick daughter. Clara got worse during the journey, but instead of stopping at Padua, Mary was urged on by her husband with the promise of better doctors in Venice. Mary arrived with Clara but it was too late. While Shelley went to find the doctor and bring him to the inn where Mary and her daughter were resting, Clara died in convulsions in Mary's arms.

Mary was stoic about the loss of her daughter and threw herself into the entertainments the Hoppners suggested as a distraction for her. She also worked on transcribing some of

Byron's poems, but Shelley could see that his wife was miserable. On top of this, Byron still refused to hand Allegra over to the Shelleys and so, in November, the Shelleys, with their remaining son William, and Claire, left Venice for Naples.

After passing the winter in Naples, the following year, 1819, the Shelley group moved to Rome. They liked the city, visiting the Colosseum and other attractions. Mary had a drawing tutor, Claire had a singing tutor and Shelley was writing. They were reluctant to leave, but summer was fast approaching and this always brought with it unbearable heat and the risk of fever.

The Shelleys' remaining child, William, was sickly and Mary and Shelley knew they would have to move away from Rome for his health. But they left it too late: on 27 May their beloved son fell ill. Doctors were called and Mary and Shelley desperately hoped for a recovery, but the three-year-old boy had contracted malaria from the mosquitos that infested the marshes around Rome and on 7 June 1820 he died. Both parents were devastated, more than at the deaths of their other children, since William had been a particular favourite. Mary took it hardest.

The couple were left childless but Mary must have known, or at least suspected, that she was pregnant for the fourth time. The loss of two children, one so soon after the other, was dreadful and Mary must have been anxious for her coming child. She was distraught and thrown into a deep depression, Shelley wrote:

> *My dearest Mary, wherefore hast thou gone,*
> *And left me in this dreary world alone?*
> *Thy form is here indeed—a lovely one—*
> *But thou art fled, gone down a dreary road*
> *That leads to Sorrow's most obscure abode.*
> *For thine own sake I cannot follow thee*
> *Do thou return for mine.*

Soon after William was buried in a cemetery in Rome, Mary, Shelley and Claire moved on to Livorno. However, ever

restless, a few months later, in September, they were in
Florence. Mary tried to console herself with writing, but the
only real relief from the depths of her depression came with
the birth of their fourth child, Percy Florence Shelley, on 12
November 1819.

Overall, in terms of writing, their time in Italy was
productive for both Mary and Shelley. Shelley produced *The
Cenci* in 1819 and *Prometheus Unbound* in 1820, among many
other notable works. Mary, while still in the depths of her
depression, completed a short autobiographical novel, *Matilda*,
in August or September of 1819. She sent the manuscript to
her father in London for publication but he found the subject
matter – incest and suicide – too controversial and didn't send
it to any publishers and wouldn't return it to his daughter
despite her repeated requests. The novel wasn't published
until 1959.

In early 1820, life had settled to some kind of normality
with writing, visiting friends and taking care of baby Percy.
The Shelleys were also on the move again, this time to Pisa.
But their problems were far from over. In the summer of
1820 they received a disturbing letter from Paolo Foggi, a
former servant who was trying to blackmail them over an
incident that had occurred during their time in Naples.

During the winter of 1818–19, the Shelleys and Claire had
been in Naples where a strange incident had occurred. On 27
December 1818 the birth of a child, Elena Adelaide Shelley,
was registered with the local authorities. The parents were
listed as Percy Bysshe Shelley and his wife. The child was
baptised on 27 February 1819 and died on 10 June 1820,
shortly before the blackmail letter arrived. This much is
known. Paolo's accusation was that Shelley had fathered the
child by Elise, the Shelleys' servant (whom Paolo had married).
Whatever the Shelleys' relationship with the mysterious
child, she had not accompanied them when they moved away
from Naples to Rome.

There is no mention of the adoption or birth of a child in
Mary's journal during their time at Naples, only a note of a
'tremendous fuss' being made on 28 February 1819. Neither is

there any notice of the death in 1820. The whole episode is shrouded in mystery. The child may have been adopted; Mary and Shelley had tried and failed to adopt children in the past, almost on a whim. Perhaps this time they had been successful. The accusation, however, was that Shelley had fathered the child by Elise, or perhaps by Claire. Shelley strenuously denied the charge. Mary was adamant that she would have known if Claire had delivered a second child. Others have suggested the child belonged to Elise and that Byron was the father.

The only thing that is really certain is that the child was not Mary's. Whatever happened, the rumours spread among the Shelleys' friends in Italy and dogged them for years, causing considerable stress to both Mary and Shelley even after an agreement had been reached with Paolo.

In August 1820 Mary finally succeeded in her wish of living separately from Claire. For six years the three of them had cohabited almost continuously, but a position was found for Claire in Florence as a governess. Mary was occupied with the young Percy and writing another novel, *Valperga*. This is a historical novel, which Mary researched heavily. Critics have commended the novel's historical authenticity, but at the time it was viewed more as a romantic tale with a historical setting. Godwin edited the novel between 1821 and 1823 before its publication that year.

In March 1821, Allegra, five years old and still under Byron's care, was established in a convent. In Shelley's opinion it was better than living with Byron himself as he thought Byron's lifestyle didn't provide a suitable environment for the child. Allegra wasn't about to be returned to Claire, whatever protestations she might make. A great amount of animosity still existed between Claire and Byron and there were other considerations. Byron had misgivings about the Shelleys as parents because of their vegetarian diet and atheism.

Shelley visited Allegra at the convent, though Byron never did, and the young girl asked Shelley to be remembered to her father and 'mammina', Byron's mistress; she had no recollection of her natural mother, Claire. Claire was firmly against the convent school and petitioned Shelley to remove her. Various extravagant plans were put forward by Claire for her daughter's rescue, including scenarios in which Byron and Shelley would fight a duel over custody of the child. Everyone but Claire knew it was unrealistic.

Claire was so distressed about her daughter that when news arrived of Allegra's death on 20 April 1822, from a fever, it was kept from her as long as possible. When she was finally told, 12 days later, she was remarkably calm.

At this time the Shelleys, ever restless, had decided to rent a house in Livorno for the summer of 1822. They were to move there with their great friends the Williams family – Edward, Jane and their children. It was further north, on the coast and would be cooler than their current home in Pisa. However, there were very few suitable properties available and in the end the Shelleys were forced to compromise and take on a house, Casa Magni, near Lerici, just down the coast from Livorno. It wasn't just an inconvenient location – the property would have to be shared with the Williams.

The rooms in Casa Magni were divided between the two families. It was crowded and the Williams's and Shelleys's servants fought 'like cats and dogs' in the gloomy house clinging to the shoreline battered by waves from the Ligurian Sea. Furniture and household goods had to be transported to the house by sea, there being only a footpath linking the house to Lerici. There were no other houses nearby and it was a considerable walk to anything like a town or village. Mary hated it, but Shelley was excited by the prospect of sailing and spending time with the Williams family, as well as Byron who was staying nearby.

Shelley and Edward Williams commissioned a yacht to be built so they could sail. Byron had also commissioned a yacht, and their competitive natures meant both parties tried to outdo each other with the designs. Byron of course won with his grand *Bolivar* complete with cannon. Just to rub it in, he also cheekily christened Shelley and Williams' smaller yacht *Don Juan* after his own poem, though Shelley had wanted to call it *Ariel*. Byron had had 'Don Juan' painted directly on to the sails. Shelley and Williams desperately tried to scrub it off but nothing could efface it and in the end they had to cut the name out.

The Williamses and the Shelleys would go out sailing and Mary's mood occasionally lifted. She was pregnant again, and must have been anxious about it after the loss of three of her children. Mary was increasingly withdrawn and isolated from her husband, who was spending more and more time with Jane Williams. It was a troubled time for both Shelleys though. Shelley was experiencing vivid nightmares and waking hallucinations, including visions of the recently deceased Allegra rising from the sea and walking towards him.

On 16 June Mary suffered a miscarriage and would have bled to death if it hadn't been for the intervention of her husband who bodily picked up Mary and plunged her into an ice bath. By the time a doctor arrived there was little for him to do and Mary was confined to bed to recover.

While Mary was still weak from her miscarriage, Shelley and Edward Williams sailed in their yacht to Livorno to meet the Hunts, their old friends from the Shelleys' Marlow days. The Hunts had recently arrived from England but it was also an opportunity to pick up provisions for Casa Magni. Mary and Jane Williams stayed behind at the house.

The men arrived at Livorno on 1 July and the pair set off again for their return journey to Lerici on 8 July with the 18-year-old Charles Vivian acting as their boat boy. If they noticed that there were few other boats leaving the harbour with them, it didn't put them off, and neither did the storm clouds already gathering on the horizon. Shortly after they left, the storm broke.

Back at Casa Magni Mary and Jane waited patiently for their husbands' return but there was no sign of them. On 12 July a letter arrived from Leigh Hunt saying the pair had left Livorno and asking if they had reached home safely. Something had evidently happened en route.

A frantic search began. Even Mary, in her weakened state, travelled to Pisa and Livorno in the desperate hope of news.

When this finally came it was the worst kind: somewhere on their return journey, Shelley and Williams' boat had sunk.

On 19 July, Mary learnt that two badly decomposed bodies had been washed up. The first one could only be identified by a scarf and a boot. It was Edward Williams. The second body, Shelley, was found a mile further down the coast at Viareggio (about halfway between Livorno and Lerici). Shelley's body was so badly decayed that he could only be identified by his jacket and a book of poems stuffed into the pocket. Both bodies were immediately buried on the beach in accordance with local quarantine laws to prevent the spread of disease.

A friend of both families, Edward John Trelawny, made the funeral arrangements. The Hunts also travelled from Pisa to attend the funerals. On 13 August, Edward Williams' body was exhumed from the sands and burnt on a funeral pyre. The following day, Shelley's body too was placed on a pyre and burnt to ashes. Mary was too traumatised to attend. Even those who had travelled to the beach for the cremation found it too much. Trelawny remained in his carriage, and even Byron's calm failed him and he swam out to the Bolivar to watch the flames from a distance. Shelley's heart stubbornly refused to burn and it was removed from the ashes entire. Trelawny wanted to keep the relic for himself but he was prevailed upon by Byron that the proper person to have care of Shelley's heart was Mary. When Mary died many years later the relic was found in her writing desk among her papers.

And so it was that at the age of 25 Mary Shelley was widowed, penniless, with a two-year-old son and a father-in-law hundreds of miles away who hated her and refused to support her. She had had five pregnancies and one miscarriage that almost killed her. She had supported Claire through the loss of her child and another child had died in Naples under mysterious circumstances. Now she had to find a way to support herself and her young son.

For a time Mary lived with the Hunts in Florence, but she had little money. Mary found the Hunts' chaotic household stressful, but she could not afford to live separately. Her father, Godwin, was in no position to support her financially. Lord

Byron thus loaned her money and gave her work to do in making fair copies of his poems. He might not have needed Mary, or anyone, to do the work but it made an acceptable cover for Mary to receive money from him without either side losing face. But it was not sustainable. Byron had already made attempts to persuade Sir Timothy Shelley to support his daughter-in-law and grandchild on Mary's behalf, but without success. Mary needed to return to England to negotiate financial support from him. Byron paid for her return trip.

Mary returned to England on 25 August 1823 after more than five years abroad. Initially she stayed with her father in the family home at 195 The Strand (Godwin had moved out of Skinner Street after a court case over unpaid rent had determined against him). However, the old tensions soon resurfaced. Negotiations with Mary's father-in-law had begun through his lawyers and though no conclusion had been reached she was advanced £100 (around £10,000 purchasing power today), enough for her to move out of the Godwin house into cheap lodgings. However, there was some good news, *Frankenstein* had made her name. She wrote to a friend, 'But lo & behold! I find myself famous!'

The first theatrical version of *Frankenstein* was playing at the Lyceum Theatre and brought knowledge of the story to a much wider audience than would have been reached by reading the book alone. This popularisation of the novel set the tone for all future productions both on the stage and screen. The novel had been dramatised by Richard Brinsley Peake and was titled *Presumption; or, the fate of Frankenstein*. He took considerable liberties with the general plot but the main points were retained. The role of the creature was given to T. P. Cooke, who went on to make a career out of his portrayal of the creature. In much the same way that Boris Karloff's name became synonymous with the monster in the twentieth century, Cooke would be associated with the creature throughout the nineteenth century.

The play was a success, delighting and terrifying audiences. Stories of women fainting at the sight of the creature stumbling down the stairs from Victor's laboratory were probably exaggerated, and perhaps deliberately so to help ticket sales. Surprising perhaps to modern theatre-goers, this adaptation included songs. Mary herself went along to see the production only four days after her arrival back in England, then in the fourth week of its run, and was delighted.

The production set many of the stereotypes that have become attached to *Frankenstein*, not just the physical appearance of the creature as discussed in the previous chapter: the monster was dumb and lumbering, rather than being the articulate and agile creature of the book; the name of the scientist and creature started to be confused; Victor acquired a hapless assistant; and both the monster and his creator are seen to die at the end of the drama rather than ending with the inconclusive disappearance of the creature with Victor's body that concludes the novel.

To capitalise on the success of the theatre production, Godwin published another two-volume edition of *Frankenstein* in 1823. The following year there were two theatrical revivals and by the end of 1825 there were five separate productions of the *Frankenstein* story on the stage. In 1824 the drama had moved to Paris where T. P. Cooke went to revive his role as the creature.

The success and popularisation of the stage productions made Mary famous but it didn't give her a penny in return for her feats of imagination. At the time, dramatists and theatres were under no obligation to pay the original author for their work. Despite this, there were some small benefits for Mary: even though the novel had been published anonymously, Mary's name was now firmly attached to the work and she could use the association to promote her other writing.

Despite fame and acclaim for her writing, Mary was still ostracised by her husband's family. The small amount she was eventually able to secure from her father-in-law, initially just

£100 per annum, was given to her as a loan for the maintenance of her son that would be repaid out of the Shelley estate when her son eventually inherited. And there were other conditions attached to the loan.

The agreement with Sir Timothy Shelley through his lawyers meant Mary had to stay in England, though she would have much preferred to travel back to Italy where she had friends, a lifestyle that suited her and where her small income would have stretched much further.

Her father-in-law also prohibited her from using the Shelley name to publicise her work. He was outraged at the infamy that had surrounded Shelley's life and his relationship with Mary. She was also banned from publishing a biography of the poet, which Mary had planned to do to honour her beloved husband, to promote his literary work and in some way set the record straight. It might also have brought her some valuable income.

Mary used whatever tricks she could to work around the conditions imposed on her. When it came to publishing her own work, Mary could not use her married name and would not consider using her maiden name; she was Shelley's widow and forever bound to him. Yet she could at least fall back on her own literary fame and was able to publish as 'the author of Frankenstein' to increase the readership of the novels she continued to produce.

Her situation with respect to her father-in-law improved slightly when Percy Shelley's eldest son, Charles, from his first marriage to Harriet, died in 1826. Mary negotiated with lawyers for more money to support her son Percy, who was now heir to the Shelley title, and wrote for magazines and publishers to subsidise her meagre income, contributing articles and essays to *The Westminster Review* and the annual *The Keepsake* as well as writing short biographies or 'lives' for inclusion in Lardener's *Cabinet Cyclopaedia*.

Whatever time wasn't devoted to writing and researching these contributions, Mary spent writing and researching for her novels. In 1826 *The Last Man* was published. In 1830 she received £150 (just over £12,000 today) for the publication of *The Fortunes of Perkin Warbeck*, a fictional account of a man who claimed to be Richard of Shrewsbury – one of the princes in the tower said to have been killed by Richard III – and heir to the English throne. In 1835 *Lodore* was published, followed by *Falkner* in 1837. Slowly her allowance from Sir Timothy was increased and her financial position eased, but she was far from rich.

In 1831 *Frankenstein* was included in a series of popular classics published by Richard Bentley as part of a series of Standard English Novels. Mary was paid £60 (just over £5,000 today) and given the opportunity to edit her work before publication. The 1818 edition was written with significant input from her husband, but this later edition is all Mary's own and has become the most read and enjoyed. The 1831 edition is a considerable rewrite with significant changes to the 1818 text and it garnered more publicity and reviews, which were generally more positive than those of the 1818 edition.

Some of the changes between the original and 1831 editions are quite significant. Victor married a family friend rather than his cousin – to remove any suggestion of incest, a topic Shelley had been heavily criticised for when it featured in some of his own work. To clearly show that Victor's family had no guilt or part in his downfall, and are truly innocent victims of the monster's revenge, it was no longer his father who introduced Victor to the wonders of electricity and modern science, it was a family friend. Professor Waldman also became a more influential figure. The science itself was little changed, though some of the details of Victor's early scientific education were removed. The switch from alchemy to modern scientific interests is much clearer in the later edition.

Galvanism is explicitly mentioned in the 1831 text, but not in the 1818 version. Though this strengthens the links between Aldini's experiments as a possible influence for the reanimation of Victor's creation, the reference is not made during this crucial passage in the text. Instead, galvanism is specifically mentioned in the Introduction to the 1831 edition and again fleetingly when Victor was first introduced to the science of electricity after lightning struck the tree near the family house. This incident now forms a clear break from his alchemical past to modern science

The addition of an Introduction to the 1831 edition was an opportunity for Mary to describe the genesis of the novel, and set out her version of events at Villa Diodati, safe in the knowledge that no one would contradict her if she chose to embellish a few details. Byron's death in 1824 meant that only eight years after the famous literary gathering, of the five people who had been at Villa Diodati in 1816, only herself and Claire Clairmont were still living.

Mary was gratified to learn that of the 3,500 copies of *Frankenstein* that had been printed, 3,000 had been sold in the first year, but financially she was obliged to keep working. Mary continued to support herself and her son through writing, though of all the subsequent written work she produced nothing ever quite matched *Frankenstein*. Mary lodged cheaply, worked hard and made significant sacrifices to economise. Any money she had to spare often went to other members of her family or friends. After her father's death in 1836, Mary was still working to support her stepmother despite a lifetime of animosity between the two.

In 1839, still under the ban from Sir Timothy, Mary published a collection of Shelley's poetry with long explanatory notes in which she was able to incorporate certain biographical details to give context to the work. It was the best she could do to get round the ban on publishing Shelley's biography. This is still an invaluable resource to Shelley scholars everywhere.

She also assisted others who wrote biographies of her husband. Moreover, when Lord Byron died she was again sought out by biographers who wished to hear her personal recollections of the great poet. However, she refused payment for her contributions.

Most of Mary's time and energy went into providing the best she could for her son. Though Mary sent her son to Harrow

(she could not face sending him to Eton, Shelley's school that he had hated so much) she lived nearby to avoid the costs of lodging her son at the school. This meant she was cut off from her friends in London, but she had little choice financially.

Occasional news of Sir Timothy Shelley's poor health raised Mary's hopes but as her stepsister commented, 'His jumps towards the grave and then his quick returns to life are too comical ... You say he has lived long enough to ruin you.' In 1833 Sir Timothy appeared to be suffering from what was thought to be a terminal illness, but despite all prognostications 'that undying ... undyable Sir Tim!' made a full recovery.

Mary's son Percy had occasionally been invited to Field Place to meet his grandfather, which perhaps Mary saw as a way of increasing familial affection and thereby improving her chances of an increased income from Sir Timothy. Mary herself never met her father-in-law.

In 1844, at the grand age of 90, Sir Timothy died. Percy Florence Shelley inherited the baronetcy and his grandfather's estates, but it did little to relieve the financial difficulties he and his mother had been living under. The post-obit loans Shelley had obtained during his lifetime had swelled thanks to high interest rates his creditors had demanded. The money Mary had been given to raise young Percy also had to be repaid to the estate from her son's inheritance and there were other debts to be cleared. There was not much left for Percy to inherit.

Though the estate and lands brought in substantial money, there were also substantial outgoings. Field Place, the childhood home of Percy Shelley, was damp and in need of repair. Mary and her son instead moved into a smaller rented house nearby and let the Field Place property. Years of poor weather contributed to losses on the estate's farms, lowering the rents that could be collected.

Mary had high hopes for the young Percy Shelley and educated him to the best of her ability. He went to Cambridge University but was an unremarkable student. In spite of everything, Percy showed none of his father's or mother's literary flair. Attempts to lure him into a career in politics failed and Percy spent his life listlessly engaged in amateur dramatics and sailing, at which he excelled, much to Mary's distress. His only real literary contribution was the preservation of his parents' work and memories.

On 1 February 1851, at the age of 53, Mary Shelley died from a brain tumour. She had been suffering from crippling headaches for several years and her writing had suffered as a consequence. Shortly before her death she experienced a series of fits and lapsed into a coma. The case was hopeless. After her death her son and daughter-in-law dedicated much of their lives to the promotion and preservation of Mary and Shelley's name and literary contributions. A shrine was erected at their family home, to which only a few of the most dedicated friends and followers were permitted access.

Mary's diary was edited and a biography commissioned to reflect most favourably on her. When Thomas Jefferson Hogg, Shelley's friend from his university days, began writing his memoirs of Shelley he was initially loaned materials from the estate in the form of Percy's correspondence, but these were withdrawn when the published work did not reflect favourably on Shelley's memory. Hogg only published two of a planned five volumes.

Mary was buried at St Peter's churchyard in Bournemouth. Later, when the development of St Pancras railway station in London threatened the graves of her parents Mary Wollstonecraft and William Godwin, their bodies were moved to the same churchyard. Mary Jane Clairmont, Godwin's second wife, was left behind. After a lifetime of upheaval and turmoil, Mary Wollstonecraft Godwin Shelley now rests between the graves of her parents.

Epilogue

Frankenstein continues to outlive its author and has spawned its own 'hideous progeny' in the form of plays, ballets, books and films. The green-skinned, square-headed, lumbering creature has become a mainstay of Halloween and horror films. Mary Shelley's fictional creature really has populated the world with its offspring, though not quite as she predicted.

From early on in its life, the idea and image of Victor Frankenstein and his monster has produced a greater impression on the public mind than the reality of the novel. Familiarity with the story and its main ideas are widespread, but far fewer people have read the book.

Reading the novel today is a different experience to that which contemporary readers had. Stories of bodysnatchers, as well as terrifying and powerful scientific experiments, would have given the book a very different context and impact. The novel has been reshaped in our minds through stage and silver-screen adaptations to reflect scientific ideas of the times. The monster has been appropriated to make political, as well as scientific, comments, but he has mostly been used to entertain.

As we have seen from the 1823 stage productions of *Frankenstein*, the novel was soon being adapted and reinvented for public consumption. Further evidence that *Frankenstein* had made it into the popular consciousness is demonstrated by the allusion to *Frankenstein* made by George Canning when he addressed the UK Parliament on the issue of the emancipation of slaves. He suggested that freeing rebel West Indian slaves 'would be to raise up a creature resembling the splendid fiction of a recent romance'. Mary was said to be pleased to have her book acknowledged but must have been disappointed at the interpretation it had been given. Mary's novel advocated for better care of our fellow creatures, not their suppression.

In 1843 a cartoon in *Punch* magazine showed a towering, threatening figure labelled 'The Irish Frankenstein'. In 1882 the same magazine showed another cartoon, with the same caption, depicting the Irish Fenian Movement as a Frankenstein's monster figure after the Phoenix Park murders. These references also show how the name 'Frankenstein' and the novel have been twisted to suit an agenda. *Frankenstein* is still occasionally used in political cartoons and debates, though today it is more commonly associated with scientific matters such as discussions on genetic modification or stem cell research.

The use of the name Frankenstein as short-hand for monstrous behaviour or 'dangerous science' shows how completely the novel has infiltrated popular culture. But it doesn't stop there. *Frankenstein* was the first work of science fiction and it also inspired the first horror film in 1910. The novel has been adapted for the silver screen many times over as well as being the source of inspiration for many other science-fiction and horror films since then.

Victor Frankenstein has been the inspiration for countless 'mad scientists' and their hapless sidekicks. The creature has morphed into robotic forms, such as in Fritz Lang's 1927 film *Metropolis*, to a stop-motion dog in Tim Burton's 2012 film *Frankenweenie*. It is estimated that there were more than 400 film derivations of the classic 1931 *Frankenstein* film. Victor and his creature have also appeared on the small screen in comedies, dramas and cartoons for kids. The image of the creature has been utilised to promote everything from sweets to hairspray.

Mary Shelley's contribution to popular culture is enormous but her work of science fiction has also had an influence on science fact, certainly in relation to its public perception. *Frankenstein* may not be very credible in terms of the practicalities of the science Victor was engaged in, but Mary had a thorough understanding of the scientific concepts and implications of Enlightenment science.

The word Frankenstein is now perhaps most associated with science gone mad or very wrong. For example, genetically modified crops have been labelled 'Frankenfoods' – a word that has been appropriated to demonise and terrify even before discussions of the safety of such products has been debated. As I hope this book has shown, this was not how the science was presented in the original novel. However, it is not all bad: *Frankenstein* and the science that inspired it also has a positive legacy.

Giovanni Aldini's experiments on dead bodies from Chapter 11 may seem grotesque and far from the interests of science but he was genuinely interested in the effects and applications of electrical phenomena. As well as experiments on dead subjects, Aldini conducted electrical experiments on the living. In his best-documented case, he used electrical stimulation to treat a farm worker, Luigi Lanzarini, who had been institutionalised suffering from 'melancholy madness' or clinical depression. Aldini believed Lanzarini's illness was caused by an electrical disturbance in the brain and proposed treating it with electric shocks from a galvanic battery. Slowly Lanzarini improved. He said that Aldini's treatments didn't hurt him and soon he was smiling and eating well. His pain evaporated and he was well enough to be released. Aldini had laid the groundwork for what would become electroconvulsive therapy or ECT.

ECT's reputation has been tarnished by poorly conducted experiments carried out in the 1950s through to the 1970s. Patients would be strapped to beds and have electric shocks applied across the temples, sometimes without anaesthetic or even the patient's consent. The portrayal of ECT in films such as *One Flew Over the Cuckoo's Nest* did little to help the image of what can be a hugely beneficial treatment. Today, with patient consent, anaesthetics and muscle relaxants, electric shocks have been found to help many people with life-threatening depression who do not respond to the usual drug treatments.

In addition, there have been many more developments in medical electricity since the Enlightenment. In the 1950s, Earl Bakken, founder of Medtronic, was apparently inspired by memories of the 1931 film of *Frankenstein*. He had a recollection of being terrified as a child seeing Boris Karloff's hand twitch after receiving bolts of electricity and thought perhaps electricity could be of medical benefit. Could Victor's lab filled with electrical equipment be refined and miniaturised to control the natural rhythms of the heart? Bakken went on to develop the first portable, battery-powered pacemaker.

Today, electronic devices are implanted not just to control heart rhythms, but also into brains to control the tremors of Parkinson's disease as well as to treat depression. Those who, through brain injury from a stroke or accident, lose control over their limbs can regain mobility through sensors and electric stimulation of nerves in the legs. Increasingly sophisticated prosthetic limbs can use nerve signals from other parts of the body to animate robotic arms.

Some 200 years after its first publication the reality of *Frankenstein*'s science is still the stuff of fiction. But perhaps it is getting a little closer to science fact.

Appendix: Timeline of Events

Year	Important historical event	Important Personal Event for Mary Wollstonecraft Godwin
1280	Death of Albertus Magnus (born 1200)	
1535	Death of Heinrich Cornelius Agrippa von Nettesheim (born 1486)	
1541	Death of Philippus Aureolus Theophrastus Bombastus von Hohenheim (Paracelsus) (born 1493)	
1650	Anne Greene survives hanging	
1666	Attempt to transfuse blood into a human, Arthur Coga	
1673	Johann Konrad Dippel born 10 August	
1705	Francis Hauksbee's experiments with static electricity	
1724	Peter the Wild Boy discovered near Hamlin	
1727	Isaac Newton dies 20 (or 31 depending on whether you are using the old- or new-style calendar) March	
1728	John Hunter born 13 February	
1731	Erasmus Darwin born 12 December	
1732	Stephen Gray's experiments on electricity	

Year	Important historical event	Important Personal Event for Mary Wollstonecraft Godwin
1733	Joseph Priestley born 24 March	
1734	Dippel dies 25 April	
1737	Luigi Galvani born 9 September	
1739	Jacques de Vaucanson makes a mechanical 'digesting duck'	
1743	Antoine Lavoisier born 26 August	
1744	Britain is at war with France (King George's War 1744–48)	
1745	Alessandro Volta born 18 February	
	Benjamin Franklin begins his electrical experiments	
	Discovery of the Leyden jar	
1751	Hogarth paints *The Four Stages of Cruelty*	
1752	Murder Act allows the bodies of murderers to be dissected	
	Thomas-François Dalibard carries out Franklin's lightning experiment in France 10 May	
	Franklin flies a kite into a thunderstorm June	
1756	Start of the Seven Years' War	William Godwin born 3 March
1759		Mary Wollstonecraft born 27 April
1760	Accession of George III	

Year	Important historical event	Important Personal Event for Mary Wollstonecraft Godwin
1765	Stamp Act imposes tax in American colonies	
1767	Joseph Priestley publishes *The History and Present State of Electricity*	
1768	Joseph Wright paints *An Experiment on a Bird in the Air Pump*	
1771	John Hunter publishes *The Natural History of the Human Teeth*	
	Carl Wilhelm Scheele discovers 'fire air' (oxygen)	
1772	John Walsh proves torpedo fish give electric shocks	
	Johann Wolfgang Goethe publishes *The Sorrows of Young Werther*	
1773	Boston Tea Party protest	
1774	Priestley discovers 'dephlogisticated air' (oxygen)	
1775	American War of Independence begins	
1776	American Declaration of Independence	
1777	Hunter attempts to revive Revd Dr William Dodd after he is hanged	
	Antoine Lavoisier names 'vital air' oxygen and comes up with theory of combustion	
1778	Anglo-French war begins (1778–1783)	

Year	Important historical event	Important Personal Event for Mary Wollstonecraft Godwin
	Humphry Davy born 17 December	
1780	Galvani begins his electrical experiments on frogs	
1781	James Graham opens the Temple of Health in London	
1782	Charles Byrne 'The Irish Giant' arrives in London	
1783	Treaty of Versailles	
	William Lawrence born 16 July	
	John Hunter steals the body of Charles Byrne	
	John Hunter moves his anatomical collection to Leicester Square	
1785	Thomas Love Peacock born 18 October	
1787	Antoine Lavoisier and Pierre-Simon Laplace publish *Method of Chemical Nomenclature*	Mary Wollstonecraft publishes *Thoughts on the Education of Daughters*
	Antoine Lavoisier publishes *Elementary Treatise on Chemistry*	
1788	Byron born 22 January	Mary Wollstonecraft publishes *Mary* and *Original Stories*
	John Hunter's collection opened as a museum	
1789	Storming of the Bastille	
	Erasmus Darwin writes *The Loves of the Plants*	
1790	Edmund Burke writes *Reflections on the Revolution in France*	Mary Wollstonecraft writes *A Vindication of the Rights of Men*

Year	Important historical event	Important Personal Event for Mary Wollstonecraft Godwin
1791	Thomas Paine publishes *Rights of Man*	Mary Wollstonecraft and William Godwin first meet
	Luigi Galvani publishes *De viribus electricitatis in motu musculari*	
	C. F. Volney publishes *Ruins of Empires*	
	Priestley's home and laboratory destroyed by rioters	
1792	First use of the guillotine	Wollstonecraft publishes *Vindication of the Rights of Women*
	France declared a Republic	Percy Bysshe Shelley born 4 August
		Mary Wollstonecraft moves to Paris
1793	Execution of Louis XVI	Mary Wollstonecraft meets Gilbert Imlay
	France declares war on British	William Godwin publishes *Enquiry Concerning Political Justice: And Its Influence on Morals and Happiness*
	John Hunter dies 16 October	
1794	Lavoisier guillotined in Paris 8 May	Fanny Imlay born 14 May
	Erasmus Darwin publishes *Zoonomia*	William Godwin publishes *Caleb Williams*
	Priestley emigrates to America	
1795	John William Polidori born 7 September	Mary Wollstonecraft makes two separate suicide attempts

Year	Important historical event	Important Personal Event for Mary Wollstonecraft Godwin
1796	Anglo–Spanish war begins	Mary Wollstonecraft publishes *Letters Written during a Short Residence in Sweden, Norway and Denmark*
		Wollstonecraft and Godwin meet again
1797	Erasmus Darwin publishes *Female Education*	William Godwin and Mary Wollstonecraft marry in secret 29 March
	John Robison publishes *Proofs of a Conspiracy*	Mary Wollstonecraft Godwin born 30 August
		Mary Wollstonecraft dies 10 September
1798	Beddoes Pneumatic Institution opens	William Godwin publishes *Memoirs of the Author of A Vindication of the Rights of Women*
	Abbé Barruel publishes *Memoirs Illustrating the History of Jacobinism*	Jane (Claire) Clairmont born 27 April
	Luigi Galvani dies 4 December	
	Samuel Taylor Coleridge publishes *The Rime of the Ancient Mariner*	
1799	Goya, *Los Caprichos*	William Godwin publishes *St. Leon*
1800	Humphry Davy publishes *Researches, Chemical and Philosophical, chiefly concerning Nitrous Oxide and its Respiration*	
	Allessandro Volta announces invention of the 'pile'	

Year	Important historical event	Important Personal Event for Mary Wollstonecraft Godwin
	Royal Institution opens	
	Victor of Aveyron found living wild	
1801	Humphry Davy appointed assistant lecturer in chemistry at Royal Institution	William Godwin and Mary Jane Clairmont marry, twice, 21 December
1802	Treaty of Amiens	
	Erasmus Darwin dies 18 April	
1803	Aldini conducts electrical experiments on the body of George Forster 19 January	William Godwin junior born 28 March
	Erasmus Darwin publishes *The Temple of Nature*	
	War resumes between Britain and France	
1804	Napoleon proclaimed Emperor	
	Priestley dies 6 February	
1805	Battle of Trafalgar	William Godwin and Jane Godwin open a publishing firm for children's books
		William Godwin publishes *Fleetwood*
1806	John Hunter's museum moves to RCS new headquarters at Lincoln's Inn Fields	
1807	Abolition of Slave Trade	Godwin family move to Skinner Street
	Davy discovers the elements sodium and potassium	

Year	Important historical event	Important Personal Event for Mary Wollstonecraft Godwin
1808	Peninsular War begins	*Mounseer Nongtongpaw is published*
	Goethe publishes *Faust (Part 1)*	
1809	Lamarck proposes a theory of inherited animal characteristics	
1810		Percy Bysshe Shelley publishes *Zastrozzi*
1811		Percy Bysshe Shelley publishes *St. Irvyne*
		Shelley is sent down from Oxford 25 March
		Shelley marries Harriet Westbrook 25 August
1812	Napoleon invades Russia	Mary travels to Dundee to stay with the Baxter family
	Humphry Davy publishes *Elements of Chemical Philosophy*	Possible first meeting of Mary and Shelley 11 November
1813	Anglo–American War begins	Percy Bysshe Shelley publishes *Queen Mab*
1814	Napoleon abdicates	William Godwin publishes *The Pantheon*
		Mary returns to Skinner Street, meets Shelley 13 May
		Mary and Shelley elope accompanied by Claire Clairmont 28 July
		July to August: Journey through France, Switzerland and along the Rhine past Castle Frankenstein
		Mary, Shelley and Claire return to England 14 September

Year	Important historical event	Important Personal Event for Mary Wollstonecraft Godwin
		Charles Shelley born 30 November to Harriet
1815	Napoleon escapes from Elba	Mary gives birth to premature daughter 22 February, who dies 6 March
	Battle of Waterloo	Mary and Shelley tour south coast of England and Devon
	Mount Tambora erupts 10 April	Mary and Shelley move to Bishopsgate in August
	Thomas Love Peacock publishes *Headlong Hall*	
1816	Vitalism debate between William Lawrence and John Abernethy	William 'Willmouse' Shelley born 24 January
		April: Claire becomes Byron's mistress
		Mary, Shelley and Claire depart for Geneva 2 May
		June: Ghost story challenge – Mary begins *Frankenstein*
		July: Expedition to Chamonix and the Mer de Glace
		Shelley party returns to England 8 September
		Fanny Godwin commits suicide 10 October
		Harriet Shelley commits suicide early December
		Mary and Shelley marry 30 December
1817	Thomas Love Peacock publishes *Melincourt*	Claire gives birth to Allegra 12 January
		March: Shelleys move to Marlow

Year	Important historical event	Important Personal Event for Mary Wollstonecraft Godwin
		Mary finishes *Frankenstein* 14 May
		Clara Everina Shelley born 22 September
		Mary Shelley publishes *History of a Six Weeks' Tour*
1818	Successful human-to-human blood transfusion carried out by James Blundell	Mary Shelley publishes *Frankenstein* 11 March
	Thomas Love Peacock publishes *Nightmare Abbey*	Shelleys depart for Italy 11 March
	Andrew Ure conducts electrical experiments on the body of Matthew Clydesdale 4 November	April: Allegra handed over to Byron
		Clara Everina Shelley dies 24 September
		December: Shelleys travel to Rome then Naples
		Elena Adelaide Shelley born 28 December
1819	Invention of the stethoscope	March: Shelleys move to Rome
	William Lawrence publishes *Lectures on Physiology, Zoology, and the Natural History of Man*	John Polidori publishes *The Vampyre*
		William 'Wilmouse' Shelley dies 7 June
		August: Mary begins *Mathilda*
		Percy Florence Shelley born 12 November
1820	Accession of George IV	Percy Shelley publishes *Prometheus Unbound*

Year	Important historical event	Important Personal Event for Mary Wollstonecraft Godwin
		Elena Adelaide Shelley dies 10 June
1821	Napoleon dies on St. Helena	The Shelleys meet Edward and Jane Williams
		John Polidori dies 21 August of cyanide poisoning
1822		Allegra dies 19 April
		May: Shelleys move to Casa Magni with the Williams
		Mary miscarries 16 June
		Shelley and Williams drown 8 July
		Shelley and Williams cremated 16 August
1823		Mary returns to London 25 August
		Mary sees stage adaptation of *Frankenstein, Presumption* 29 August
		Mary Shelley publishes *Valperga*
1824		*Posthumous Poems of Percy Bysshe Shelley* published
		Byron dies 19 April
1826		Mary Shelley publishes *The Last Man*
		Charles Bysshe Shelley dies 14 September, Percy Florence becomes heir to the baronetcy
1827	Volta dies 5 March	
1829	Davy dies 29 May	
1830	Accession of William IV	Mary Shelley publishes *The Fortunes of Perkin Warbeck*
1831		Revised edition of *Frankenstein* published

Year	Important historical event	Important Personal Event for Mary Wollstonecraft Godwin
1832	Anatomy Act ends body-snatching	William Godwin junior dies 8 September
1833		Mary moves to Harrow, Percy attends as a day pupil
1834		William Godwin publishes *Lives of the Necromancers*
1835		Mary Shelley publishes *Lodore*
		Lives of the Most Eminent Literary and Scientific Men of Italy, Spain and Portugal, Vol I and II published
1836		Godwin dies 7 April
1837		Mary Shelley publishes *Falkner*
		Percy goes to Trinity College, Cambridge
1838		*Lives of the Most Eminent Literary and Scientific Men of France Vol I* published
1839		*Poetical works of Percy Bysshe Shelley* published
		Essays, Letters from Abroad and Fragments published
		Lives of the Most Eminent Literary and Scientific Men of France Vol II published
1841		Mary Jane Godwin dies 17 June
1844		Mary Shelley publishes *Rambles in Germany and Italy*
		Sir Timothy Shelley dies 24 April, Percy Florence inherits the baronetcy
1848		Sir Percy Florence Shelley marries Jane St John 22 June
1851		Mary Shelley dies 1 February

Bibliography

1800. *The Juvenile Library, Including a Complete Course of Instruction on Every Useful Subject*. R. Philips, London.

1823. *The Drama; Or, Theatrical Pocket Magazine*. T. & J. Elvey, London.

Aeschylus. 1961. *Prometheus Bound and Other Plays*. Penguin Books, London.

Aldini, G. 1819. *General Views on the Application of Galvanism to Medical Purposes: Principally in Cases of Suspended Animation*. J. Callow, London.

Allen, G. 2012. *Inflation: The Value of the Pound 1750–2011*. RP12-31. House of Commons Library.

Al-Khalili, J. 2010. *Pathfinders: The Golden Age of Arabic Science*. Allen Lane, London.

Ashcroft, F. 2012. *The Spark of Life: Electricity and the Human Body*. Penguin Books, London.

Aynsley, E. E. & Campbell, W. A. 1962. 'Johann Konrad Dippel 1673–1743' *Medical History* 6(2): 281–86.

Ball, P. *The Elements: A Very Short Introduction*. Oxford University Press, Oxford.

Bailey, J. B. 2012. *The Diary of a Resurrectionist 1811–1812*. Digi-Media-Apps, www.digimediaapps.com

Barrington, D. 1775. *The Probability of Reaching the North Pole*. C. Heydinger, London.

Barruel, The Abbé. 1799. *Memoirs, Illustrating the History of Jacobism*. Cornelius Davis, New York.

Bartholomew, M., Brown, S., Clennell, S., Emsley, C., Furbank, P. N. & Lentin, A. 1990. *Units 13–14: The French Enlightenment*. The Open University, Milton Keynes.

Bertucci, P. 2007. *Therapeutic Attractions: Early Applications of Electricity to the Art of Healing*.

Blundell, J. 1828. *Some Remarks on the Operation of Transfusion*. Thomas Tegg, London.

Bondeson, J. 2001. *Buried Alive: The Terrifying History of Our Most Primal Fear*. W. W. Norton & Company, New York.

Bynum, W. & Bynum, H. (eds). 2011. *Great Discoveries in Medicine*. Thames & Hudson, London.

Carr, K. 2013. 'Saints and Sinners: Johann Konrad Dippel'. *The Royal College of Surgeons of England Bulletin* 95(1): 21–22.

Clemit, P. 2009. 'William Godwin's Juvenile Library'. *The Charles Lamb Bulletin* 147: 90–99.

Coghlan, A. 2015. 'World's First Biolimb: Rat Forelimb Grown in the Lab'. *New Scientist* 3 June.

Coleridge, S. T. 1798. *The Rime of the Ancient Mariner*. Gutenburg.

Coleridge, S. T. 1816. *Christabel; Kubla Khan, a vision; The Pains of Sleep: Volume 1*. John Murray, London.

Cresswell, R. (translated). 1862. *Aristotle's History of Animals*. Henry G. Bohn, London.

Crosse, A. & Crosse, C. A. H. 1857. *Memorials, Scientific and Literary, of Andrew Crosse, the Electrician*. Longman, Brown, Green, Longmans, & Roberts, London.

Crouch, L. E. 1978. 'Davy's "A Discourse, Introductory to a Course of Lectures on Chemistry": A Possible Scientific Source of *Frankenstein*'. *Keats–Shelley Journal*, 27: 35–44.

Darwin, E. 1807. *The Botanic Garden: A Poem, in Two Parts: Part 1 Containing The Economy of Vegetation. Part II. The Loves of the Plants*. T. & J. Swords, New York.

Darwin, E. 1800. *Zoonomia; or the Laws of Organic Life*. P. Byrne, Dublin.

Darwin, E. 1803. *The Temple of Nature; or, The Origin of Society: A Poem, with Philosophical Notes*. J. Johnson, London.

Davy, H. 1800. *Researches, Chemical and Philosophical; Chiefly Concerning Nitrous Oxide, or Dephlogisticated Nitrous Air, and its Respiration*. J. Johnson & Co, London.

Davy, H. 1812. *Elements of Chemical Philosophy*. J. Johnson & Co., London

Domini, N. J. & Yeakel, J. D. 2017. '*Frankenstein* and the Horrors of Competitive Exclusion'. *Bioscience* 67 (2): 107–110.

Doren, C. Van. 1911. *The Life of Thomas Love Peacock*. J. M. Dent & Sons, London.

Dougan, A. 2008. *Raising the Dead: The Men Who Created Frankenstein*. Birlinn, Edinburgh.

Doyle, W. 2001. *The French Revolution: A Very Short Introduction*. Oxford University Press, Oxford.

Elsom, D. M. 2015. *Lightning: Nature and Culture*. Reaktion Books, London.

Fara, P. 2002. *An Entertainment for Angels*. Icon books, Cambridge.

Feldman, P. R. & Scott-Kilvert, D. 1995. *The Journals of Mary Shelley*. The John Hopkins Press, London.

Finger, F. & Law, M. B. 1998. 'Science in the era of Mary Shelley's *Frankenstein*'. *Journal of the History of Medicine*, 53 (April): 161–180.

Fisher, L. 2005. *Weighing the Soul: The Evolution of Scientific Beliefs*. Orion Books, London.

Florescu, R. 1977. *In Search of Frankenstein*. New England Library, London.

Frayling, C. 2005. *Mad, Bad and Dangerous to Know? The Scientists in the Cinema*. Reaktion Books, London.

Gagliardo, J. G. 1968. *Enlightened Despotism*. Routledge & Kegan Paul, London.

Gannal, J. N. (translated from the French by Harlan, R.). 1840. *History of Embalming, and of Preparations in Anatomy, Pathology, and Natural History; Including a New Process of Embalming*. Judah Dobson, Philadelphia.

Gigante, D. 2002. 'The Monster in the Rainbow: Keats and the Science of Life'. *PMLA* 117 (3): 433–448.

Godwin, W. 1798. *Enquiry Concerning Political Justice: And its Influence on Morals and Happiness*. G. G. & J. Robinson, London.

Godwin, W. 1798. *Memoirs of the Author of A Vindication of the Rights of Woman*. J. Johnson, London.

Godwin, W. 1814. *The Pantheon: or Ancient History of the Gods of Greece and Rome*. M. J. Godwin, London.

Godwin, W. 1832. *Fleetwood: Or, The New Man of Feeling*. R. Bentley, London.

Godwin, W. 1835. *St. Leon: A Tale of the Sixteenth Century*. R. Bentley, London.

Godwin, W. 1835. *Lives of the Necromancers or, An Account of the Most Eminent Persons in Successive Ages, Who Have Claimed for Themselves, or to Whom has been Imputed by Others, the Exercise of Magical Power*. Harper & Brothers, New York.

Goethe, J. W. von. 1780. *The Sorrows of Young Werter: A German Story*. J. Dodsley, London.

Goethe, J. W. von. Translated by Hayward, A. 1859. *Faust: A Dramatic Poem*. Ticknor & Fields, Boston.

Golinski, J. 1992. *Science as Public Culture: Chemistry and Enlightenment in Britain, 1760–1820*. Cambridge University Press, Cambridge.

Goulding, C. 2002. 'The Real Doctor Frankenstein?' *Journal of the Royal Society of Medicine* 95: 257–259.

Harris, R. W. 1975. *Absolutism and Enlightenment*. Blandford Press, Poole, Dorset.

Hartley, H. 1972. *Humphry Davy*. EP Publishing Limited, Wakefield.

Hawke, D. F. 1976. *Franklin*. Harper & Row, New York, San Francisco, London.

Hayman, J. & Oxenham, M. 2016. *Human Body Decomposition*. Elsevier, London.

Hesiod. 2016. *The Complete Hesiod Collection*. Amazon, Great Britain.

Hofer, P. 1969. *Los Caprichos, Francisco Goya*. Dover Publications, New York.

Hogg, J. T. 1888. *The Life of Percy Bysshe Shelley*. Volumes 1 and 2. Edward Moxon, London.

Holmes, F. L. 1993. 'The Old Martyr of Science: The Frog in Experimental Physiology'. *Journal of the History of Biology* 26(2): 311–328.

Holmes, R. 2005. *Shelley: The Pursuit*. Harper Perennial, London.

Holmes, R. 2009. *The Age of Wonder: How the Romantic Generation Discovered the Beauty and Terror of Science*. HarperPress, London.

Itard, E. M. 1802. *An Historical Account of the Discovery and Education of a Savage Man, or of the First Developments, Physical and Moral, of the Young Savage Caught in the Woods Near Aveyron, in the Year 1798*. Richard Phillips, London.

Jungnickel, C. & McCormmack, R. 2001. *Cavendish: The Experimental Life*. Bucknell, Pennsylvania.

Katznelson, L. MD; Atkinson, J. L. D. MD; Cook, D. M. MD, FACE; Ezzat, S. Z. MD, FRCPC; Hamrahian, A. H. MD, FACE; & Miller, K. K. MD. 2011. 'American Association for Clinical Endocrinologists Medical Guidelines for Clinical Practice for the Diagnosis and Treatment of Acromegaly'. *Endocrine Practice* 17 (Suppl 4).

Knellwolf, C. & Goodall, J. (eds.). 2009. *Frankenstein's Science: Experimentation and Discovery in Romantic Culture, 1780–1830*. Ashgate Publishing, Surrey.

Knox, F. J. 1836. *The Anatomist's Instructor, and Museum Companion: Being Practical Instructions for the Formation and Subsequent Management of Anatomical Museums*. Adam & Charles Black, Edinburgh.

Kragh, H. 2003. 'Volta's apostle: Christoph Heinrich Pfaff, champion of the contact theory'. Kirjassa F. B. & E. A. Giannetto (eds.) *Volta and the History of Electricity*. Universita degli studi di Pavia. Hoepli. Milano, 37–50.

Lavater, J. C. 1810. *Essays on Physiognomy; for the Promotion of the Knowledge and the Love of Mankind*. G. G. J. & J. Robinson, London.

Lawrence, W. 1819. *Lectures on Physiology, Zoology, and the Natural History of Man*. J. Callow, London.

Lewis, M. G. 1832. *The Monk, Printed Verbatim from the First London Edition*. Baudry's Foreign Library, Paris.

Locke, D. 1980. *A Fantasy of Reason: The Life & Thought of William Godwin*. Routledge & Kegan Paul, London.

Luke, H. J. 1965. 'Sir William Lawrence: Physician to Shelley and Mary'. *Papers on English Language and Literature*, 2: 141–152.

MacCarthy, F. 2003. *Byron: Life and Legend*. Faber & Faber, England.

Macilwain, G. 1853. *Memoirs of John Abernethy, R. R. S. with a View of His Lectures, Writings and Character*. Harper & Brothers, New York.

Marcet, J. 1809. *Conversations on Chemistry: In Which the Elements of that Science are Familiarly Explained and Illustrated by Experiments and Plates: to Which are Added, Some Late*

Discoveries on the Subject of the Fixed Alkalies. Increase Cooke & Co., N. Haven.

Mellor, A. K., 1989. *Mary Shelley: Her Life, Her Fiction, Her Monsters.* Routledge, Chapman & Hall Inc, New York.

Milton, J. 1996. *Paradise Lost.* Penguin Books, London.

Montillo, R. 2013. *The Lady and Her Monsters: A Tale of Dissections, Real-Life Dr. Frankensteins, and the Creation of Mary Shelley's Masterpiece.* HarperCollins Publishers, New York.

Moore, T. 1860. *The Life, Letters and Journals of Lord Byron.* John Murray, London.

Moore, W. 2005. *The Knife Man: Blood, Body-Snatching and the Birth of Modern Surgery.* Bantam Books, London.

Moores Ball, J. 1928. *The Sack-'Em-Up Men: An Account of the Rise and Fall of the Modern Resurrectionists.* Oliver & Boyd, London.

Morley, H. 1856. *The Life of Cornelius Agrippa von Nettesheim. Doctor and Knight, Commonly Known as Magician.* Chapman & Hall, London.

Murray, E. B. 1978. 'Shelley's Contribution to Mary's *Frankenstein*'. *The Keats–Shelley Memorial Bulletin*, 29: 50–68.

Newmann, W. R. 2005. *Promethean Ambitions: Alchemy and the Quest to Perfect Nature.* The University of Chicago Press, Chicago.

Pancaldi, G. 2003. *Volta: Science and Culture in the Age of Enlightenment.* Princeton University Press, Oxfordshire.

Paracelsus (translated into English by Turner, R.). 1657. *Paracelsus of The Chymical Transmutation of Metals & Geneology and Generation of Minerals.* Rich: Monn at the Seven Stars, and Hen: Fletcher at the three gilt Cups, London.

Parent, A. 2004. 'Giovanni Aldini: From Animal Electricity to Human Brain Stimulation'. *The Canadian Journal of Neurological Sciences*, 31(4): 576–584.

Peacock, T. L. 1816. *Headlong Hall.* T. Hookham, Jun. & Co, London.

Peacock, T. L. 1817. *Melincourt.* T. Hookham, Jun. & Co, London.

Peacock, T. L. 1818. *Nightmare Abbey.* T. Hookham & Baldwin, Cradock & Joy, London.

Pera, M. & Mandelbaum, J. 1992. *The Ambiguous Frog: The Galvani–Volta Controversy on Animal Electricity*. Princeton University Press, Oxford.

Piccolino, M. & Bresadola, M. 2013. *Shocking Frogs: Galvani, Volta, and the Electric Origins of Neuroscience*. Oxford University Press, Oxford.

Plutarch, Langhorne, J. & Langhorne W. 1850. *Plutarch's Lives of the Noble Greeks and Romans, Translated from the Original Greek: With Notes, Critical and Historical and a Life of Plutarch*. R. S. & J. Applegate, Cincinnati.

Pole, T. 1813. *The Anatomical Instructor: Or, An Illustration of the Modern and Most Approved Methods of Preparing and Preserving the Different Parts of the Human Body, and of Quadrupeds, by Injection, Corrosion, Maceration, Distention, Articulation, Modelling, &c., with a Variety of Copper Plates*. J. Calow & T. Underwood, London.

Polidori, J. W. & Rossetti, W. M. (eds). 1911. *The Diary of Dr. John William Polidori, 1816*. Elkin Matthews, London.

Priestley, J. 1767. *The History and Present State of Electricity, with Original Experiments*. J. Johnson & B. Davenport, London.

Priestley, J. 1808. *Memoirs of Dr. Joseph Priestley, to the Year 1795, Written by Himself; With a Continuation to the Time of his Decease, by his Son, Joseph Priestley; and Observations on His Writings, by Thomas Cooper, President, Judge of the 4th District of Pennsylvania; and the Rev. William Christie*. J. Johnson, London.

Principe, L. M. 2013. *The Secrets of Alchemy*. The University of Chicago Press, Chicago & London.

Rapport, R. 2005. *Nerve Endings: The Discovery of the Synapse*. W. W. Norton & Company, New York.

Rees, A. 1819. *The Cyclopædia; Or, Universal Dictionary of Arts, Sciences and Literature, Volume 24*. Longman, Hurst, Rees, Orme & Brown, London.

Reiger, J. 1963. 'Dr Polidori and the Genesis of Frankenstein'. *Studies in English Literature 1500-1900*, 3(4): 461.

Richardson, R. 1987. *Death, Dissection and the Destitute*. Routledge & Kegan Paul, London.

Rivera, A. M., Strauss, K. W., van Zundert, A. & Mortier, E. 2005. 'The history of peripheral intravenous catheters:

How little plastic tubes revolutionized medicine'. *Acta. Anaesth. Belg.*, 56: 271–282.

Roach, M. 2004. *Stiff: The Curious Lives of Human Cadavers.* Penguin Books, London.

Saeed, M., Rufai, A. A. & Elsayed, S. E. 2001. 'Mummification to Plastination Revisited'. *Saudi Med. J.* Vol. 22 (11): 956-959.

Schlesinger, H. 2010. *The Battery.* HarperCollins, New York.

Seymour, M. 2000. *Mary Shelley.* John Murray (Publishers), London.

Shelley, M. 1817. *History of a Six Weeks' Tour Through a Part of France, Switzerland, Germany and Holland.* T. Hookham & C. & J. Ollier, London.

Shelley, M. 1818. *Frankenstein: Or, The Modern Prometheus.* Oxford University Press, Oxford. Lackington, Hughes, Harding, Mavor & Jones, London.

Shelley, M. 1823. *Frankenstein: Or, The Modern Prometheus.* G. & W. B. Whittaker, London.

Shelley, M. 1823. *Valperga: or the Life and Adventures of Castruccio, Prince of Lucca.* G. & W. B. Whittaker, London.

Shelley, M. 1831. *Frankenstein: Or, The Modern Prometheus.* Puffin Books, London. Henry Colburn & Richard Bentley, London.

Shelley, M. 1835. *Lodore.* Richard Bentley, London.

Shelley, M. 1837. *Falkner.* Saunders & Otley, London.

Shelley, M. 1844. *Rambles in Germany and Italy 1840, 1842 and 1843.* Edward Moxon, London.

Shelley, M. 1857. *The Fortunes of Perkin Warbeck, A Romance.* G. Routledge & Co., London.

Shelley, M. 2004. *The Last Man.* Wordsworth Editions, Hertfordshire.

Shelley, M. 2013. *Mathilda and Other Stories.* Wordsworth Editions, Hertfordshire.

Shelley, P. B. 1810. *Zastrozzi, A Romance.* G. Wilkie & J. Robinson, London.

Shelley, P. B. 1811. *St. Irvyne; Or, The Rosicrucian: A Romance.* J. J. Stockdale, London.

Shelley, P. B. 1840. *Essays, Letters from Abroad, Translations and Fragments.* Edward Moxon, London.

Shelley, P. B. 1994. *The Works of P. B. Shelley.* Wordsworth Editions, Hertfordshire.

Smartt Bell, M. 2005. *Lavoisier in the Year One: The Birth of a New Science in an Age of Revolution.* W. W. Norton & Company, New York.

Sompayrac, L. 2008. *How the Immune System Works, Third Edition.* Blackwell Publishing, Massachusetts.

Spark, M. 1987. *Mary Shelley: A Biography.* NAL Penguin, New York.

Stocking, M. K. (ed.). 1968. *The Journals of Claire Clairmont.* Harvard University Press, Cambridge, Massachusetts.

Sunstein, E. W. 1991. *Mary Shelley: Romance and Reality.* John Hopkins University Press, Maryland.

Swan, J. 1835. *An Account of a New Method of Making Dried Anatomical Preparations.* E. Cox & Son, London.

Teresi, D. 2012. *The Undead.* Vintage Books, New York.

Thomson, H. 2015. 'First Human Head Transplant Could Happen in Two Years'. *New Scientist*, 25 February.

Thomson, H. 2016. 'Ark of the Immortals: The Future-Proof Plan to Freeze Out Death'. *New Scientist*, 29 June.

Thornton, R. J. 1800. *The Philosophy of Medicine, or Medical Extracts on the Nature of Health and Disease, Including the Laws of the Animal Economy, and the Doctrines of Pneumatic Medicine: Volume 3.* C. Whittingham, London.

Tilney, N. L. 2003. *Transplant: From Myth to Reality.* Yale University Press, New Haven & London.

Tomalin, C. 1992. *The Life and Death of Mary Wollstonecraft.* Penguin Books, London.

Ure, A. 1819. 'An Account of Some Experiments made on the Body of a Criminal immediately after Execution, with Physiological and Practical Observations'. *Quart. J. Science* 6: 283–294.

Uglow, J. 2003. *The Lunar Men: The Friends Who Made the Future.* Faber & Faber, London.

Vickery, A. 1999. *The Gentleman's Daughter.* Yale University Press.

Volney, C. F. 1796. *The Ruins, Or, A Survey of the Revolutions of Empires.* J. Johnson, London.

Walker, A. 1771. *Syllabus of a Course of Lectures on Natural and Experimental Philosophy.* W. Nevett & Co, Edinburgh.

Wollstonecraft, M. 1891. *A Vindication of the Rights of Woman: With Strictures on Political and Moral Subjects.* T. F. Unwin, London.

Wood, G. D. 2014. *Tambora: The Eruption that Changed the World.* Princeton University Press, Princeton.

Wulf, A. 2016. *The Invention of Nature: The Adventures of Alexander von Humboldt, The Lost Hero of Science.* John Murray, London.

Zimmer, C. 2005. *Soul Made Flesh: How the Secrets of the Brain were Uncovered in Seventeenth-Century England.* Arrow Books, London.

Websites

William Godwin's Diary – http://godwindiary.bodleian.ox.ac.uk/index2.html

Shelley Archive – http://shelleysghost.bodleian.ox.ac.uk

Peter Collinson – www.quakersintheworld.org/quakers-in-action/249

Execution of George Forster – www.exclassics.com/newgate/ng464.htm

Rackstrow's Museum – http://blog.wellcomelibrary.org/2009/10/rackstrows-museum

The History of Golden Syrup – www.lylesgoldensyrup.com/our-story

Portable Pacemaker Inspiration – www.medcitynews.com/2014/10/frankenstein-inspired-medtronic-founder-earl-bakken

Tapping the Admiral – www.tappingtheadmiral.co.uk/history

Acknowledgements

Thanks first of all to Jim Martin for not learning his lesson the first time round and letting me write another book. Thanks also to Anna MacDiarmid for her fantastic feedback and support.

Many people have generously taken the time to read and give comments and constructive criticism on what I have written. In particular I would like to thank my parents, who have taken much better care of their own hideous progeny than Victor Frankenstein did of his creation. Their ceaseless enthusiasm for proofreading has made the writing process much easier and the final book is considerably better for their suggestions.

I am enormously grateful to Carla Valentine, for her excellent help and feedback on aspects of grave robbing and anatomical preservation. Thanks also to Claire Benson, David and Sharon Harkup, Helen Johnston, Matthew May, Ashley Pearson, Helen Skinner, Richard and Violet Stutely and Mark Whiting. Their contributions have been invaluable. Thank you to all of them. Special thanks must also go to Bill Backhouse for endless tea and putting up with far too many conversations about dead frogs.

Any errors, badly constructed sections or ugly scars in the finished work are all down to me. There is much I have had to leave out. Mary Shelley lived an extraordinary and full life and I would encourage everyone to read one of the excellent biographies about her as well as her brilliant creations, not just *Frankenstein*.

Index